PARTY TIME

Shaun Attwood is the author of *Hard Time: A Brit in America's Toughest Jail*. He regularly speaks to audiences of young people about the perils of drugs and the horrors of prison life.

PARTY TIME

SHAUN ATTWOOD

MAINSTREAM
PUBLISHING

EDINBURGH AND LONDON

First published in Great Britain in 2013 by
MAINSTREAM PUBLISHING company
(EDINBURGH) LTD
7 Albany Street
Edinburgh EH1 3UG

ISBN 9781780576138

A catalogue record for this book is available
from the British Library

5 7 9 10 8 6 4

The Random House Group Limited supports The Forest Stewardship
Council® (FSC®), the leading international forest-certification organisation.
Our books carrying the FSC label are printed on FSC®-certified paper.
FSC is the only forest-certification scheme supported by the leading
environmental organisations, including Greenpeace. Our
paper procurement policy can be found at
www.randomhouse.co.uk/environment

MIX
Paper from
responsible sources
FSC® C016897

Printed and bound in Great Britain by Clays Ltd, St Ives plc

For my Koestler Trust mentor, Sally Hinchcliffe,
and all of the staff at the Koestler Trust
and Prisoners Abroad.

The world would be a better place with more
people like you in it – helping prisoners
to a second chance in life.

AUTHOR'S NOTE

WRITING MY AUTOBIOGRAPHY in a cell, after sobering up from years of drug use, I thought, *How lucky you are to be alive.* In prison, Gerard Gravano – the son of Salvatore 'Sammy the Bull' Gravano, a Mafia mass murderer – told me he'd once headed an armed crew dispatched to take me out to the desert. I credit incarceration with sending my life in a whole new positive direction. I now tell my story to students across the UK and Europe to educate them about the consequences of drugs and crime. I mention people in this book who lived fast and died young. Almost daily, I get emails from young people:

> You came into my school this week to talk about your life so far. Firstly, your talk was amazing. It was the highlight of almost everyone's day. Secondly, I have recently started taking some of the less hardcore drugs as a follow-on from smoking. I didn't really see how a few highs here and there could cause a problem, but your story really spoke to me. Thanks for taking the time to come to my school.
>
> Sarah

> I'd just like to say that your story really got to me and many other people unlike any speech or advice we've ever had. It was enjoyable, but also a very important lesson for all young people. I think it's great that you are trying to teach people not to make the same mistakes. You are an inspiration, and I'd like to thank you for spending your valuable time speaking to us because it was certainly a reality check for many people. Yours is a story I will never forget. Thanks again.
>
> James

Some names and other details in this book have been changed to protect people.

If you'd like to send feedback on any of my books or ask a question, here's my email address: attwood.shaun@hotmail.co.uk.

QUIZ

THE FIRST PERSON to email attwood.shaun@hotmail.co.uk the correct answers will win a signed first-edition of *Hard Time* plus an original postcard I mailed from the maximum-security Madison Street jail in Phoenix, Arizona. Two runners-up will receive signed copies of the UK paperback of *Hard Time*. The winners will be annouced on at my blog, Jon's Jail Journal.

1. Which name in this book sounds like the part of prison that houses inmates awaiting execution?
2. Identify three sentences in this book that contain the words 'hard' and 'time', not including mentions of my previous book.
3. T-Bone – an ex-Marine who used his fighting skills to stop prison rape – shares his stories at Jon's Jail Journal. Which catchphrase of T-Bone's is used in this book?
4. In my previous book, *Hard Time*, to which this is the prequel, if you take the first letter of each name (excluding surnames) in the order in which they appear in the eighth paragraph of the acknowledgements, the names of two philosophers will appear. Who are they?

CHAPTER 1

WE APPROACH TWO drug dealers, lads about our age, 20, skulking in a corner of a dark nightclub, skulls shaved.

'Can we get two hits of Ecstasy and two grams of speed?' my friend asks.

My fingers and legs start to shake.

'E's twenty quid. Tenner a wrap of Billy Whizz.'

'Here you go.' My friend offers our money.

The dealers exchange looks as if pondering whether to rob us. My body stiffens like plaster setting in a cast. The biggest snatches our cash. The other passes the drugs imperceptibly. They vanish. I worry about getting arrested for possession. It's 1989, and drug deals rarely end happily on my TV. Bracing for undercover cops to grab us, I spin my eyes around the room.

My friend yanks my arm, rushes us to the toilets, locks us in a stall. He reveals two white pills and speed meticulously wrapped in little paper rectangles. 'You put the Billy Whizz in your drink,' he whispers, tipping white powder into a bottle, 'and neck the White Dove.'

Buying drugs is one thing, taking them another. *Will I be hooked for the rest of my life?* My fear of ending up in an ambulance and my parents finding out recedes as the thrill rises. *I can experiment a few times, have fun, quit whenever I want . . .*

'Come on, get on with it,' he says, having taken his.

I dump the speed into a bottle of Lucozade, pop the pill, take a swig and gag on the chemical aftertaste. *Oh my God! What happens now?* I turn to my friend. 'How long before I feel it?'

'Within the hour.'

My friend is a fellow student at the University of Liverpool, where I'm doing business studies. Raves are making headline news, so I'm at The Thunderdome in Manchester to find out what all the fuss is about. The bare square room with a stage at the front is unimpressive. Only a few people are dancing to music that makes no sense. Repetitive beats and beeps like signals from outer space. Most of the ravers are stood by the walls, gazing at the dance floor as if expecting an elephant to materialise. Nightclubs intimidate me. I feel shy in them. I don't dare talk to anyone other than my friend. Convinced I'm about to overdose – die, even – I spend the next half-hour checking my pulse, timing the beats per minute.

An expression blossoms on my friend's face as if he's having an orgasm. Exuding the kind of bliss seen on angels in medieval paintings, he can't stop smiling or stand still. He asks me to dance. I haven't enjoyed dancing since the days of punk rock. I say no. He bounces off. I regret letting him down. Frustrated that the drugs aren't affecting me, I finish my drink. I walk towards the bar. My knees buckle and the strength drains from my legs. I try to soldier on but wobble as if on sinking sand and have to sit down.

Someone kicks me. 'Sorry, mate.'

Staring up at a happy raver in baggy jeans, I break into a smile that wraps around my face and refuses to go away. There's a strange feeling on my back. *Has a bug landed there?* I reach over my shoulder to slap it off. *No bug.* It's the sensation of my T-shirt against my skin. Running my fingertips up and down the nape of my neck feels like feathers are tickling my skin. *Or are my fingers melting into my skin?* A sensation so pleasurable, I massage myself. Breathing feels different, too. Each inhalation pulses pleasure through my body as if I'm getting fondled by an invisible woman. Smiling at the forest of legs growing around me, I remember I was going to the bar – but that doesn't matter any more, nor does losing my girlfriend, the engine problems with my car, the calculus-heavy 5,000-word balance-of-payments essay due on Monday morning . . . The high is demolishing every worry in my life, leaving me no choice but to be happy with the way things are.

The club fills. Time is irrelevant. Ravers are everywhere, a kaleidoscope of coloured clothing. Hugging, grinning, grooving, jumping happiness machines, raising the temperature with their body heat. My desire to join them gains strength; it's just a matter of time. My high keeps rising, interrupting the flow of my thoughts, making my eyeballs flutter upwards as if under the influence of the moon's magnetic pull. Hot, I want to take my T-shirt off; pondering the urge melts it away. The music and beeping noises are making sense now. They're saying, *Get off your arse and dance!*

I'm bobbing my head, playing the piano on my thighs, when my friend finds me. He smiles. Our eyes sparkle in recognition of each other's highs.

'Come on,' he says.

I follow him into the thicket of bodies. He starts to dance. I jump from side to side, trying to find my groove, and settle into the same rocking motion as everyone else. I'm dancing, loving dancing, surprised by how natural it feels, experimenting with moves copied from those around me. My heart is beating hard and in time with the *boom-boom-boom* blasting from giant black speakers. My arms are jerking up and down as if I'm throwing boulders at the ceiling when everyone stops dancing. *Has someone turned the music off? No.* Only the beat has stopped, leaving a soothing sound. Hands shoot up. Whistles blow. A machine hisses out smoke. A black woman sings with beauty bordering on spiritual, tingling my skin all over. Piano notes are struck. We sway, our fingers reaching into the beams of the sun laser. An air horn sounds. Bracing for a lorry to plough through the club, I jump. The absurdity of the notion makes me laugh aloud. The soulful woman's voice fades as DJ Jay Wearden mixes in a Guru Josh track: '1990s . . . Time for the Guru'. A saxophone solo sends a tremor through my body. My eyeballs shiver. In the square room that had bored me earlier, I feel as if I'm at one with God. I never want the party to end.

CHAPTER 2

I'M 12 AND the lunch bell just rang at St Joseph's. The herd drifts to the canteen.

In a black blazer, grey pullover, white shirt and yellow-and-blue-striped tie, I jog to a corner shop, burst through the door – *jingle-jingle* goes the entry bell – rest my hands on a glass counter and ask, short of breath, 'Can I get two ounces of pear-drops and two ounces of strawberry bonbons, please?'

Weighing the sweets, the shopkeeper wafts a smell of powdered sugar that wets my mouth. He puts them in bags and hands them over.

I pay and dash down the road and across a field back to school. My customers are waiting. I sell sweets individually for twice the price, delighting in haggling. I accept a lunch coupon for pear-drops. All sold out, I strut to the canteen for fish fingers and chips, the joy of profit jangling in my brain like the coins in my pocket.

Thirteen and my parents – a secretary studying to be a teacher, and an insurance salesman – move from a terraced house near the centre of Widnes, a small chemical-manufacturing town, to a semi-detached in a neighbourhood where they believe the children are better behaved.

I befriend four lads addicted to watching the same American street-gang movies. We christen ourselves The Sweats; the other boys in our neighbourhood are The Wets. When we encounter The Wets, we rough them up. When we don't see them, we throw rosebuds at their windows to get their parents to chase us.

We amuse ourselves in a variety of ways. We dash across motorways in a game of chicken, flipping off drivers. We stick our legs out of carriage windows in the path of oncoming trains, pulling them back in at the last possible minute. Whenever we find a dead cat on a road, we put it in a plastic bag and show it to local girls, animal lovers, claiming to have killed it in a satanic ritual. We find videos stashed in parents' bedrooms. Watching horror movies, we get blazed on Southern Comfort. We masturbate to pornography, keeping an eye on the size of each other's penises. We steal knickers from the washing lines of beautiful women, sniff them and wear them on our heads. We occasionally shoplift, even though we have money to pay.

I don't tell The Sweats that I watch birds, play chess, programme computers and collect coins and stamps.

The leader of The Sweats is Dez. Tall. Curly-haired. The oldest. He specialises in tormenting his younger brother, Peter.

I'm with The Sweats outside a pub called the Black Horse when Peter approaches.

'Put some of that dog shit in your mouth, Peter, if you wanna join The Sweats!' Dez barks, pointing at the ground.

Peter spots the dog dirt on the pavement at the foot of a red telephone box. A lengthy central coil, tapering off at both ends, surrounded by sausage-like chunks, all light brown. 'Any piece?'

'Just put some in your mouth if you wanna be a Sweat!'

Peter squats and pokes each piece as if prioritising them by consistency. 'I'll be a Sweat, right?'

Revolted by what he is about to do, yet in awe, I step closer to get a better look, but the smell shoves me back.

'Put some in your mouth, for fuck's sake!'

Peter picks up a piece, examines it, puffs. He chucks it into his mouth. His face puckers until he looks cross-eyed. 'It's fucking horrible,' he mutters. 'Is this good enough, Dez? Can I spit it out now?'

'If you wanna be a Sweat, you've gotta swallow it,' Dez cackles.

'Yeah, swallow it, Peter Patheticus, or you'll never be a Sweat!'

Determination appears on Peter's face. He gulps as if clearing a rock from his throat. He opens his mouth. Empty. '*Urghhhhh* . . . It's nasty! I did it! I did it! I swallowed it! I'm a Sweat now!' Scratching his throat, he stares at Dez.

'You daft fucking bastard! I tricked you, you stupid git! Now fuck off home. You're no brother of mine. You eat dog shit and you fucking stink. Get home before I beat the shit out of you.'

Peter's brown eyes glaze over in a sad way. He hangs his head and tries to leave. Dez trips him up. They stick their boots in.

Feeling sorry for Peter – so young and vulnerable – I don't contribute my Dr Martens.

After that incident, Peter knocks on my door a lot. Two years his senior, I take him under my wing. We hang out at a local petrol station, blasting Bronski Beat on his boombox, harassing The Wets and boys straying in from other neighbourhoods. At weekends, we offer a car-washing service at a pub. Peter gambles his earnings on slot machines, whereas I save mine.

At fourteen, I elect to do economics. My teacher, Mr Dillon, gives me extra classes on my own. He explains how to read the *Financial Times* and follow the stock market. From the library, I order dozens of books on the subject. I spend less time playing computer games and more dreaming of becoming a millionaire on Wall Street.

The Sweats are on the prowl up Pex Hill, a patch of countryside at the top of Widnes. It's a clear day, but I don't care much for the view: buildings all the way to Liverpool, including two cathedrals in the city centre; on the banks of the River Mersey, eight giant cooling towers blotting out the sky above Fiddlers Ferry Power Station as if manufacturing clouds; in the distance, the mild slopes of the Clwydian Mountains in North Wales.

Under an oak, Dez hawks phlegm, spits a green ball accompanied by considerable spray at a cloud of midges, scattering them, and tells us to forge tunnels through the bracken. We arm ourselves with acorns, pelt girls on horseback and take off into the tunnels on all fours like a pack of wild dogs.

When the novelty wears off, Dez says, 'Let's go see who's in the quarry.'

We follow him along a footpath, winding around heather bushes and hawthorn and elderberry trees giving off a musky perfume that refreshes my lungs. We squeeze through a gap in the railings around the quarry. I'm gazing at the graffiti on the sandstone cliffs – RAFFY, SEAN, NEZ AND NIGE – when The Sweats grab me. They force me to the edge and dangle me off.

Staring down – *I'll die or break my spine if I fall* – I clench my sphincter, barely able to hold in what's trying to come out. Terrified to struggle in case they lose their grip, I shout, 'Stop! Stop! Stop!'

'Teach you to hang out with my brother!' Dez yells. 'Let's just drop him.'

'Make sure he hits the rocks. We don't want him to live to tell the tale.'

They swing me back and forth for what feels like half a lifetime. Tears leak out; reluctant to add to their satisfaction, I scrunch my face to retain the rest. Eventually, they yank me up. Walking down Pex Hill, I swear my days of being a Sweat are over.

Sixteen, but Mo, an aunt I worship – every time she gets a windfall, she flies me to Arizona and spoils me with endless shopping sprees – is changing the age on my passport to twenty-one. Mo busts people trying to embezzle banks, earning her a reputation for being one of the toughest fraud officers in the Wild West. Through this work, she understands the ways of criminals.

'Almost done,' Mo says, running a pen over sticky tape attached to the curves on the left-hand side of the 8 in my year of birth, 1968. She lifts the tape. The 8 is now a 3.

'I just aged five years!' I say.

'Now you can get into bars.'

Later, Mo takes me to a nightclub, Zazoo's.

'ID!' the bouncer yells over a Prince track.

Trembling at the prospect of the alteration being detected, I surrender my passport.

He examines it, hands it back. 'All the way from England! How cool.'

Mo smiles at me.

Inside is a wonderland of neon lights, disco balls, adults dancing, well-manicured hands flaunting glitzy cocktails.

Mo goes to the bathroom and reappears with a blonde beauty. 'This is Alexis, Shaun. She's dying to meet you.'

'Hi, Alexis,' I say, blushing. *Why on earth is she so keen to meet me?*

'Your accent's *so* cute,' Alexis says, intensifying my embarrassment. 'Mo's been telling me about you being Paul McCartney's nephew.'

I look at Mo. She winks.

I stifle a grin. 'Er . . . yeah. Ever been to Liverpool?'

'I've never been out of America.'

'Would you like to visit?'

'Hell, yeah! C'mon, let's dance . . .'

In England, over Sunday dinner, I ask my parents for money to invest in British Telecom shares.

'What do you think?' Mum says, turning to Dad.

'Bugger off,' Dad says. 'I'm not supporting Margaret bloody Thatcher's privatisation programme.'

'It's only fifty pence a share,' I say in my best salesman's voice. 'Mr Dillon thinks it'll start trading much higher.'

'No!' Dad says. 'We've got a Tory in the house now, have we? Just like your grandmother.'

'Of course – Nan! Why didn't I think of that? Thanks, Dad!'

After eating, I jog to Nan's for a second Sunday dinner. The smell of Grandfather Fred's chicken gravy rekindles my hunger. After mmmming and ahhhing over the meal, I tell Nan about British Telecom shares. She gives me £50 to invest. When the news reports that BT shares have doubled on their first day of dealings, I pogo like a punk rocker up and down in the living room in front of my family, yelling, 'Yes! Yes! Yes!' I sell the shares, and keep the profit for the next privatisation.

Seventeen and I'm up Pex Hill with my two best friends, Hammy – formerly of The Sweats, a year younger than me but built more solidly, and much sought after by the girls – and Dez's brother, Peter, who never made it into The Sweats and whom we now call Wild Man, a nickname bestowed on him – based on misbehaviour – by his uncle Bob, a whisky-nosed old-timer. We're sat on a tree that leans over the quarry; we call it the Thinking Tree.

Marvelling at the drop below, I ask, 'What're you two gonna do when you finish school?'

'I'm going to prison,' Wild Man says.

'Why's that?' I ask.

'I see these red and white dots.'

'Red and white dots! Why'd you see them?' I ask.

'White dots are fine. They're normal everyman's anger. Red dots are slaughter.'

'How often do you see the red ones?' Hammy asks.

'More than enough.'

Hammy's laugh declares how proud he is of Peter's ability to see dots.

'Are the red dots because of Dez beating you up?' I ask.

'I can't even have a wank without getting punched in the face by our Sweat, Dez,' Wild Man says.

'But look at the size of you!' I say. 'I'm surprised you haven't thrown him through a window by now.'

'The teachers at Fairfield are so scared of Peter,' Hammy says, 'they've stuck him outside, raking leaves with the caretaker.' Hammy and Wild Man attend the same Protestant school, Fairfield, whereas I'm at Widnes Sixth Form College doing A levels.

'What about when you finish school, Hammy?' I ask.

'I don't know. What about you, Atty?'

'I'm going to be a millionaire in America.'

'You probably will, with all that stock-market stuff,' Hammy says.

'Will you take us with you?' Wild Man asks.

'Deffo. I'm not going to stop until I buy my own island. When I make enough money, I'll fly you two over.' I have it all figured out: I'm going to repeat the success of the legendary investors I worship.

'If you bring Wild Man over, you'd better build a cage for him first. We'll give him grub but won't let him out. When he misbehaves, we'll poke him with sticks.'

Wild Man snaps a branch off. His eyes search below. 'What's it like in America, Atty?' He hurls the branch at hikers in the quarry. It misses. They spot us, scowl, shake fists. Wild Man smiles and waves.

'The people talk funny, but they're dead friendly,' I say. 'The birds buzz off our accents. Everything's massive. Roads. Houses. Cars. And they've all got swimming pools in their back yards.'

'In their back yards!' Wild Man says.

'Like on *The Beverly Hillbillies*?' Hammy asks.

'Yes, exactly,' I say.

'Bloody hell!' Hammy says.

'How come they all have swimming pools in their back yards?' Wild Man asks.

'When the plane comes in to land, you see all the swimming pools. America's the richest country in the world. That's why it's easy to be a millionaire there. Even you can get a job as a wrestler or something, and you won't end up in prison.' *I'll see to it that Wild Man has a good life in America.* 'There's no hope for you in Widnes.'

'There's no hope for any of us in Widnes, Atty,' Wild Man says. 'That's why you're going to America.'

*

Eighteen and I'm visiting Aunt Mo in Phoenix.

Along a desert road, torrential rain pounds her car, overwhelming the squeaky windscreen wipers. She parks at a video store. Getting out, I slip in my flip-flops, cutting my foot.

The sight of blood widens Mo's eyes – but not with alarm. 'Listen to me, beloved nephew. Do exactly as I say if you want to make a ton of money from an insurance claim. Go in the store, slip again and fall. I'll do all the talking. Can you handle that?'

'Er, yeah. Sure. I think so,' I say.

I push the door open, walk in, fall theatrically and end up face down.

Mo takes charge. 'Did you see what just happened to my nephew? How can you have a wet floor with no warning sign or anything to prevent slips? I want to see the manager!'

The clerk's round, rosy face pales into a full moon. She fetches the manager, who agrees – in the tone of someone trying to placate a bomb-strapped terrorist – with everything Mo says and surrenders the insurance information.

Mo speeds to a hospital. The doctor says the cut doesn't need stitches.

Thank God!

'He's here on holiday from England. We can't take any chances. He needs stitches . . .' Mo all but puts the doctor in a headlock until he produces a needle and thread.

On a sore foot, I limp from the hospital

Mo puts a reassuring hand on my shoulder. 'The bigger the medical bills, the bigger the compensation.' She coaches me on what to say to the insurance adjuster.

I get $5,000 from the insurer and £1,500 on a claim from my travel insurance. After the crash of '87, I invest the money in drugs by way of shares in Glaxo Pharmaceuticals.

Twenty and I'm driving home with Wild Man from a rave at the Eclipse club in Coventry; we're dancing in our seats to the acid-house beat of DJ Stu Allan. The engine warning light turns on in the old Talbot Horizon I inherited from Mum. I park on the shoulder. In the early-morning chill, Wild Man and I shiver off our Ecstasy highs. I use a screwdriver to jemmy the bonnet open. As usual, the car needs water. We wander off with an empty bottle and stop at a canal hemmed in by steep walls.

'There's no way we can get to that water,' Wild Man says.

'Yes there is: if you hold one of my arms tight and dangle me over the edge.'

'If I drop you, you're fucked. Look how deep and fast it is.'

'Then don't drop me. If we drive for much longer with no water, it'll destroy the engine.'

'OK.'

Holding out an arm, I say, 'Grab me and lower me down.'

Wild Man's big hands fasten around my wrist with the strength of a gorilla. I flash him a look that says, *Don't let go*. Digging my sneakers into gaps in the wall, I work my legs down, descending steadily, leaning my arm out with the bottle, gagging on the smell of chemicals ascending with mist from the canal surface, my heartbeat vibrating in my ears louder than the water whooshing.

'You're almost there. Try it now!' Wild Man says, my weight destabilising him.

Tilting as far as possible, I feel blood rush to my head. I submerge the bottle. 'It's full! OK. Please get me up.'

'Yes, la'.'

The force of his pull almost wrenches my arm from its socket.

'Thanks, la',' I say. 'We did it.'

'You've got the brains and I've got the brawn,' Wild Man says.

Twenty-one. I graduate from the University of Liverpool with a BA in business studies, a 2:1. Researching employment in America, I discover it takes years to get a work visa – shattering my dream. I apply to be an investment analyst in London, convinced the American brokerages can magically transfer me over to Wall Street. Certain of being hired on the spot because of my passion for the stock market, I go through months of gruelling interviews. Each rejection crushes my optimism. I call Mo for advice.

'Phoenix is booming. It's expanding so fast, the city limits are like shifting sand. Ten thousand people moved here last winter. It's the place to be for good jobs in every field. Why don't you move in with us and give yourself a year to see if things work out? Worst-case scenario you'll get a suntan.'

'But I have no work visa.'

'I know one of the top immigration attorneys in Phoenix. If you come on a visitor's visa, we can apply to change it to a temporary work visa or another visa allowing you to work in a specific field.

Just jump on a plane and we'll sort all that out when you get here.'

She's right. I can go a long way in Arizona with my English accent.

In 1991, Mum waves me off from Runcorn train station. 'My whole life's in that suitcase,' I tell her, sad to leave but buzzing at the prospect of conquering the stock market. *I'll make my first million within five years. Nothing will stop me. Nothing at all.*

CHAPTER 3

'WHAT'S YOUR REASON for coming to America, Mr Attwood?' asks a stern-faced immigration officer in May 1991.

'Visiting my aunt and uncle.' My heart somersaults over the lie.

'How long do you intend to stay in America?'

'A month.'

'How much cash have you brought?'

'Not much.'

'Then how do you intend to support yourself in America?' he asks, grimacing.

Unnerved, I fish my credit-card holder from my pocket and open it like a concertina. 'With these.'

He nods and stamps a visa. 'Have a good stay in America, Mr Attwood.'

Oh, yes, in America money is king!

I fly from Chicago to Phoenix. Getting off the plane, I'm ambushed by heat. My dazzled eyes slam shut. Opening them partially, I see desert air shimmering on the runways. As I walk towards the building, the sun stings my shaved head and a gust of wind deposits dust in my mouth. I spit and switch to breathing through my nose. By the time I get to the terminal, my brains are boiling like an egg. I hug Mo and retrieve my luggage.

On the drive home, Mo stops at a Circle K convenience store. My excitement at being in America somehow blows the lid off my 54-oz ThirstBuster. Pink lemonade spreads across the counter and drips on the floor.

'I'm so sorry,' I say, throwing my hands up.

'I'll clean it up, dude,' the clerk says.

Mo shakes her head. Outside, she yells, 'Don't ever fucking

apologise! Blame the cup! Blame the lid! Blame the staff! Demand fucking compensation!'

'You're so right. What was I thinking?'

From Mo's house, I mail my résumé to the stockbrokerages in the phone book. In a race to make money before I run out of credit, I must find work fast. Days later, I find a letter from Kruger Financial in the mailbox. I dash inside, tear it open and announce to Mo that I have an interview.

A week later, speeding down the I-10, Mo says, 'If they ask to see your Social Security card, tell them your aunt has it in safe keeping, but you'll be happy to bring them a photocopy for their records.' On a previous visit, Mo had guided me through getting various other forms of ID.

'But it has "NOT VALID FOR EMPLOYMENT" printed on it,' I say, perspiring in my shirt, suit and tie.

'I'll fade that out of the copy.' A car cuts us off. Mo lowers her window and offers a middle finger. 'Motherfucking daft git!'

'And what if they ask for a work visa?'

'We'll get a printing set from Toys R Us or any stationery store, and stamp "H-1B professional-level job visa" into your passport. That should satisfy employers. I did the same in Chicago. I had no work visa. My immigration attorney advised me to file my tax returns correctly and on time. I did and the government left me alone. If you don't mess with the IRS, you'll be just fine.'

'You've got it all figured out,' I say, elevating her up the ranks of business geniuses. *It'll all be so easy with her guidance.*

'And just remember when you go into this interview: *it's fuck or be fucked in the business world.* Be honest about your abilities. The Americans have no time for the British attitude of being reserved. Build yourself up to the hilt, so they'd feel pretty fucking stupid if they didn't hire you.'

We sign in at a security desk and take the elevator to the 13th floor. Mo stays on a sofa. I'm shown into a conference room.

I stride past a long mahogany table and stop at full-length windows, impressed by the view. Below a sky so clear it looks like a window into outer space, palm trees and buildings are scattered across the desert, shrunk to the size of matchsticks and boxes. Nearby is a cluster of high-rises – monuments to financial success, my kind of Stonehenge – and, further away, a mountain shaped like a camel, mansions riding its humps. *I belong there. It's just a matter of time.* The height gives me a sense of power over everything below.

A broad, chubby man swaggers in with the air of a Mafia don. Olive skin. Slicked hair. Silky cashmere suit. Facial shape and eyes like a Saint Bernard's. 'I'm Johnny Brasi, the boss of Kruger's Phoenix office,' he says in a New York Italian accent.

'Pleased to meet you,' I say, accentuating my Englishness.

Grinning, he gives my hand a few firm pumps. 'Take a seat. So, Shaun, tell me, why do you wanna be a stockbroker?' He rests his elbows on the table, leans forward and gazes at me as if reading my thoughts.

I launch into describing my adventures in the stock market, convinced my enthusiasm will win him over.

He listens patiently. 'Analysing stocks and selling them are two entirely different things. Do you have what it takes to be a salesperson?'

'I can succeed at anything I put my mind to.'

'I like your attitude, and I like your accent. That accent will really help you on the phone. So here's what I'm willing to do for you: I'm gonna offer you a job as a stockbroker with Kruger Financial.'

'Thanks very much,' I say, delighted. *Everything's falling into place so quickly.* 'When can I start?'

'To work as a stockbroker, you need a Series 7 licence. To get a Series 7, you need to pass an exam. To pass the exam, I recommend you sign up for the classes the next bunch of trainees are attending. If you do the classes and pass the test, you could have your licence as early as two months from now.'

'That sounds fine,' I say, unfazed.

'What you need to understand about Kruger Financial is that you'll be employed as an independent contractor. That means you'll not be making any money until you begin to generate commissions from selling stocks.'

Here's the catch.

''Cause you'll not be on any fixed salary, the amount of money you can make is unlimited. It all depends on how hard you work and the commissions you generate.'

'I like the sound of that, but I want to start earning commissions right away. How hard is this test? Maybe I can do it without the classes.'

'It's not the policy of this firm to enter a trainee for the test without doing the classes. There's a lotta math in it.'

'My degree involved loads of calculus and statistics. This test can't be any harder than that.'

'There's a lotta options questions in it.'

'I've traded options.'

Johnny laughs. 'I'll show you the study book. It's a big book. Then you'll see you need the classes.' He fetches the book.

Opening it, I say, 'You've got to be kidding!'

'I told you so.'

'No, not the size of it. It's all multiple-choice questions. This is easy. How soon can you put me in for the test?'

He narrows his eyes as if assessing whether I'm worth taking the risk. 'If you're that confident, I may be willing to let you skip the classes. Are you sure you won't let me down?'

'I definitely won't.'

'When I put my trust in someone, I'm not the kind of guy who likes being let down.'

'It's not going to happen,' I say, trying not to imagine what he does to people who disappoint him.

He smiles. 'The earliest I can get you in for the test is about two weeks.'

'No problem.'

'Take this book home with you.'

'Thanks, boss.'

Johnny tells me to study at Kruger to absorb the atmosphere. The brokers, about 30 power-dressed men, arrive before 6 a.m., sporting sleep creases on their faces. They greet the secretaries and join the battle for the coffee-maker. From the vending machines, they load up on candy and Mountain Dew. The workplace is mostly open plan. The majority of the brokers are sat four to a quad: a cross-shaped table with corkboard divides. As 6.30 a.m. nears, their rate of caffeine consumption rises exponentially, as do their spirits. When the opening bell rings on the New York Stock Exchange, the brokers spring from their chairs and yell into their phones at volumes normally reserved for the hard of hearing.

'Dow's up twenty-seven!'

'Techs are on the move again!'

'Market or limit order?'

'It's ten and a sixteenth. Crap! They just raised the offer to an eighth!'

'ASA International's off three thirty-seconds on low volume.'

'I'm telling you, it's a dead-cat bounce.'

'Dump that dog!'

'It just bust through its year high!'

'You bought ten thousand at a buck fifty!'

The phones ring constantly. Each handset has a 24-foot curly cord, enabling the brokers to pace. Gripped by the action and unable to study because of the noise, I long to be on a phone, converting words into cash, laying the foundations of my empire.

Next to the conference room, Johnny is in a glass-walled office, sitting heavily on a black chair resembling a throne. Every so often, he emerges to lord it over the brokers. 'I wanna see everyone stand up! If you pace, your enthusiasm will travel down the phone lines, energise whoever you're pitching to, and they'll wanna piece of what you're excited about. You'll open more accounts and close more sales. Grab your mirrors and look at yourselves smiling while you're on the phone. Smiling brokers close more sales.'

His words excite the brokers. They stand and pace, criss-crossing the room with curly cords. To get around the cords, brokers duck, swerve and limbo dance.

In the middle of each quad is a Quotron: a rotating metal box with a screen flashing green stock quotes. Competition for the Quotrons is fierce, priority going to brokers writing trade tickets. The mood of the brokers goes up and down with the numbers on the Quotrons. With their own Quotrons, the biggest producers occupy four offices at the back. Every so often, one dashes to Johnny's office waving a trade ticket – usually an investment so large that the floor brokers watch enviously. It's noisy until the trading session ends. Then the producers swagger home, abandoning the cold-calling floor brokers to a workplace redolent of trashcans overflowing with polystyrene coffee cups and sweat seeping through starched shirts.

Two weeks later, I ace the Series 7, boosting my confidence. I strut into the 6 a.m. sales meeting, take a seat and cock my head back.

Stood by a whiteboard displaying brokers' names, commissions and new accounts for the month, Johnny and two young men loom over the brokers. My fellow rookies look half asleep, but the men with Johnny have the wide, alert eyes of ravers on speed. The taller one has thick, curly hair; the other has a crew cut and is chewing gum aggressively.

'All of you know that to make it in this business,' Johnny says, 'you've gotta stay on the phone. And I don't mean taking personal calls from your wives and girlfriends. That's gotta stop. You need to be on the phone generating trades and opening new accounts.'

Fixing us with stares fit to melt our eyeballs, the two men nod.

'Producing brokers should be calling their clients and asking for referrals.' Johnny raises a pretend phone to his ear. '"Mr Jones, who else do you know who'd be interested in taking advantage of this stock while it's still cheap?" It's as easy as that, but some of you seem to be afraid of your phones. Well, I've got news for you: it's been scientifically proven that people cannot travel down phone lines to hurt you. Maybe Mr Jones' stock has gone down from where you bought it. If it has, then you pick up your phone, and say, "Mr Jones, we thought ASA International was a good buy at one dollar. Well, it's an even better buy at fifty cents. You bought ten thousand shares before. Let's go in and buy another twenty thousand at fifty cents, and that'll get your average price right down."'

The gum-chewer punches a quad divide. A few of us jump in our seats. 'You should be asking for a hundred thousand shares and then settling for fifty!' His eyes find mine. Feeling a threat to my existence, I look away.

'That's right,' Johnny says. 'I brought these two here today so you, especially the rookie brokers, can meet the two top-producing brokers from Bezner Securities. Some of you older brokers know Jimmy Shargal and Len Gleeson. Jimmy here's gonna give you new brokers some advice.'

Jimmy spits his gum into a trashcan. He scans the audience sneeringly. With the conviction of a religious fanatic, he recounts his rise as a stockbroker from rookie to Tyrannosaurus rex. I'm spellbound. *He's got the military discipline to build an empire.* Every so often he punches a tabletop or quad divide. 'How many calls does a rookie have to make? At least five hundred cold calls a day! That'll get you ten to twenty leads! From those leads, you'll open one new account! That's thirty new accounts a month! How many of you have ever opened thirty accounts in one month in your miserable lives?' Sighting us down his nose, he inhales in a way that says *he* owns the air around us. 'You should be in here before the market opens cold-calling the East Coast! You should be in here late at night cold-calling the West Coast and Hawaii! You should be in here on the weekends catching local business owners while they're relaxing in their homes in Paradise Valley and Scottsdale! Johnny has given you everything you need to succeed like me and Len!'

Lapping it up, we nod. My veins swell, pumping my body up.

Len spins an arm and slams the board with a fist, nearly knocking it off the wall. 'Don't ever, ever forget, you're only as big as where your numbers on this board are at for the month!'

At fever pitch, I'm ready to tear people to pieces on the phone. *They'll buy stocks or else.*

After the meeting, Johnny takes me aside. 'I'm not gonna seat you in a quad with the other rookies at the front of the office. They've had no investment experience before coming here. They're pitching certain stocks. You're different. I'm gonna let you pitch whatever you wanna pitch.'

I feel special. 'Where should I sit?' I ask, searching for the youngest and friendliest faces, which are mostly near the front.

'There's a space in the quad at the very back.'

I crane my neck to get a better look at the three men sat there. Anxiety shoots up from my guts, collapsing my high. With hard, menacing faces, they look like convicts in suits.

'Just grab yourself a phone book and start cold-calling. To get used to cold-calling, try pitching Salt River Project bonds to numbers in Sun City. That's where the old people with money live. They trust Salt River Project.' Johnny hastens to his office and greets a big man, bald and eyebrowless, leaning on a cane topped with a silver skull.

I take my seat and open the phone book near the back, afraid to talk to my quadmates or make eye contact with them.

'Good morning, Mr Washington! This is Shaun Attwood calling from Kruger Financial to see if you'd be interested in some 7 per cent Salt River Project bonds.'

'I'm eating my freaking breakfast right now!'

'You do want to make money, don't you?'

Click.

'Good morning, Mrs Washko! This is Shaun Attwood calling from Kruger Financial to see if you'd be interested in some Salt River Project bonds yielding 7 per cent.'

'Our son handles our investments.' *Click.*

'Good morning, Mrs Washnock! This is Shaun Attwood calling from Kruger Financial to see if you'd be interested in some 7 per cent Salt River Project bonds.'

'Take my name off your list or I'll sue your goddam ass!' *Click.*

Mocked, sworn at, hung up on, I eavesdrop on my quadmates, hoping to learn what to say on the phone.

Jason Park – a brawny New Yorker of Irish and Korean descent with striking smoke-grey eyes and facial muscles that ripple as he talks – is fresh from the big house. He was sentenced to two years for breaking a man's nose with a pool cue in a bar fight. To explain his absence, he tells his clients he was in chemotherapy, battling a disease that almost killed him multiple times. He calls cancer survivors, bonds with them through their shared suffering and sells them stocks.

Troy Ireland – a gaunt and grizzled ex-Marine with bulging shell-shocked eyes and scars across his face so deep his stubble fails to disguise them – snorts crystal meth off the desk and hangs out with Hell's Angels.

Curt Pritchett – a brilliant salesperson with an icy disposition, whose elongated head and deep-set eyes lend him the look of an underwater predator – keeps a bottle of Smirnoff in his briefcase at all times. His vocal inflection ranges from army-general commands to sing-song whispers that would put a baby to sleep.

These three have christened our table 'the criminal quad'. I spend hours trying to absorb their sales pitches. For the first few weeks, they offer me little by way of conversation other than an occasional grunt and appear to be contemplating doing me harm. But, over time, they start schooling me, including putting their clients on speakerphone. I listen, thrilled, to entire conversations, filing away for future use how they respond to objections.

Far more approachable is Kruger's youngest broker, Matt Bedford, 19, greyhound lean with a friendly face and big eyes. Even when the stock market is falling, he oozes enthusiasm, making stocks sound like tickets guaranteed to win the lottery. He's adept at pacing. When his curly cord reaches its maximum extension, he about-faces with the agility of a guardsman on parade. Matt and I work the latest. Our friendship blossoms. Over drinks, I tell him how much I miss English raves and he promises to find a local party.

*

My first few months, I generate no commission. I use most of my credit to get an apartment by the office. Local family members donate a hodgepodge of furniture. With little money and no time to cook, I live off cheese on toast, and bananas. Poor diet, financial stress and fear of having to return to England cause ulcers in my mouth. *Am I cut out for this?*

I change my strategy to pitching America West Airlines' junk bonds. Trading at ten cents on the dollar, they offer a 900 per cent return if the company doesn't default. Having read that Asians have high incomes and like to gamble, I look them up in the phone book. The strategy works. My first customers are Chens and Mengs. Opening accounts lifts me from a mini-depression to a high like when I lost my virginity. That people send thousands to invest based on a few brief telephone conversations astounds me. *Now I have numbers on the board, I matter in here!* Johnny applauds me at the sales meeting for being 'shit-hot definite millionaire class', turbo-charging my morale.

A month later, Jason – whom I've grown closest to in the criminal quad – confides that nothing at Kruger is as it seems. Most of my colleagues worked for a defunct firm that defrauded investors. The National Association of Securities Dealers banned Johnny from stockbroking. He's operating under a false name. Shocked, I don't know what to do. I feel naive for trusting Johnny, for allowing enthusiasm to blind me into working for a telemarketing operation rather than the reputable firm I dreamt of.

Most of the rookies hired at the same time as me have quit or been fired. But Johnny keeps recruiting more. He likes to say, 'I just love throwing people against the wall to see how many stick.' The brokers with the biggest numbers on the board cannibalise the clients and sales leads of each broker who leaves. Thanks to my rising new-account numbers, Johnny starts to cut me in on the action.

Ron McDaniel was Johnny's boss in the '80s. The oldest stockbroker in our office, Ron has the tough air of a New Yorker and seems unlikely to get preyed on. He urges me to ignore what the rest are buying and invest in a stock I've never heard of called Microsoft.

A rumour starts that Ron has fallen out of favour with Johnny and that the business he's spent decades building – hundreds of clients, thousands of leads – is on the verge of cannibalisation. To hasten Ron's demise, Curt starts a rumour that Ron is a sex offender in financial difficulty, living out of a car with an underage girlfriend he pretends is his niece.

Johnny summons Ron to see him. As Ron enters Johnny's office, Johnny nods at the criminal quad. When Ron sits down, my quadmates leap up and descend on his workspace like wild beasts. The rookies watch the ransacking from a safe distance. Silent. Still. Wary. Like zebras observing lions devour one of their lame.

'Get over here, Shaun! Getcha some sales leads!' is all I need to hear from Jason.

I spring from my seat and join the frenzy. Intoxicated by the aura of my quadmates' ruthlessness and the value of what I'm about to take, I rifle a drawer and seize paperwork. It takes minutes to cannibalise a lifetime's work. A security guard arrives at the reception.

Ron emerges from Johnny's office. 'Can I just grab my lunch box?'

'No way!' Johnny says.

The security guard, whom Ron has greeted daily for years, yells at Ron as if arresting a murderer: 'You need to come with me!'

My quadmates quarrel over Ron's lunch. Chewing a sandwich, Curt starts dialling Ron's clients.

Ron befriended me, yet all I can think about is exploiting his demise. I call his leads and open my biggest account yet. *There's no stopping me now. I'm applying Mo's advice: it's fuck or be fucked in the business world.*

Working late, Matt and I discuss the rumour that the National Association of Securities Dealers is about to close Kruger down.

'Maybe we should jump ship,' I say, slumped in my chair after pacing all day.

'If we try to get hired by another firm and Johnny finds out,' Matt says, stood up, staring at me, 'God knows what he'll do to us.'

'One thing's for sure: they'll raid our clients.'

'How can we stop them doing that?' Matt asks.

'We can't. But I've got an idea. The account paperwork for everyone's clients is in those drawers by the secretaries. If we photocopy it, then when they call our clients, we can call *all* of theirs.'

'Dude, that's brilliant!' Matt says, reaching out to shake my shoulder. 'There must be thousands of accounts in there! Imagine all the new accounts we could open.'

'There's no way we can photocopy them all in one night. We'll have to do it slowly, over a few weeks, and hope no one shows up and catches us red-handed.'

We photocopy so many accounts, we run out of paper. We have to use the fax machine to keep going.

'Would any of you like to tell me what's been going on with *my* photocopier late at night?' Johnny asks at the sales meeting, his eyes bouncing from broker to broker. 'The counter's showing hundreds of copies have been made.'

The damn machine has a counter! Afraid to look at Matt, I imagine the guard on his way up to show us out.

'Someone in here must have an explanation,' Johnny says, scowling.

Troy and Curt titter.

Johnny marches towards the criminal quad. 'Does someone at the back there know something I don't?'

Radiating guilt, I pray my expression doesn't betray me. My upper body freezes, but my legs shake below the desk. I press my knees together.

'Nope.' Troy juts his chin.

'Look, if no one has an honest explanation, then I'm left with no choice but to assume something dishonest's going on.' Johnny stops by Matt.

Patting Matt's shoulder in a fatherly way, Johnny says, 'Let me tell you what I think's going on.'

The guard appears at the reception.

It's all over! Pressure rises in my body. My face heats up. I feel my pulse in my throat. My eyes dart to the back door. I swivel my chair, ready to dash out.

'Someone here has secured a job at another brokerage.' Johnny takes his hand off Matt, and struts to soft-spoken Paul Lines. 'That someone is photocopying accounts and leads. That someone is not happy here. And who's been whining the most about Kruger Financial? We all know who: Paul Whines.'

My quadmates laugh. Relief washes over me, but tinged with guilt because of Paul.

'My name's Lines,' Paul says, blushing. 'And I certainly haven't been in at nights photocopying or –'

'But you did recently go for a job interview at Yorba Securities.' Johnny smiles with satisfaction at his own omniscience.

Paul's face stiffens. 'You've got the –'

'What you don't understand is,' Johnny says, wagging a finger, 'the stockbrokerage community in Phoenix is a very small one, and I've been around for a *very, very long time*. If something's going on in this community, I know about it. Immediately! Paul Whines, you're fired! Let this be a lesson to the rest of you.' Johnny's eyes range the room and return to Paul. 'And, Whines, don't even think about grabbing your files. The security guard is here to show you out.'

CHAPTER 4

'**I'M BEN COLLINS.** Come through to my office,' says a junior manager at Yorba, where Paul Lines, out to get revenge on Johnny, has arranged an interview for Matt and me in a drab first-floor building with tiny windows overlooking a parking lot. With pockmarked skin and protruding eyes, Ben looks half lizard. He enquires about our backgrounds.

'What can you tell us about Yorba?' I ask.

'Yorba's a small firm, but not a bucket shop like Kruger,' Ben says. 'We have an in-house trader, Jim Detherow, so you won't have to call out of Arizona to place your trades. The manager here's Tim Ford and, unlike Johnny Brasi, he's a class act.'

'Are you pushing house stocks?' Matt asks, referring to the high-commission stocks Kruger specialises in.

'No. You'll be allowed to buy whatever you want. Whatever you feel will make your clients the most money.'

Pleased, I ask, 'Will you provide sales leads?'

'Not really. You'll have to generate your own. But there are a bunch of old accounts you can call.'

'We've got plenty of leads,' I say, alluding to the Kruger accounts we photocopied.

Matt giggles.

'How soon can we start?' I ask.

'Soon as you like.'

Wary of running into co-workers, we enter Kruger late at night to fetch our files. I turn the lights on. We search for boxes to pack our stuff in.

'Let's get out of here fast. Johnny might see the lights on and drive over here. He'd probably kneecap us on the spot,' I say, bracing for him to appear at the reception.

'What would you do if he showed up?'

'Probably fall at his feet, beg for mercy, offer to cut a little finger off.'

'Yeah, me too. Seriously, though, when Johnny finds out, he's gonna kill us,' Matt says, dumping brochures from a box.

'I know. Now that we're actually doing it, I'm shitting myself. Is he really backed by the Mafia or what?'

'That big bald dude that comes to see him with the fancy cane,' Matt says, 'that's one of his gangster backers.'

'Great. Hopefully, they'll take you out to the desert first, then I'll know to leave town. After all, you're his star account opener.'

'Johnny liked you from the get-go,' Matt says. 'That's why he put you in the criminal quad, dude.'

I feel slight guilt. *Mo has blessed our plan. We must be doing the right thing.* 'I've got an idea,' I say, loading a box. 'Seeing as we're moving to Yorba together, why don't we form a partnership?'

'Like how?'

'Like we merge our books, keep putting long hours in and split everything we make. Teaming up will give us more strength to do battle. We can watch out for each other,' I say, gazing at Matt's eyes, willing him to saying yes.

'Sounds good to me.'

While Matt empties a drawer, I structure our roles in the partnership. *He started before me and is a better closer, but I have more experience in analysis and investing.* 'We've got to try to make our clients money. That means you'll have to stop putting them in penny stocks.'

'But that's all I know,' Matt says. 'Johnny's got me programmed with sales pitches for the penny stocks Kruger's making a market in. Look at all of the accounts I just opened with Ryan Murphy.'

'But Ryan Murphy's going to tank, and your clients are going to lose money.'

'What should I do?' Matt asks.

'Ryan Murphy's an environmental company. Let's look at that sector and see if there are any safer companies available. Then you can just vary your sales pitch.'

'I think this partnership's gonna work.'

'Me too.'

We shake hands and hug.

'We can keep each other motivated,' Matt says. 'Let's get the hell outta here!'

'Wish we didn't have to lose this view,' I say, ogling the city lights.

Our first day at Yorba, we scramble to inform our clients about our move. We brace for Kruger to attack. No shots are fired in the morning. War breaks out in the afternoon. Kruger brokers bombard our clients, demanding they keep their accounts with them. Overwhelmed by calls, we juggle the multiple clients we have on hold. I tell them that Kruger is doomed, their brokers are penny-stock outlaws and Yorba is in a position of financial strength, stirring fear of their accounts sinking with the Kruger ship.

Most of my customers transfer. As do Matt's. But Kruger brokers keep calling them. We employ our secret weapon: the accounts we photocopied. Out of fear and respect, we don't call the accounts of the criminal quad. We target the clients of the Kruger brokers who are pestering our clients the most. Our calls are well received. Dozens of Kruger clients accept account-transfer forms and newspaper articles warning about the stocks Kruger specialises in. We wage war at night, when most Kruger brokers are at home. The battle focuses our minds, sharpens our senses. I feel alive. When our back offices begin to process the transfer forms, it becomes apparent we're liberating clients from Kruger that aren't ours. We know Johnny's onto us, that he knows we used his photocopier to steal account information. Expecting him to hit back hard, we do the unthinkable: we call Johnny's clients.

Immediately afterwards, out of fear for both of our lives, Matt insists we go to a pawnshop to buy handguns. Holding a 9mm with a silver barrel and a black grip, I'm shocked and nervous, yet hopeful it will protect me from Johnny. After the purchase, I ask Matt how to load it.

He inserts bullets into a clip that slots into the gun. 'I've put the safety switch on so you won't shoot your nuts off.'

A few days later, our branch manager, Tim Ford – a lanky redhead with an aquiline nose and a ginger moustache who speaks with Southern eloquence – summons us to his office. 'Are you guys calling Kruger accounts that don't belong to you?'

'They're calling our clients,' I say.

'Technically, they have a responsibility to inform your clients that you've left Kruger.'

'But they're talking shit about us,' Matt says.

'Look, I just had a call from Johnny Brasi and he's threatening legal action.'

The prospect of a court case, of getting sued out of the business, quickens my heartbeat.

'I don't know what you guys are up to, and it's probably best we keep it that way, but for the time being I'd like you guys to back off. If Kruger does go out of business, then I don't see how Johnny can bring any legal action against Yorba. So back off and wait it out. On a more positive note, you guys have done a great job opening so many new accounts.'

The truce with Kruger makes time drag. Every day I arrive at work hoping to hear Kruger has folded. It takes two months.

Ben Collins gives us permission to resume calling Kruger accounts. We swoop, like ravens on a warm carcass. It's even easier pickings. The clients we forewarned of Kruger's downfall credit us with fortune-telling powers and transfer their accounts.

Tim Ford calls us into his office.

We're in trouble again.

'I've got something important to tell you.'

'Yes,' I say, tensing up.

'The Yorba Phoenix office is closing down.'

'Oh no,' I say, rolling my eyes.

'But the good news is I'm offering you both jobs with the new firm I'm founding, Detherow & Ford.'

'But we've just transferred all our customers here,' I say, disappointed. 'Are you saying we're going to have to move them again?'

'Yes. We're opening a brand-new office. Paul Lines is moving with us. You guys should check it out.'

We inspect the stockbrokerage but are unhappy with the payout schedule. The more commission we gross, the higher percentage we take home, and Detherow & Ford's schedule implies a 10 per cent pay cut.

Unacceptable. I'm barely making ends meet.

We move, but not to Detherow & Ford.

We're contacted by Radcliff Financial, whose payout schedule is superior to Detherow & Ford's. High up in a skyscraper, Radcliff's manager, Nick Solari, interviews us. We say we don't want to work at a firm like Kruger. Nick insists Radcliff is reputable, we can buy whatever stocks we want and there'll be no pressure to do our clients wrong. Our first day at Radcliff, we're delighted to have a view of the mountains back.

CHAPTER 5

COOLING OFF AFTER work, I go to a yuppie bar and await Matt. Perched on a stool at a circular table, I'm taken by surprise when a tall Japanese woman in a black pencil dress showcasing long, toned legs smiles at me. *Have I intercepted a smile aimed at someone else?* Looking over my shoulder, I see no possible recipients. *The smile's a call to action, but what should I do?* As if my glass of pink wine contains the answer, I guzzle half of it. My face flushes as I prepare for action. I ponder introductions: *Hi! I'm Shaun. I'm here from England. How're you?*

Flicking back long, straight dark hair, streaked blonde and red, she turns her porcelain face slightly and stares at me invitingly. *It's now or never.* I smile, take a deep breath, puff out my chest, grow taller, strut over. But her presence deflates my bravado. 'Er . . . hello. My name's, er, Shaun.'

'My name Sumiko.'

Her smile puts me at ease. 'Where are you from, Sumiko?'

'Japan.'

I jump straight into questions about Japan and tell her about England. Her English is poor, my Japanese nil, but we manage to converse, assisted by body language. She's a fitness instructor from Fukuoka.

Ten minutes later, Matt walks in, winks and positions himself at the bar.

'I've got to go now,' I say.

We exchange numbers. She asks if I'll help move her pool table.

'Sure. No problem.' *What a strange request, but I'd like to see her again.*

'You help, I cook for you.'

'Sounds like a fair trade.'

'What food you like?'

'Curry. Chicken curry.'

'You like spicy?'

'I love it. It's my favourite.'

'You tried kimchi?'

'No. What's that?'

'Surprise,' she says, beaming.

On Saturday, I head for Sumiko's in a Ford Tempo on loan from Mo. I turn into a resort. Tall palms line the entrance. I feel as if I'm driving through a column of giants. I pass fancy flower gardens, an English-style roundabout, buildings reminiscent of an old Spanish village. Stucco facades. Red roof tiles. Plants in terracotta pots. I go up a hill, past a water park, tennis courts, horse stables and a golf course. I park, knock at a second-floor apartment and wait, fidgeting with my clothes.

Sumiko answers, smiling. 'Take shoes off, please.'

Entering, I admire the thick white carpet, her dainty feet swallowed up by its glow. I stop myself short of kicking my shoes off and try to remove them like an English gentleman, relieved today's socks have no holes. My eyes dart all over the place and linger on paintings with the intricate detail prevalent in the Orient. At the foot of each wall are cabinets – black, lacquered and laden with emerald and jade statuettes – with tiny drawer handles suitable for a baby's fingers. Something smells delicious.

'Nice place.' I walk to the pool table and give it a shove. It doesn't budge. 'There's no way I can move this!'

'I call other people. They no show up,' she says, shaking her head.

'Do you want me to help you some other time, then, when there's more of us to move it?'

'Yes. Anyway, I cook.'

'For me?'

'Yes.'

'What did you cook?'

'It's surprise. You hungry?'

'I'm always hungry.'

'Come. Sit. Eat.' She seats me at a glass dining table and lays out food.

'What's that you've got the rice in?' I ask, my stomach rumbling like the mating call of a frog.

'A rice cooker.'

'I've never seen one before. Warm rice all day. That's amazing!'

The most complex recipe I've cooked so far in America is beans on toast. The presence of so much home cooking makes me lose control. I pile a mountain of rice onto my plate and add a pool of curry until my meal resembles a volcano. I shovel heaped forkfuls into my mouth and swallow with minimal chewing, resenting having to stop eating to drink water to dislodge the logjam of rice from my throat. Three plates later, I'm stuffed.

'Try this,' she says.

'What is it?' I ask.

'Kimchi. Here, try some.' Sumiko stabs the kimchi – which looks like the least appetising vegetables on earth mangled together and bathed in blood – with chopsticks and drops some on my plate.

I fork the dollop and budge it around, trying to ascertain its consistency. *Mostly cabbage?*

Radiating encouragement, Sumiko studies my face.

If I don't eat it, I'll break her heart. Mustering enthusiasm, I lift the kimchi, catching a whiff of mildew. I drop my smile but raise it fast. Gingerly, I put the kimchi in my mouth. Cold. Sour. Pickled. Hoping to minimise its contact with my taste buds, I swallow it in one gulp. *Good riddance. Oh shit! Now what?* My tongue starts to burn. While straining to maintain my smile, my cheeks contort. I emit a half-hearted *mmmmm*. I chug water, hoping to wash away the aftertaste. 'It's OK, but I prefer these,' I say, reaching for a fried sweet potato.

Next up is plum wine. Claiming she's allergic to alcohol, Sumiko serves me a glass. It slides down my throat like fruit juice. I glug it greedily. About ten minutes later, the euphoria hits. My face flushes. My smile expands. I talk and talk.

Two more glasses slow my brain down. My thoughts collide. I can't speak. I stare at Sumiko, the walls, the decor . . . The room lurches like a ship. The food in my stomach attempts to escape. I swallow it back down, but the kimchi taste returns with a vengeance.

Sumiko says I'm too drunk to drive and suggests I stay the night. I stagger to her room, undress and get in bed. She joins me. We slide closer. I put my arm around her. Our kimchi breath meets before our lips.

Over the next few months, we date. I refrain from kimchi but not plum wine. Sumiko asks me to move in with her. Dazzled by her company and surroundings, I say yes.

Sumiko looks younger than me but is seven years older. Harmless- and delicate-looking on the surface, she works out for hours with military aggression. Every weekend, she marches up Squaw Peak Mountain. I stumble behind her, panting, begging to rest. She recently divorced an American she met in Japan. From him, she got a green card and a $100,000 settlement, fuel for constant shopping trips to luxury malls. She claims her father, a farmer, prospered from the bubble in Japanese land prices. That she came home from school and saw him and his workers gut, pepper and eat her pet dog. That he was abusive and beat her mother to death with a stick. She weeps as she says these things. I listen, shocked, sad. Her stories make me want to take care of her, but she takes care of me. She replaces my shirts and ties from Ross Dress for Less with designer attire. When she doesn't cook, we dine at expensive restaurants. I drive her sports car to work. When I come home, she massages me and walks on my back. We enjoy living at the resort so much, we plan to buy a house there. To save up, we move to a cheap apartment near my work.

We fall in love, and Sumiko gives me a Japanese name, Satoru. I learn a love song in Japanese and sing it to her often. I recite passages from *Romeo and Juliet* that I learnt in high school, which moves her deeply. Happy at home and work, the rave scene and drugs are far from my mind.

Sumiko says that, because of her bad luck with men, she'll feel more secure if we're married. Emotionally immature, besotted and wanting to make her happy, I agree even though we've only been together for five months.

Sat in a deckchair on the porch overlooking Mo's swimming pool, I tell my aunt I'm engaged.

'I can tell you love Sumiko and want to make her happy,' Mo says, opening a can of Budweiser. 'You have a tendency to want to make people happy – at times to your own detriment. But from a more practical perspective, have you thought about how this may benefit you?'

'No. What do you mean?'

'You can never visit your mum and dad because they won't let you back in the country when they see you've overstayed your visitor's visa. If you're married on paper for three years, then you have the right to a green card. You can also apply for naturalisation and become a legal alien.'

'How does that work?'

'Immigration calls you for interviews from time to time. Provided they're convinced that you're a couple living together with mail and bills in joint names, there shouldn't be any problems.'

'Then I won't have to worry about being deported,' I say.

'I'll run everything by a lawyer and get back to you.'

I tell Sumiko what Mo said, and she agrees that I should apply for a green card so we can travel overseas and I no longer have to work illegally.

Before marrying Sumiko, I want my parents' approval. With Mum, Dad and my sister, Karen, visiting at Christmas, I plan a New Year's Eve party to celebrate our engagement.

On the way to pick them up at the airport, I worry about them finding fault with Sumiko. Despite her limited vocabulary, Sumiko charms them with her demure smile and respectful nature. Entering our apartment, my family admire the decor and Asian artwork.

Later on, when Sumiko's cooking, Mum says, 'She's lovely. So beautiful.'

'I'm so glad you like her,' I say, smiling with relief.

'Yes,' Karen says, 'she's stunning, but I wish I could have a proper conversation with her. And, Shaun, you speaking pidgin English all the time won't improve her language skills. She'll only learn if you speak properly to her.'

'I know, but it's easier this way,' I say.

Sumiko goes out of her way to make them welcome. She discovers Mum loves sweet pancakes and makes them daily for breakfast. Dad says he likes savoury pancakes with bacon, and the next morning they're there.

Sumiko studies Mum and Dad cooking traditional English Sunday dinner. A whole chicken. A tray laden with yellow roast potatoes. Dad making gravy with Oxo cubes. Mum putting plates in the oven puzzles Sumiko.

'You cook plates?' Sumiko asks, making us laugh.

'England's so cold, we put plates in the oven to keep the food warm,' Mum says.

The following week, Sumiko cooks English style.

'She'll do anything to please,' Mum says in the living room. 'You're lucky. You've found a good woman there.'

'Yes, that's what most men want,' Karen says, 'someone to slave on them.'

'Whenever I offer to help with the cooking, she scowls at me!' I say.

In the evenings, Sumiko massages Mum. At first, Mum is delighted, but the massage lasts longer each night, stretching over an hour. Getting massaged, ticklish Mum starts to laugh, offending Sumiko.

'Why you laugh? You no like massa?' Sumiko asks, frowning.

'It's so embarrassing. The more I try not to laugh, the more I want to laugh.'

Aware of Mum's interest in herbal remedies, Sumiko decides to brew a tonic to pep us up on Christmas Eve. She purchases fresh ginseng root and boils it in a large saucepan with various herbs and spices, filling the house with a stale-sweat smell.

'Ginseng good. Clean blood. Make happy. Good for man. Good for woman.'

'Anything that smells that vile must be good for you,' Dad says. 'But I'll probably give it a miss.'

'Hush,' Mum whispers. 'You'll have to have some or she'll be offended.'

'I'll give it a go,' Karen says. 'I'm into herbal stuff. But it does smell bad.'

We watch, fascinated, as she tends to the brew, stirring, tasting, adding more ingredients for two days, until she feels it's ready.

Before going to a Christmas Eve open house at Mo's, happily anticipating the festivities, we gather in the kitchen. Sumiko spoons out the brew as an aperitif. As they sip, Karen's and Mum's faces contort.

Can it be as bad as kimchi?

Forcing a smile, Mum says, 'It's nice. Thank you, Sumiko.'

Dad barely touches it and says, 'I can feel it working already.' We laugh at him.

'Yes, it's interesting,' Karen says, trying not to grimace.

I pretend to drink. When Sumiko turns her back, I pour mine down the sink. Sumiko drinks a large glass.

Mo puts on a lavish spread. We listen to records and reminisce about Christmases past. While everyone is having fun, Sumiko whispers that she wants to leave. Pointing at her sickly expression and face dappled with pink blotches, I tell my family she's unwell. On the way home, she starts yelling and screaming in Japanese, ignoring me.

'I think you drank too much ginseng,' I say, concerned. 'You'll have to wait for it to wear off.'

'*Damare konoyarou!*' She repeatedly punches the windshield with a bejewelled fist, so hard it cracks the glass.

'Jesus! Sumiko, calm down. Do you want me take you to a hospital?' I ask.

'No hospital! Home!'

Hours later, my family arrives in a taxi.

'What happened to the car window?' Mum asks, entering the apartment.

Can't tell them about Sumiko. They'll worry, and might want me to call the wedding off. I better take the blame. 'Er . . . we had a bit of a row and I smashed it.'

'Some row,' Dad says. 'Smashing a window's a bit extreme.'

Accepting my lie, they shake their heads and tut. The next day, trading thankful expressions, we watch Sumiko tip the tonic down the sink, declaring it made her crazy. Sumiko becomes more attentive. She takes Mum and Karen to the Phoenician resort for pancakes with strawberries and cream. In the evening, she cooks sumptuous Japanese dishes, and stops scolding Mum for laughing during the massage.

My family help us prepare for the New Year's Eve party and have no objections to our engagement. My American relatives and few friends congratulate us, and when it strikes twelve we celebrate the New Year, listening to gunshots outside. In Dad's speech, he says meeting Sumiko was the highlight of his visit and she's 'a very special lady'.

Six months into our relationship, we marry at a courthouse in Glendale. With local family members, we celebrate at TGI Friday's. In our honeymoon hotel, the lack of TV channels upsets Sumiko. She throws things around, generating a noise complaint. The manageress threatens to chuck us out. Sumiko doesn't care. It takes hours to calm her down. Hurt and disappointed, I put the outburst down to her emotions running high that day.

CHAPTER 6

NICK SOLARI, MY new boss, is a tall, sincere man with a wispy beard and owlish eyes. At the 6 a.m. sales meeting, he opens a book, *Rhinoceros Success* by Scott Alexander. We gaze in worshipful silence as he reads.

'Somewhere, deep in the jungle where few dare venture, there lives a wild animal called success. It is rare and much sought after, but only a few ever risk tracking it down to capture it. The hunt is long, hard, and risky. There are many hardships along the way that tear at your heart and soul. The jungle brush throws up an almost impenetrable barrier. Bugs constantly bite and bore into your skin. Poisonous snakes, crocodiles, and other dangerous animals present very real dangers to your safety. The incessant, burning sun is your constant, relentless companion until nightfall. Then the temperature drops to near freezing and you long for the burning sun against your already reddened, blistered skin.'

The quote is so pertinent to my life that the other brokers in the room fade from existence. *Nick knows exactly how I feel. Becoming a millionaire is going to take longer than anticipated because of the hardships I've encountered. Every time I start to do well, I'm forced to change firms and rebuild. I'm making some money but spending more and relying on Sumiko too much. Despite setbacks, I'm determined to succeed.*

'At times you feel weak and dizzy from exhaustion. Success seems at times an imaginary creature, impossible to capture. But you continue on, because you are too deep in the jungle now to head back without your prize.'

I'm exhausted from long days of cold-calling, but I have a solid pipeline of leads and a growing client book. I'm deep in the jungle. I can't stand the thought of quitting, of everything I've worked for getting cannibalised.

'Months go by, maybe years. Still, no sign of success. It is a clever animal, rarely exposing itself, always quick to flee should it sense danger of being caught. Success is so uncommon, so unique, and so challenging that you must have it! No other animal requires so much skill to hunt and capture.'

My second year. I don't want to change firms any more. I need stability to succeed.

'As rare as the animal is, even more rare are the men and women who set up their own expeditions in its pursuit. You and I are part of that group who must have success. The rewards are great. We know that. We also know that the hunt is difficult, at best. We know the odds are against us. We know many have failed and few will even attempt the expedition. When we know all this, we know that success is for us!'

Johnny did me a favour forcing me to cold-call from the phone book. Being thrown against his wall strengthened me to take on anything in stockbroking.

'Success is not easy. It is a truly difficult animal to capture, requiring lots of work, quick thinking, desire, and persistence on the part of the hunter. This, then, is your "rhinoceros manual" for your greatest hunt. Use it and you will not only achieve more success quicker, but you will also have the greatest time of your life charging through the jungle. Let's go! Right now is the season for success!'

Yes, I have the qualities of the hunter. And manic energy to work longer than my colleagues, guaranteeing I will eventually rise above them.

'Are you stockbrokers rhinos whose thick skin can't be affected by petty rejections on the phone?'

'Yes!'

'I can't hear you! Are you rhinos?'

'Yes!' we roar like jungle animals.

'Then let's break some records dialling for dollars today!'

We leap from our seats and attack our phones, buzzing with the energy of a new firm on the rise.

Radcliff's top producer is Max Purcell, a short, fair-haired man with long ginger eyelashes and a bulbous nose, who speaks in a deep, threatening Texan drawl. His territory is the biggest office at the back. Every so often, he emerges with a trade ticket and dashes past the quads, his body tilted as if leaning into a strong wind. His smarmy manner makes me dislike him. I want to earn a back office, to outdo him. But how?

CHAPTER 7

I HEAR ON the radio that 808 State – a rave group from Manchester – is playing in Las Vegas. Sumiko agrees to go. The six-hour drive whizzes by in a whirl of excitement. Spotting Las Vegas, I'm amazed by the skyscrapers and the unnatural glow in the sky, as if something extraterrestrial is happening. I park at the venue. The techno *boom-boom-boom* raises goose-pimples on my forearms.

Walking to the club, Sumiko glowers at the glitter girls in the queue, all skimpy clothes and leg flesh. Pouting like a petulant child, she folds her arms. 'We not going in there!'

'What do you mean?' I ask. 'Are you joking?'

'Don't want you round those women!'

'What? I just drove all this way!' I yell, anger heating my face up.

'We not going in!'

'I'm here to see 808 State, not the women. I love you! I haven't come all this way with my wife to find another woman. That's ridiculous!'

'We not go in, Shaun!'

We argue for 15 minutes. She grows enraged. Fed up, I agree to go home.

Stewing in disappointment, I speed along the freeway, wary of Sumiko, her stiff body radiating heat with a kimchi tang. Afraid of provoking her, I say nothing.

I'm concentrating on the road when she screams and claws my face. My skin burns. Amid the yelling and shoving, the wheel is knocked. The car shoots off the freeway – my body braces – and bumps over the desert. I pump the brakes. Expecting a rollover, I lock my arms, grit my teeth, push my back against the seat. The car spins out of control across the Mojave, kicking up plumes of sand like a dust devil. My head whirls as if I'm on a waltzer ride.

Time stretches, each second unfolding with a chance of death. When the spinning slows, relief creeps in. The car skids past a boulder and stops short of a tree that looks half cactus. My body goes limp.

'What the fuck! You almost got us killed!'

Sumiko stares at me like a sad animal, tears in her eyes. My anger softens. I blame myself for taking her to a nightclub.

After that, every few weeks she explodes in the house. She throws things around and smashes plates. Young, naive, I don't know how to handle her. Remembering how Ecstasy melted my stress away, I crave that feeling.

I tell Matt, 'Sumiko's going to Japan soon. I've gone so long without raving, I'm starting to hear *wolves* howling for me to come out and party.'

On the Saturday Sumiko leaves, Matt drives me to Phoenix's run-down warehouse district.

On a street corner, a hobo accosts us. 'Got any change?'

'Here's a dollar,' I say. 'Don't spend it on drugs.'

We walk past the Madison Street jail, a tall, bleak building with tiny bulletproof windows. The music leaking from the Silver Dollar Club tingles the skin on my forearms, bringing something inside of me alive. We pay and enter a large, dark room packed with people dancing. When the house music slows down, hundreds of arms shoot up.

I laugh at a large face projected onto a wall: a camp old man in Goth make-up. He peeps at me, grins and stares ahead as if nothing happened.

'Did you see that?' I say, hoping the face peeps again.

'What?' Matt asks.

'That face just looked at me and smiled.'

'Did you take drugs already and not tell me?'

'I wish. Let's get some Ecstasy, shall we?' I say.

'I'll ask around.'

'I like it. It's like an English club only much smaller. Maybe there's hope for raves in Phoenix after all. I'll be right back. I've got to take a piss.' I leave Matt at the bar. In the stall I try to enter, two muscle boys in wife-beaters are having sex.

'Sorry,' I say.

'Join us or get out. Either way, close the goddam door!' one says.

The next stall is empty. All done, I find Matt chatting to a bull of a Mexican American dressed in black with a steel nose-ring.

'This is Moo,' Matt says.

'Hello, Moo,' I say.

'Hi,' Moo says in a high-pitched whisper.

'Moo's got X,' Matt says.

'How much for?' I ask, excited.

'Twenty-five,' Matt says.

'I'll take one,' I say.

'Two,' Matt says.

'Fifty dollars first,' Moo says in the voice of a little girl. Moo does the deal and leaves. Familiar with the taste of Ecstasy, I chew it.

'Why're you chewing it?' Matt asks.

'So I know if it's bunk or not.'

'It's gotta taste gross! If they're bunk, I'll beat that Moo's ass.'

'No, it's good. It tastes right. We'll be off our heads here soon. Me before you, because it hits you faster when you chew it.'

'Now you tell me! Gee, thanks!'

We hover around the bar, waiting for our highs to arrive. It takes 30 minutes for my knees to buckle. I lean against Matt.

'Y'all right?' Matt asks.

'Never felt better.' The sides of my head tingle, warmth inches in. It sweeps across my face, the nape of my neck and creeps down my spine. My diaphragm and chest move in harmony as my breathing slows down. Each exhalation releases more tension. I grow hot but relaxed. 'It's great . . . that we met,' I say, my eyeballs flickering upwards. 'I would never have had the balls to steal those Kruger accounts without you.'

'At the rate we're opening new accounts, we'll be millionaires in a few years.'

'Isn't it great?' I say.

'Fucking A!'

We high-five.

'Five years from now, we'll be at Merrill Lynch, living in mansions in Paradise Valley.'

'Driving BMWs and badass Japanese sports cars,' Matt says.

'Taking holidays all over the world.'

We laugh.

'You know what else I'm going to do when I have the money?' I ask.

'Move to Utah, convert to Mormonism and have ten wives,' Matt says.

'No, silly. I'm going to throw proper raves in Arizona so people can experience how I felt when I started raving.'

'It's all country and western and metal and rap out here. There's not enough interest.'

'By the time we're rich, it'll be more popular. I'll figure it out. Raves for thousands of people, not a few hundred like this.'

'Raves would be awesome out in the desert.'

'I'm getting . . . like . . . a rush of energy,' I say. 'Ready to dance?'

'Hell, yeah!'

The dancers on a raised area pull us up. Inhibitions gone, I move effortlessly to the music. I close my eyes and let the music move me. I seem to float. Rush after rush sweeps my body like electricity.

Are you ready? goes the song. *Jump everybody jump everybody jump . . .*

We leap from platform to platform. When DJ Sandra Collins plays The Prodigy's 'Charly', I close my eyes and imagine I'm at an English rave. We dance our way to the front of the main stage, dripping sweat, hands in the air, eyeballs rolling towards heaven, hugging the strangers around us, grinning at the throng of freaks below. I feel right at home.

CHAPTER 8

'I'VE GOT AN idea that might get us investors that doesn't involve cold-calling,' I say to Matt one evening, exhausted from dialling more than 500 numbers.

'What?' Matt says, hanging up the phone.

'Dumpster diving,' I say.

'Dumpster diving!' Matt frowns. 'You're crazy.'

'Have you ever thought how much client info there must be in the trash brokerages throw away?'

'No,' Matt says.

'Watch this.' I stick my hand in a garbage can, pull out a pile of paperwork and wave it at Matt. 'Imagine if our competitors got their hands on this. Names. Addresses. Telephone numbers.'

'That makes sense,' Matt says, nodding.

'We can cold-call five hundred people a day all month long in the hope some are looking to invest in the stock market and convert a tiny fraction into new accounts, or we can find people who're already investing by going through trash.'

'It'll be like those brokerages did all the legwork, the cold-calling, the bullshit, for us.'

'Exactly. If it works out, we won't have to bust our arses on the phones so much.'

'Where do we dumpster-dive at?'

'Local brokerages listed in the phone book.'

We buy garbage gloves, trash bags, box cutters. We target Bezner Securities because Len Gleeson and Jimmy Shargal – the two brokers who gave the motivational speech at Kruger – recently threatened to blow Matt's car up over a mutual client.

Matt drives us to Bezner, on a street by Metrocenter Mall. From the car, we survey the dumpster, enclosed by three walls, with a gate at the front.

'No one'll notice us with all these shoppers,' I say.

'Let's go for it,' Matt says.

We rush to the gate. I push it open. 'If security comes, let's say we're looking for something we threw away by accident.'

'We're wearing suits. They're not gonna fuck with us.' Matt snaps his gloves on.

Peering in the dumpster, I say, 'At least it's full of trash.'

We grab bags and slice them open. The stink of coffee and putrefying fast food assaults us. I search six bags. Find nothing. Grow disappointed.

Matt climbs in and passes out more bags. 'Bezner's trash has gotta be in here somewhere.'

A man and woman peep over the wall. Imagining they're security guards, I freeze.

'Ignore them,' Matt whispers. 'Just nosy-ass shoppers.'

They walk away.

I slash a bag open and sift through the contents. Spotting account info, I smile. 'Yes! We're in business.'

'No shit! Lemme see.' Matt's eyes widen as if admiring treasure. We high-five. Encouraged, we tear through bags and find more paperwork. We stash everything in the car and take off.

Poaching clients who've written letters of complaint to Bezner is easy. One transfers a six-figure portfolio to me. We return to that dumpster many times.

Our next target is Detherow & Ford, occupied by our former co-workers. I relish the mission, thinking of it as payback for them trying to shaft us on the payout schedule.

At night, we park in an empty lot. The dumpster looks like an easy target. But approaching it, I spot a padlock. 'Shit. It's locked.'

'Fuck, dude! Now what?' Matt says.

Noticing the cleaners at work, I say, 'Let's scope this out. Follow me.' When I can see into the entrance, I stop. A cleaner is pushing a trolley; others are putting trash by the door.

'Check those bags out!' Matt says.

'There's no way we can grab them with these cleaners around,' I say, salivating at the sight of the bags. My thoughts gallop, searching for a solution. 'At least we know how they operate. I say we sit in the car and wait to see what they do next.'

We spy for two hours. The cleaners put the bags in the dumpster – but lock it. We decide to return the following night, hoping to snatch the bags before the cleaners dump them. Matt times my journey from the car to the office and back: 42 seconds. To get the bags into the car should take three snatches, so we need the cleaners to be absent for longer than two minutes.

The next night, we watch the cleaners. When they disappear into the building, we rush to the entrance, grab bags and chuck them in the car. A cleaner spots our second snatch and shouts. A posse of cleaners pursues us, all yelling in Spanish.

'Let's get the fuck out of here!' I say, sprinting to the car. Basking in the fun, thrill and danger of it all, I can't stop laughing.

Matt screeches away. The car fills with the stink of burnt tyres.

'Now they know what we look like, we'd better leave that one for a while,' I say.

Not all of our dumpster missions are successful. Many are locked. Some are accessible but the paperwork is shredded. Security patrols chase us from others. However, the dumpster diving boosts my numbers on the board – numbers my life increasingly revolves around.

CHAPTER 9

'DID YOU FUCK blonde pussy?' Sumiko yells when I walk through the door after work.

'What're you talking about?' I ask, frowning.

'Every American guy, they love blonde pussy,' she says, wagging a finger. 'England guy probably same.'

'I've been at the office all day, making money so we can save up and get a house.' Exasperated, I stomp up the stairs and take a shower. I hear her destroying the kitchen, yelling in Japanese.

The next day, she apologises, and smothers me with kindness. But every few weeks, the cycle repeats. Afraid for her health and our marriage, I urge her to see a doctor. He prescribes Zoloft. Much to my relief, her anger disappears and we start behaving like newlyweds.

Sumiko's sister, Shuzuko, flies in from Fukuoka. Wearing a white suit, a veil and enough rosary beads and crucifix necklaces to deck out a nunnery, Shuzuko floats towards us in the airport like an apparition of the Virgin Mary with a Japanese face. She speaks no English, so I greet her in Japanese. The sisters hug, chat and giggle like schoolgirls. In our apartment, they cook miso soup. At night, they pray in the living room. I appreciate Shuzuko's calming influence on Sumiko.

A few days later, I arrive home at night, ravenous, open the door and step inside.

Sumiko leaps at me and blocks my way. 'You fucking asshole! You motherfucker!'

'What've I done?' I ask, my stomach tightening. 'Sumiko, please calm down. Tell me what's wrong.'

Yelling in Japanese, she chases me around the coffee table. Shuzuko drops to her knees, closes her eyes and prays.

'Why're you mad at me? What's going on?'

'Shuzuko told me my medicine Western poison. You and the doctor sending me to heaven to join my mom. Shaun, why you try kill me?' She starts bawling.

I turn to Shuzuko. 'What the fuck did you do that for?'

Shuzuko shuts her eyes tighter.

'I'm not trying to kill you! The medicine is supposed to help you! I think you need some right now!'

'Shuzuko put medicine down food disposer. Medicine gone. How could you, you bastard?'

Sumiko marches to the kitchenette, tears cupboards open and launches dishes. One almost hits my head. Another crash-lands on the coffee table, breaking the top into jagged pieces of glass. Terrified, I dance around the living room, dodging plates.

'Why you try kill me, Shaun?' she yells, throwing a can opener at me.

'Your sister's wrong. I'm not trying to kill you,' I say.

Whispering in Japanese, Shuzuko fondles rosary beads, shards of glass bouncing around her like hail.

'Bastard!' Sumiko charges at me.

I run around the coffee table. She closes in, clawing me at every opportunity, ripping skin off my neck and chest. Hoping to lock myself in the bedroom, I dash inside but fail to shut the door in time. Sumiko hurtles in and flushes me out. Hoping to trick her into following me to the far end of the living room, I head in that direction. She falls for it. I sprint back to the bedroom, lock the door and heave a chest of drawers behind it. She pounds on the door but can't get in. I sit on the bed, my heartbeat rapid. When the banging and yelling stops, I go to sleep.

At 5 a.m., my alarm beeps, startling me back to reality. *It's going to wake the sisters!* My arm lashes out to turn it off. I listen. Silence. *It must be safe.* I put my suit on and shift the chest of drawers. I open the door, cautiously, scanning every inch coming into view – no sign of hostilities. I step out, surprised by the sight that greets me. It's an apartment-cum-chapel: Christian artefacts on the carpet; rosary beads and crucifixes on the walls; a poster of the Virgin Mary cradling the baby Jesus, their heads emitting an eerie yellow glow; flames flickering from rows of candles adjacent to the sleeping women, illuminating two pale faces so at peace with the world they appear to have the auras of angels; Sumiko, wearing a jade rosary and gold crucifix, a flame casting the shadow of a bottle of holy water down one side of her face. Praying not to wake them, I tiptoe towards the front door. I reach for the knob, vigilant for signs of life.

Sumiko springs her eyes open like a vampire getting staked through the heart. She yells something in Japanese akin to a battle-cry and pounces like a cat. I spin around. As her face lands between my legs, I feel her teeth graze my skin as they clamp shut. Wanting to get my penis out of harm's way, I recoil. She falls on the floor, a piece of cloth dangling from her mouth.

My eyes shoot to my trousers where my boxers are visible. 'Look what you did!' I yell, pointing at the hole. 'I can't go to work now!'

Shuzuko opens her eyes and makes the sign of the cross. Sumiko springs at me again. Sprinting for the bedroom, I bump into Shuzuko, knocking her over. Sumiko catches up, grabs my collar and rips my shirt, the buttons flying off like tiddlywinks. Feeling her nails dig in and strip away skin, I wince. I push her away.

At my wits' end, I lock myself in the bedroom and dial 911. 'My wife's out of control. I'm worried she might hurt herself. I don't know how to stop her . . .'

'You no call police!' Sumiko yells, thundering on the door.

When I hear a radio crackling, I emerge to two policemen, stood stunned, watching Sumiko wriggling on the floor like a demented worm, sobbing, slobbering on the carpet, slurring in Japanese, and Shuzuko praying over her, hands together, kneeling, eyes closed, swaying.

'Goddam!' says a policeman, shaking his head.

I explain recent events. The police disapprove of Shuzuko disposing of the Zoloft. When questioned, the sisters say nothing, but Sumiko eventually provides some basic answers. The police take the sisters to cool off at a friend of Sumiko's.

Thank God it's all over! I sink into the sofa, flop my arms down and try to stabilise my breathing. *Her behaviour makes no sense. Maybe she'll get back on Zoloft and things will normalise. Need to call the office. Tell them I'm running late.* I pick up the phone and start to dial.

The door bursts open. Sumiko charges in, her face contorting as if she's in the throes of satanic possession. Everything happens in slow motion. Starting to rise, I drop the phone. Sumiko swerves and grabs the iron from the countertop. She careers straight at me, raising the iron to strike my head. Hemmed in by two walls, I only have seconds to act. *Running to the bedroom will expose the side of my head to the iron.* Staying put, I raise my forearms to shield myself.

'You no kill me, *bastard*!' she yells, thrusting the iron at my head.

As I duck, the iron glances off my shoulder. Sumiko runs into me, bounces off, loses her footing and collapses onto the coffee table. Jagged pieces of glass puncture her body. We both stare, paralysed by the sight of blood gushing from her limbs.

If the bleeding isn't stopped, she's going to die. I want to do something but don't know what.

The two policemen from earlier rush in, radio for help and order me outside. Siren noises grow louder.

Come on, Sumiko, pull through. You'll be OK.

Emergency vehicles fill the parking lot. Police surround me.

'What did you do to her?'

'Why'd you do it?'

'You attacked her, didn't you?'

'What made you do it?'

The firestorm of questions frazzles my brain. Over and over, I sputter the truth: 'I called you out so something like this wouldn't happen. The two cops let her give them the slip and look what happened. How's this my fault?' No matter what I say, they insist I assaulted Sumiko and that it's in my best interests to come clean. I reiterate my innocence. They don't believe me. *I'll soon be joining Jason Park in jail.*

A policewoman steps forward. 'Take your shirt off.'

I comply, embarrassed by the scratches.

She examines my body while the rest remain silent. 'Look at those marks. This man's obviously a victim of domestic violence.'

Familiar with the term from the news – used to describe women – I blush. A policeman confirms I made the emergency call.

'You're free to go,' the policewoman says.

'Is she OK?' I ask.

'A few severe cuts, but she'll be all right,' she says.

At least I'm not going to jail! I trudge away, grateful to her, relieved, a headache setting in. *Shit. I'm so late for work, the boss'll be mad.* I rush into the apartment, put clean clothes on and dash out.

In the office, my colleagues see the scratches on my face and neck, clearly the work of a woman's fingernails. Mockery rains down upon me. Only the secretaries offer sympathy. They advise me not to see any clients.

When the stock market closes, I go home for lunch. The door opens, surprising me. Sumiko limps in, her legs bandaged. Shuzuko takes one look at me and her eyes widen as if I've grown horns. She hisses something in Japanese, grabs a bottle of holy water, rips the top off, splashes me, collapses on the floor and starts wriggling around, weeping. I'm wiping holy water off my face when Sumiko yells her battle-cry. She chases me out of the apartment, but she can only hobble, so it's easy to keep her at bay. Determined to catch up, she almost tumbles down the stairs. We end up in the parking lot, looping around cars, her swearing in Japanese. We're playing cat and mouse when her ex-husband screeches into the lot. He jumps out of his car. Burly. Bearded. Grinning slyly.

'What're you doing here?' I ask.

Sumiko yells at him in Japanese.

'Sumiko called me from the hospital and explained what'd happened.'

'She's still wild. Why don't you take her to your place till she calms down?' I say.

His laugh destroys my hope. 'Hell, no! I don't want her back. I've got a refill for her medication, and I'm gonna take her sister straight to the airport and put her on the next flight back to Japan. Look at those injuries. This is ridiculous, man! Her sister shoulda never told her to stop taking her medication. Look, Sumiko, you've gotta take your medication!'

'Go to hell!' Sumiko yells.

He coaxes Sumiko inside and insists she take the Zoloft.

'I feel so bad about all this,' I say.

'Don't sweat it,' he says. 'The cops used to come out all the time when I was married to her.'

'What?'

'Yeah, I'd call them or the neighbours'd call them. The cops used to say, "Oh no, not her again." She used to break all our most expensive shit.'

I'm shocked, yet relieved that I haven't caused Sumiko's anger. But the more I think about it, the more I fear it can't be fixed.

CHAPTER 10

TWO HOURS AFTER the opening of the stock market, Matt shows up for work.

Exhausted from fielding calls from both of our clients, I say, 'If you're not going to respond to my wake-up calls, I've got a better idea.'

'What?' Matt asks, making a cup of coffee.

'Why don't you move from your mum's to a place near the office? That way I can bang on your door in the morning and we can walk to work together.'

'And then I don't have to be bothered with my piece-of-shit car,' Matt says, nodding.

'The rent's dirt cheap round here, too. Being right by the office makes it much easier for me to be in here more. No commute. None of that shit.'

Matt moves, and for a while everything seems fine. He shows up at work one morning in a new convertible BMW, wearing an Armani suit.

'Where's all that come from?' I ask.

'I struck gold,' Matt says, flaunting a Motorola cellphone the size of a house brick. 'I'm dating Amelia Guss.'

'Who?'

'Dr Guss's daughter!' he says, referring to his biggest client.

'Does Dr Guss know?'

'Yeah, he's all good with it.' Matt pulls a piece of paper from his pocket. 'Check this account statement out.'

'*Wow!*' I say, ogling the seven-digit balance.

Matt beams. 'He's gonna transfer that money to his account with me. Not only is he a doctor, he owns a printing company, businesses, property all over the freaking place.'

'Good job, Matt!' We high-five. 'How soon are you marrying his daughter?'

'Asshole!' he says, punching my arm.

I'm pleased until Matt starts disappearing for days on end, gallivanting with Amelia. When he does show up, he parks the BMW at the foot of the building, blazes into the office, places some massive trades and takes off. His production remains high, but his behaviour upsets our boss – and me. He's no longer building the pipeline of leads brokers need to replenish their business. I can't express my frustration because his contribution to our partnership has nudged above mine, and he barely spends time with me any more. Getting pushed out of his social life is hurting me, too.

A few months later, the fling with Amelia ends. Matt loses his new toys. He stops coming to work altogether. Worried, I go and bang on his door.

A woman answers, tanned, barely clothed, wide-eyed, her bright-red lipstick smudged. 'What do you want?'

'I'm Shaun. I work with Matt.'

'He's . . . er . . .' She casts a sly look over her shoulder and frowns at me. 'He's feeling . . . sick and doesn't want to talk to anyone right now.' Before I can respond, she slams the door.

Hurt, disappointed, I walk away.

Days later, I spot Matt leaving his apartment. Excited, I increase my stride. 'How's it going, Matt?'

His face tightens. 'I've gotta level with you, Shaun. I've been fucking off work to do crystal meth and party.'

'What?' Shocked, I pause to think of an appropriate response. 'Matt, I like to party just as much as anyone, but I'm not going to throw away all the hard work I've done just to get high all the time.'

'I'm just not motivated to come to work any more.'

'Matt, how can you give up so easily?' I ask, my disappointment boiling into anger. 'Look at everything we've been through since Kruger! I can't believe you're letting our friendship and partnership down like this!' Focused on success, I don't understand the nature of his burn-out or how he can drop our goal. 'All we've got to do is stick to the programme and we're going to be rich, for fuck's sake!'

'I'm so sorry, Shaun. I just don't know what to tell you,' he says, unable to look me in the eye.

'Tell me you're going to stop doing drugs and come to work!'

'I can't.'

'You're going to throw your career down the toilet just to get high? I can't believe I'm hearing this from you, the best closer I've ever met!' I say, waving my arms like a madman.

Matt stares at his sneakers, a yellow tint in his eyes, their brightness gone.

'What am I supposed to tell our boss?'

'I don't care,' he says in a resolute tone.

His answer stings like a jab to the nose. But I still want to help him. 'Well, I do care! I'm going to tell Nick you're sick. That'll give you time to snap out of this,' I say, feeling helpless, unable to come to terms with losing my friend, my partner.

Matt doesn't return to work. I beg Nick to give him more time and I pay to keep Matt licensed. After a few months, Nick officially fires Matt. The battle for our partnership is over. I suffer a kind of relationship break-up heartache. I worry about Matt and dream about what could have been. The reality crushes me for a few days. I emerge resolved to work solo.

Matt gets evicted. He telephones sporadically.

'Shaun, I need your help, man.'

'What is it, Matt?'

'Some dudes from the west side are trying to kill me.'

'How did that happen?'

'Over dope. I need you to call this number and tell them I've left town.'

'Bloody hell!' I'm shocked, but our bond is so strong, I keep helping him. 'All right. Give me the number.'

Months go by before the next call: 'I can't speak to you on the phone. Meet me at the George & Dragon at two.'

'Is everything OK?'

'I'll tell you what happened when I see you.'

In the British pub, I almost don't recognise the man limping towards me, wearing glasses, his face gaunt, his skin jaundiced. I'm shocked and saddened by what drugs have reduced Matt to.

'What happened?' I ask, dropping off a stool to give him a hug.

'I just got outta jail.'

'Oh no! What for?'

'I got in a car chase with the cops,' he says.

'You're shitting me!'

'They rammed my vehicle. I crashed and ended up in hospital. That's why I'm limping.'

'What're you going to do now?'

'I'm gonna move to Georgia. Try living with my dad down there. I just wanted to meet you one last time, say goodbye and thank you for everything.' Matt's tired eyes glaze over with emotion and I feel his pain.

'Matt, I don't know what to say. This is so fucking sad.' I hug him tightly, squeezing my eyes shut, tears welling. *I hoped to still hang out as friends. No chance now.* I'm too emotional to speak; the highlights of our two years together flow through my mind.

He calls from Georgia to tell me he's made it OK. I never hear from him again.

Partying destroyed Matt's career, yet I don't perceive any danger. *I'm too strong-minded to end up like Matt. I'm only taking Ecstasy every now and then when clubbing. No big deal. I'm a functional, recreational drug user. My habit will never get out of control.*

CHAPTER 11

RESOLVED TO SUCCEED on my own, I set my sights on ousting Max as the biggest producer. Six months later, all the records on the board are Max's and mine. In '94, Goldstein & Associates buy out Radcliff Financial. I flourish at the bigger firm.

FOR THE RECORD

MOST # DIALS/DAY	590 SHAUN ATTWOOD
MOST # LEADS/DAY	31 SHAUN ATTWOOD
MOST # NEW ACCOUNTS/DAY	9 SHAUN ATTWOOD
MOST # NEW ACCOUNTS/MONTH	19 SHAUN ATTWOOD
HIGHEST GROSS PRODUCTION/DAY	$10,000 MAX PURCELL
HIGHEST GROSS PRODUCTION/MONTH	$27,500 MAX PURCELL
LARGEST TICKET (GROSS)	$10,000 MAX PURCELL
LARGEST TICKET (INVESTMENT)	$1 MILLION MAX PURCELL
MOST CONSECUTIVE TICKETS/DAY	SHAUN ATTWOOD
LARGEST NEW ACCOUNT	1.2 MILLION MAX PURCELL

For a year, Sumiko has been stable on Zoloft – convincing me she's cured. We go clubbing, but I stop taking drugs. We buy a two-storey house in Ahwatukee, an urban village by the Pointe South Mountain Resort, where she lived when we first met. Moving to the area she loves makes her happier.

To generate more business, I unleash Sumiko's cooking on my clients. Before they arrive, Sumiko stays up all night, pacing from pot to pan like the commander of a war room, stinking the house up with seafood recipes. When my clients arrive, she serves too many dishes to fit on our dining table. After eating, my clients loosen their clothes, invite us to their homes and more business follows. With my career and marriage flourishing, I'm high on life. Drugs slip further from my mind.

I dumpster-dive less, but it's still lucrative. Targeting a brokerage in Mesa run by Kruger refugees, I set off at dusk. The dumpster is full of client paperwork. With no one around, I take my time loading bags into the Toyota Celica. *It's all so easy.*

Driving home on the US-60, revelling in the thrill of stealing clients from ex-colleagues, tapping the wheel, bobbing my head, crooning to radio tunes, I'm oblivious to the car behind. I accelerate – Sumiko's chicken curry is waiting, and the nightly massage that leads to other things. The speedometer hits 100 mph. I'm lost in a daydream revolving around converting the garbage stinking up my car into thousands of dollars – until a bright light smothers the Toyota as if a spacecraft is trying to land on it. I come to my senses. Fast. My eyes lock onto a police car, its lightbar on, flashing me to pull over. *Oh shit! How do I explain a car full of trash from Mesa when I work in Phoenix?* I pull over, drop the window and tremble.

The police vehicle parks and floods my car with light. The driver gets out and approaches my side. 'Driver's licence, insurance and registration.' He shines his flashlight on the bags on the back seat.

'Here you go,' I say in a weak voice.

'I'll be right back.' He takes my documents to his car.

For a few minutes, I worry about getting busted for industrial espionage.

The cop marches back to my car. 'Why're you in such a hurry, Mr Attwood?'

'Late for dinner. Wife's cooking. You know how it is.'

'No, I don't know how it is. Food that good you'd risk your life and the lives of others by speeding? We've been following you zigzagging in and out of the traffic for four miles.'

'I'm terribly sorry, officer.'

His partner materialises at the passenger side like a ghost, making me jump. He traces his flashlight over the bags. I see myself in handcuffs.

'Any idea how fast you were going, Mr Attwood?'

'I wasn't paying attention.'

'What do you do for a living?'

'Stockbroker.' *But not for long. This will end my career.*

'Those bags from your office, Mr Attwood?'

The lie leaps out before the consequences sink in: 'Yes.' *Great, now I've fibbed. That's probably a crime.*

'Do you mind if we take a look at those bags?'

'No. Go ahead.'

'Step out of the vehicle. Go and stand by the passenger side so you don't get run over.'

I walk around the car fast. Trucks roar by, wafting fumes and dust and heat that add to my nausea. Radiating guilt, I watch the cops extract the bags and arrange them in a row on the hard shoulder. They pop the trunk, find more bags, add them to the row. Exchanging cautious glances as if expecting to find body parts, they prod the bags with flashlights. They open a bag. My body tenses. *Surely they'll notice the paperwork's not mine and handcuff me.* They poke around inside the bags, ignoring the paperwork. *Maybe they're looking for drugs.* On finding nothing, they trade confused looks and shrug.

'Do you have anything you want to tell us?' one asks, tilting his head back and scrunching his brow as if he knows I'm up to something.

'If you let me go with a warning, I promise I won't speed again.'

They laugh and put the bags back in the car.

Driving home in the slow lane, nursing a speeding ticket on my lap, air con blasting my face, I tell myself, *No more dumpster diving.*

CHAPTER 12

CITING SIDE EFFECTS, Sumiko stops taking Zoloft. I'm having a shower when she bursts in and tries to slice my penis off with a Ginsu knife. Stopping the blade, I cut my hand. She bites my arm, leaving a wound that looks like my bicep has grown a mouth. Blaming her mental illness, and committed to marriage, I stay with her.

With Sumiko constantly angry, I feel lonely, miserable and on the verge of going berserk. More than ever, I crave the relief provided by Ecstasy. I want to rave, get high and forget about Sumiko. Listening to tapes I made in England, I close my eyes and pine for raves. As each weekend nears, I hear wolves howling for me to come out and party. The wolves represent everyone I ever partied with. Their call fills me with sadness – and longing to be reunited with my wolf pack.

A colleague agrees to join me at The Works, a nightclub in Scottsdale popular with gays and ravers. Sumiko refuses to come, so I go in her sports car.

At The Works, I buy wine from a topless pretty boy and enter the techno room. My eyes widen as I take in the sight: hundreds dancing on a wooden-plank floor and platforms of various heights; walls adorned with sailors; latex-clad females in black thongs prancing on a suspended metal catwalk; windowpane-like screens displaying psychedelic visuals. Around the edges of the club, on luxurious sofas in dimly lit balconies, people are snorting drugs, drinking and fondling each other. I spot the dealer Moo and take a hit of Ecstasy. I'm getting into the music, anticipating a good time.

Feeling a tap on my shoulder, I turn around, smiling, expecting to see my colleague – but it's Sumiko. She attacks me and the bouncers escort us out. She departs in her sports car, leaving me stranded.

I'll talk her into picking me up later on. Just then – as if it was waiting for her to leave to arrive – the Ecstasy takes effect, raising my temperature, evaporating my stress. I approach the bouncers, convinced the joy I'm radiating will penetrate their dark souls and they'll allow me back in.

'She's gone. Can I come in?'

'Fuck off!' A bouncer shoves me away with both hands, knocking the smile off my face, but only for a few seconds.

Hovering by a sculpture of a semi-naked muscular man holding a giant globe with WORKS on one side and a map of the world on the other, and basking in the pleasure of my tingling skin, I grin at strangers. Inhaling deeply, tasting the warm night air, I stroll down Scottsdale Road. With no one to smile at, I contemplate star formations. *What's life all about?* Deciding I'm a small part of something too big to understand, I get a shivery feeling. Overwhelmed by the knowledge the stars are trying to impart, I avert my eyes from them. I bob my head to dance music coming from passing cars, and my arms come to life as if conducting an orchestra. I stop outside Walgreens and call Sumiko. No answer. Tired of walking, I lurk by the payphone like a hobo, hoping for a friendly face to talk to. Hours pass. No one comes.

The novelty of solitude has long worn off by the time a decrepit pickup truck parks. The driver's dark-blue door creaks open. A tower of hair tilts out, a cinnamon-red beehive. A pair of high-heeled boots, pointy, black, suede, hit the asphalt. Dressed in black, the driver raises her head, confident and graceful, like a queen. She's tall. French-manicured fingers heavy on silver rings slam the door. Resembling a cross between a ghost and a Gothic count, the passenger emerges, also dressed in black, piercings on his face. With each stride, his long silvery-blond hair bounces, expands, contracts. He speaks to her in a feminine whisper. Sashaying towards Walgreens' entrance, she answers mockingly, all svelte brown limbs protruding from leather. Her bracelets, covering her forearms like body armour, clink as she walks. Her enormous eyes – so dilated I suspect she's high – flash in my direction. Caught admiring her, I'm stuck for words. I offer a nod and smile. They disappear into the store.

They re-emerge with drinks, whispering. I'm about to greet them when she spins around. 'Hey, mister, do you need a ride?'

'Yes. Yes please,' I say, relieved. 'I've been at The Works. I'm stranded. Trying to get to Ahwatukee.'

'Got any concealed weapons?' she says, her tone implying it's not a joke.

'No,' I say, shaking my head.

'Well, I pack at all times,' she says. 'If you try anything stupid, I'll shoot your ass.'

'I won't try anything stupid,' I say, more desperate for a ride than nervous about her weapon.

They whisper again and she says, 'We're going to Tempe. That's the direction you're going. Jump on in.'

They get in. I squeeze onto the end of the cabin seat.

'I'm Kelly. This is Poppy,' she says, gunning the engine. 'We've been at The Works too.'

I shake Poppy's limp hand.

'Hello,' he says in a protracted whisper, exposing a pierced tongue.

'How do you do?' *She's gorgeous. He's gay. They belong in* Rocky Horror.

'Why don't you tell us what you were *really* doing outside Walgreens on Scottsdale Road at three in the morning?' Kelly asks.

Having never talked to anyone about the extent of my problems with Sumiko, I unload it on them. It feels great.

'Do you really wanna go home?' Kelly asks.

'No. She's probably sharpening her Ginsu knives about now.'

'We're going to ours to drink shots of Jägermeister and listen to house music. Wanna join us?'

'You're not serial killers, are you?' I ask, smiling.

'You'll just have to find out,' Kelly says in a serious tone.

I follow them into a two-storey apartment. Poppy turns music on and puts Jägermeister on the coffee table. They sit on a small black leather sofa. I start to lower myself onto what looks like a seat.

'Not on that!' Kelly yells. 'It's just a moving box we spray-painted black.'

Laughing, I collapse onto a beanbag by a lava lamp. Kelly prepares shots of Jägermeister with the reverence priests reserve for Communion wine. Pretending to be a connoisseur in matters of alcohol, I throw back a shot. While it sets fire to my throat, I struggle to look normal. The burning subsides, leaving a pleasant cough-candy aftertaste. 'How long you been raving?'

'I guess back from before rave was rave,' Kelly says. 'I've been dancing since I was a little girl. When I was in high school in upstate New York, we'd fly down to Studio 54. That's where I met Calvin Klein and how I got my first modelling shoot.'

'You modelled for Calvin Klein!' I examine her face: the high cheekbones lend credence to her story.

'Yeah, I was making mad, mad money until I got in a car accident. They said I wasn't gonna be able to walk. That's how I got this scar on my knee,' she says, pointing.

My eyes stray from the two-inch scar up and down her smooth brown legs. Eager to steer her back to raving, I ask, 'What's the best clubbing you've done?' Our eyes connect. A warm feeling runs through me as if I just received good news.

'The Love Parade.'

'No shit! I've always wanted to go to the Love Parade.'

'First of all, I lived on the Ku'damm –'

'The what?'

'The Kurfürstendamm. It's like the Champs-Elysées of Berlin. Well, the Love Parade goes down the Ku'damm. And where the Uhlandstraße met the Ku'damm, I lived on a top-floor corner unit.'

'That must have been insane.'

She tilts her head and smiles at Poppy. 'It was intense. I remember the parties before the Love Parade. Going to the Russian side of Berlin. Watching Sven Väth in this building that was all crumbled down.'

'I listen to Sven all the time!'

'I was afraid the building was gonna fall down.'

'Maybe it had been bombed.'

'It had been bombed! It was the coolest thing. To get in you had to go down a trail, cross a rickety bridge – there was a blue neon light in the water – and down a tunnel. You didn't hear the music until you went into this dimly lit room. It just hit you like – *boom!* It was packed inch to inch, the whole room just jumping. It felt like the floor was moving up and down.'

'I know exactly what you mean. I'm getting goosebumps just thinking about it. I –'

'It was awesome. It was insane. I'd seen Mardi Gras, but this was just like – I dunno – like you got high off the music. You didn't need to do any drugs.'

We drink more Jägermeister. Poppy disappears upstairs. I grow more relaxed – until I realise it's noon. *Sumiko!*

'I'd better get going. I've stayed here so long, my wife'll think I'm off with a blonde. If you drop me off, I'll tell her I fell asleep under a bench near The Works and it's her fault for leaving me there.'

Kelly parks at the end of my road. I say goodbye, get out, wait for her to leave, drop onto the ground and wriggle in a patch of dirt and leaves. Satisfied with the look, I knock on the door, bracing to be attacked. Sumiko answers and rants.

'Look at the state of me! I fell asleep outdoors! This is all your fault for leaving me at The Works!' I say, pointing at my clothes.

Her eyes latch onto the filth. Surprisingly, her face softens. I walk in without incident.

On Monday morning, I wake up with Kelly on my mind. I call her from work. She tells me to stop by any time. I do – each visit magnifying my attraction.

CHAPTER 13

OUR CALLER ID is showing New York area codes: one number a cellphone, the other Citicorp. There's a voicemail for Sumiko from a man speaking with an East Coast accent and using a familiar tone.

'Who's this guy calling you from New York?' I ask over dinner.

'Old friend,' Sumiko says. 'No big deal.'

On Saturday, Sumiko says she's going out with some Japanese friends and sleeping over at one of their homes. I tell her to enjoy herself. With Sumiko gone, I relish the peacefulness. On Sunday afternoon, she shows up in a good mood and goes out of her way to be kind, raising my hope that her behaviour is normalising.

Midweek, Sumiko goes shopping. Spotting bags from Victoria's Secret, I fantasise about the lingerie and look forward to what she has in mind. But on Saturday she says she's staying at her friend's house again. Seeing the New York cellphone number on the caller ID, I wonder what's going on.

On Saturday night, I call the house Sumiko is staying at. Her friend says Sumiko isn't there and she doesn't know her whereabouts. I dial the Citicorp number on our caller ID.

It goes to voicemail: 'Hi, you've reached Steven Jones at Citicorp . . .'

I jot down the cellphone number and dial it from a payphone.

'Steven Jones. How can I help you?' he says in a New York accent, his voice tipsy-sounding.

He must be in town on business. 'Can I speak to Sumiko, please?'

'Who's this?' he asks.

'Her husband.'

He hangs up.

Something inside of me snaps. I feel sad and hurt and humiliated – until anger takes over. The wolves howl. I drive to The Works, take Ecstasy, dance and try to forget about Sumiko, but she haunts my high. I return to the empty house and fall asleep.

On Sunday, I confront her. She denies everything, accuses me of having an affair with one of her blonde girlfriends, arms herself with a Ginsu and chases me around, demanding to sniff my penis for vaginal secretions. She destroys the house, and the police arrest her. I call my dad's sister, Aunt Ann, pack up my belongings and leave.

Days later, Kelly asks me to move in with her. I jump at the chance to spend time with the woman who's been on my mind so much.

CHAPTER 14

'**WHEN WAS THE** first time you took Ecstasy?' I ask Kelly.

The one hundred and fifty bracelets on each arm rattle as she puts two bottles of St Pauli Girl on the coffee table. She joins me on the sofa, pressing her legs parallel to mine. 'It was in the hottest club in Houston, Fizz. My boyfriend said, "Here, open your mouth, close your eyes," gave the pill to me and handed me a Corona. I knew it was a touchy-feely drug. I was dancing and wondering how long it was gonna take to hit. My boyfriend's friends, they're all smiling, getting off. I yawned and they all started clapping and saying I'm gonna be feeling something soon. My leg buckled a little bit real quick.' Kelly bounces a hand on her thigh, drawing my eyes back to her legs. 'But I caught it and played it off like I was dancing, and then my boyfriend said, "Now it's really gonna hit you." I was dancing hard and fast. I looked like I was going one hundred miles per hour, but it felt like two miles. Literally, I heard *wahrrrrr*, like a time warp had opened up. I started smiling to the point where I couldn't dance. I took my boyfriend by the hand and sat down, grinning, like everybody else in the group. I said, "Oh my God! What do we do? I can't move. I can't go anywhere." I'm cracking up, laughing at my boyfriend's friend, this really annoying drunken Englishman.'

I tell Kelly about my first rave. 'I was raving every weekend after that. Making all kinds of friends. It was my religion. I mostly did Ecstasy and speed. We call speed Billy Whizz in England. You have to eat a gram of it. It's not like crystal meth here.'

Reaching for her beer, Kelly asks, 'What do you think of crystal meth?'

'I've never done it. What about you?' I ask.

'I prefer it to Ecstasy. Actually, crystal meth *is* my Ecstasy. It has that effect on me. I've got some if you wanna try it.'

Remembering what it did to Matt, an alarm bell goes off. 'I don't know. I saw it destroy a good stockbroker friend.'

'That's 'cause he let it.' Kelly turns her palms, which are resting on her thighs, upwards. 'The drug didn't destroy him, he abused it and used it negatively. It does have its uses. The military use speed to keep their pilots alert. It helps my creativity. I keep this townhouse spotless. I make my own furniture.'

'What's the high like?' I ask, the desire to bond dismantling my fear.

'It feels like Ecstasy when it kicks in. It's like the buckle and yawn, but instead of going from one hundred miles per hour to two miles per hour, you go from one hundred miles per hour to one hundred and eighty beats per minute. I like to go out and dance on it.'

'All right, let's do some then.' The consequences I've seen on television – before and after shots, sunken faces, open sores, blood-stained victims on stretchers, stand-offs with the police ending in suicide by gunshot, even a postman who cut his son's head off – fade as I find excuses: 'I'm so stressed out from dealing with Sumiko for so long and having to move out of my own home, maybe this'll make me feel better. Besides, it's the weekend.'

'I'll get the equipment then.' Kelly fetches paraphernalia. She dips the flared end of a straw into a tiny baggie, scoops out some yellowish rocks and powder that stink like turpentine and petroleum, and tips them onto a black octagonal plate.

'I never saw a Slurpee straw used like that before.'

'I grabbed it at work. Circle K. I'm training to be a regional district manager.' She rips a piece of paper from a magazine, places it on the rocks and rolls the lighter over. *Crunch*. Using a razor blade, she chops the crushed meth into fine powder. *Tat-tat-tat* . . .

'Wouldn't it be easier to do that with a driver's licence?' I ask.

'If you get pulled over, the cops can tell.'

'How?'

'The crystal-meth chemicals eat through the plastic.'

Eat through plastic! What will it do to my insides?

'You wanna go first?' she asks, offering a few inches of straw.

Unable to refuse – whatever the consequences – I say, 'Sure. They look like big lines.'

'Big, big Kelly lines!'

Matt's gaunt face pops up like a ghost. *That'll never happen to me. I've been doing drugs for years and I'm fine. I'm a functional, recreational drug user* . . . Hunched over, I snort a line. My nose burns as if a match has been lit inside. I wince. Leaning as far back as possible to distance myself from the pain does nothing: it gets worse. My eyes sting and gush.

'You've got crystal tears.' Leaning over the plate, Kelly lifts her eyes to mine, smiling playfully. 'How's that burn? Got you good, didn't it?' The line of meth Kelly snorts whistles up the straw.

Praying for the fire in my nose to go out, I sit rocking my head, my pulse throbbing at my temples. Kelly nurses her nose. Only our breathing is heard. When our noses recover, we chat as if nothing happened.

Half an hour later, my heartbeat accelerates. Thirsting for air, I gulp it down, relishing the sensation of my lungs filling up. My head starts trembling. A pain grips my heart that's ticklish and terrifying. Pressure builds on the left side of my chest, so I massage my pectoral. When the heart pain subsides, rushes of pleasure ripple through my body. As if operating independently, my brain begins processing everything going on in my life. My thoughts split and I end up having multiple conversations with myself. Suddenly, everything quickens. My heartbeat, my thoughts. Energy surges through my body, forcing me forward as if an internal booster rocket is activating. Ready to talk for the rest of my life, I fire out words: 'I'm rushing like crazy.' Unable to sit for a second longer, I leap up. 'I'm gonna get a Carl Cox CD outta the car. Be right back.' I snatch my keys off the table, dart out, fling open the car door, rummage around, find a CD, dash back in, shove the CD in the stereo, fidget with the buttons, turn the volume up, smile at Kelly, get on the sofa, swig beer, rock back and forth and bob my head and tap my feet and drum my fingers on my thighs . . .

'I wish I could get as high as you,' Kelly says, her eyes dilated. 'I'm always kind of hyperish without drugs, so the crystal tones me down.' She takes another swig.

'This tones you down! How does that work?'

'On it, I'm more conscious of my behaviour.'

'It's making me conscious of all kinds of things. I can see what an idiot I was for staying with Sumiko for so long!' *Am I speaking too fast for her to understand?* 'What was I thinking? It's weird how clear it all is in my head right now,' I say, powerless to slow my speech down. *How's she staying so relaxed?* I feel movements in my brain that I've never felt before – as if things that shouldn't be rubbing against each other are doing so. The feeling lasts a few seconds, scaring me, and stops. The rushing intensifies. *I feel so alive!* I rock even faster.

Admiring her French manicure and the peculiar silver rings protruding from her fingers, Kelly says, 'I had to get a restraining order against my psycho ex. He grabbed me by the hair when I was trying to leave one time. I told him, "Dude, I will shoot you dead in your own house." His aunt was there and she called the police. They took a report. I said he didn't hit me. I just wanted to leave.'

We exchange relationship stories. Happy and sad. We laugh at our mistakes. We shift closer. The next thing, I lean in and kiss her.

The meth gives me the courage to ask, 'Should we go upstairs?' I scan her face to see if I've caused offence.

She raises her bottle, takes time to drain all visible signs of beer, emits an exhalation bordering on a sigh and says, 'I don't see why not.'

CHAPTER 15

WALKING INTO CIRCLE K, I say, 'Kelly, I've got something to show you!'

'I'll be right back,' she tells the clerk, and follows me outside.

Flinging my arms open, I sing, '*Ta–da!*'

Admiring my new Toyota Supra, white with beige leather seats, Kelly asks, 'How much was it?'

'Almost fifty thou,' I say.

'Dude, with that, you could've bought a helicopter to go to work with!'

I open the door. 'Fancy sitting in it?'

She gets in. '*Wow!* It's like a spaceship.'

One month and two speeding tickets later, the dealership demands the car back, claiming to have found a problem with my credit. Perplexed by their U-turn, I refuse. Worried about repo men, I park atop a lot visible from the stockbrokerage.

A week later, I spot a man crouching behind the Supra to read the plate. He makes a call. I round up a posse of stockbrokers, mainly macho Italian New Yorkers and my friend Carson, a strapping bodybuilder from Idaho – both of us high on meth from lines we snorted earlier. We dash into the lot, take the elevator and rush to my car. Carson gets a handgun from his car. We surround the repo man.

'What're you doing messing with my car?' I yell.

The repo man's rugged face remains unmoved. 'The dealership sent me. It's their car and they wannit back.'

Irked by his attitude, I say, 'I don't think so.'

'He's probably a car thief!' Squinting like a gunslinger, Carson draws his weapon on the man. 'Don't fucking move!' he yells, his facial muscles flexed.

The man's arms shoot up as if to catch a Frisbee. 'Hey, don't fire.'

'Get away from the car!' Carson yells.

Gazing at the gun as if rethinking his occupation, the man cowers away from the Supra.

High from the altercation, I jump in the car. 'Keep him here until the police arrive!' I screech away and exit the parking lot. A car gives chase. Manoeuvring at high speeds, running red lights, I ditch it. I call Kelly: 'Repo men are hunting me down. Pack some clothes real quick and let's go to Sedona. My client who owns the Red Rock Lodge said we can have a jacuzzi room any time. If they want to play games, I'll put some miles on this car. We've got to leave in a hurry, so chop up two master-blaster lines of crystal. I'll be right there.'

With the thrill of an outlaw on the run, I take off for Sedona. On the freeway north of Phoenix, the houses disappear; sand, cacti, weeds, bushes and rocks dominate. When there's no traffic in front, I accelerate to 150 mph. The Supra trembles as if trying to take off.

Over an hour later, I park by chalets nestled into a red-rock landscape. In the fresh, cool air, I breathe more easily, as if my lungs have shed layers of insulation. My client thanks me for the rise in her Motorola stock and takes us to a jacuzzi suite behind a prickly-pear cactus whose flat green leaves and little red pods resemble table-tennis bats and balls. The sight of a jacuzzi big enough to swim in raises our spirits. We snort meth, undress and frolic in the bubbles, safe from repo men, yet excited they're hunting us down.

Half an hour later, noticing my shrivelled fingertips, I say, 'Should we get out now?'

'Why don't we go to Oak Creek, exchange blood and swear an oath of love?' Kelly says.

'Exchange blood! Like how?' I ask, climbing out of the jacuzzi, aroused by the prospect of committing a vampiric act.

Kelly gets out and begins towelling herself. 'Like Mickey and Mallory Knox,' she says, referring to the serial-killer couple in the movie *Natural Born Killers*. Kelly collects books about serial murderers.

Falling in love with Kelly, I'm ready to agree to anything. 'Let's do it!' I say, relishing the coconut scent of her skin cream.

Kelly puts on a black leather skirt with silver studs down the sides and a tight black sweater.

At Oak Creek Canyon, we get out of the car to the sound of water crashing against rocks. Cliff faces tower over thick green vegetation; the sandstone changes from white to buff to red, a red that darkens at the bottom as if the rock is leeching the lifeblood from the earth. We walk by Navajos peddling wares on tables.

Kelly stops. 'I gotta check this jewellery out.'

The Navajo trader – hair in a bun, wearing a satin skirt, velvet top and concho belt adorned with turquoise – squints at Kelly.

'Which do you like the most?' I ask, fishing a wad of dollars from my pocket.

'This is awesome!' Kelly says, fingering a sterling-silver slave bracelet: a ring connected to a bracelet by a chain, black onyx stones on the ring and bracelet. Kelly haggles the price down to $50.

As I walk towards the forest, my lungs fill with the vanilla fragrance of the ponderosa pines. We venture into the trees. Animal calls replace human sounds. I bask in the pleasure of being liberated from civilisation.

'Here's a good spot,' Kelly says, forging ahead.

A raccoon chatters, runs, disappears, swallowed up by the forest. The last rays of the day are filtering through the pines.

'It's so quiet,' I say.

'Peaceful,' Kelly says. 'The New Agers say this is a vortex site.'

I close my eyes and inhale. 'I can feel some kind of energy.'

'I should hope so with all the drugs you're on.'

I giggle. 'You want to do the ceremony here?'

'Yes.'

'You first.' *I'll give myself an itsy-bitsy cut that won't hurt.*

Kelly extracts a razor blade from her handbag. Without hesitation, she slashes her left index finger and raises it to show blood leaking from a deep gash. 'Your turn.'

Holding the blade, I have second thoughts.

As if reading my mind, Kelly says, 'Here, I'll do it.' She takes the blade.

I offer her my hand, tensing my arm to keep it steady.

'I'll be quick.' Before I can reply, she slices a finger.

'*Ow!* Fuck!'

'That's not very romantic. Here, link fingers.' She presses her finger against mine, intermingling our blood.

'Now what?' I ask.

'Now we've got to make a vow to each other.'

'OK, you first.'

'With this, we will be bonded for ever, and I shall love you as a wife. Now your turn.'

'With this, we will be bonded for ever, and I shall love you like a husband. *Till death do us part,*' I say, imitating Mickey Knox the serial killer.

'Good. Now put your jacket on the ground so I can lie down.'

'What for?' I ask.

'You know what for.'

'You mean conjugals right here?'

She arches her eyebrows and smiles in a way that leaves me little choice but to scan the ground for dangerous insects.

CHAPTER 16

HIGH ON METH, I speed to Chupa, a rave in an old warehouse building on Madison Street in downtown Phoenix run by DJs Eddie Amador and Pete 'SuperMix' Salaz. Kelly, Poppy and I get out of my new car, a twin-turbo Mazda RX7, Montego blue with sleek feminine curves and a far sexier posterior than the Supra, which I surrendered to the dealership after negotiating compensation.

On a street corner, I give $20 to hobos gathered around a fire in an industrial drum. 'If you make sure no one messes with my car, I'll give you another twenty next week.'

We weave through a zombie tribe of crackheads spilling from an alleyway, their eyes bulging unnaturally from sockets hollowed into sunken faces as if searching for the sleep they haven't had in days. We make minimal eye contact with them, and even less with the gangbangers cruising by in lowriders thumping gangsta rap. The *bap-bap-bap* of bullets firing in a building hastens our pace.

It's a relief to get off the street. Familiar faces greet us at the door. Red lights guide us down a hallway and past a room with a flooded toilet reeking of sewage. A purple strobe beckons us into the darkness like a Hindu goddess waving multiple arms. We disappear into a smoke-machine cloud that smells of burnt cotton candy and lines the insides of our noses with soot. We hug the regulars. Drag queens. Club kids. Ravers. We dance for hours to hypnotic music – trance, tribal, house – mostly without lyrics, except for phrases repeated by bizarre voices. Robotic voices. Androgynous voices. The voices of divas. Voices I hear long after they've stopped.

Like a ball of energy dropping in from another dimension, a stocky Native American dressed in black – long dark hair, baseball cap on backwards – bounces onto the dance floor. Moving as if his bones have turned into liquid, he mimics loading up a shotgun, pulls the trigger and blasts everyone dancing around him. People crowd to watch. A man bumps into him. Smiling, he dances around the man and, meticulously in sync with the beat, pretends to elbow him multiple times in the back. I suspect he's on Ecstasy, pure stuff, and I want some.

Later on, I approach him outside. 'You dance so well, you should be in music videos.'

'Thanks, dude,' he says, a peaceful quality to his voice.

'I'm Shaun. Here from England. I'm having a hard time getting Ecstasy.'

'My name's Acid Joey. I can get you anything you want.'

We grin as if a special relationship has begun. I get his number.

I'm dancing at the back when Kelly disappears down the hallway, hastening for the entrance. *She must need fresh air.* I keep an eye out for her. Minutes later, she charges in as if on the warpath. She starts to raise her Derringer .22, a small silver gun, level with the back of a massive African American.

'Kelly!' I sprint, my heartbeat bashing my eardrums, drowning the music out. 'Kelly!' I grab the cylinder of bracelets around her arm and push the gun down. 'What the fuck are you doing in here with that?'

'I'm gonna shoot that asshole!' she says, straining to raise the gun.

Worried about getting shot, I yank her towards me. 'What're you talking about?'

'That guy there!' She nods at the man. 'He gave me problems outside The Works one night. He's out to get me.'

'Are you sure it's him?' I ask, dreading having to deal with him. 'Yes.'

'What did he say? Did he threaten you?'

'It's him!'

'He looks like he's just minding his own business to me. Look, if you think it's him, then I'm going to talk to him. Maybe he'll apologise. But first we're going to put your gun back in the car. Come on.' I escort her outside, open the passenger door and toss the gun under the seat. Back inside, I say, 'You wait here. I'm going to have a word with Carson before I approach this guy.' I leave her glued to the wall.

Picking up on my agitation, Carson frowns. 'What's up?'

'I just stopped Kelly from shooting someone.'

'You're shitting me.'

'I'm serious.'

'Told you she's a gangster,' Carson says, shaking his head. 'Who's she wanna waste?'

'That guy over there,' I say, pointing at the man. 'She said he gave her problems at The Works. I said I'll go and talk to him and see if he'll apologise.'

Carson's eyes widen. 'Apologise! You're gonna get your ass beat down. Look at the size of him! He's the biggest guy in here!'

'I know. I'm not really going to ask for an apology. I'll just play it by ear. But I need you to watch my back.'

'Maybe I better get my gun,' Carson says.

'No. This is Chupa. It's a peaceful crowd. Besides, Kelly's been up all week on tweak. She might be imagining the whole thing.'

'All right. I'll watch what happens. I'll rush him if he attacks you.'

'Thanks, Carson.'

I inhale a few times, sucking courage from the air, and stride towards the man. I tap him on the shoulder. 'Excuse me, mate?' I ask, emphasising *mate* in the hope he makes allowances for foreigners.

He turns. 'Yes?' he says in a deep voice.

My body braces. I gulp. 'Don't I know you from The Works club?' I ask, hoping Carson makes his move before I get flattened.

'I've never been to The Works,' he says, smiling as if the question amuses him.

'Never been to The Works?' I say, rejoicing inside.

'Why?' he asks, beaming.

Ecstasy happy? 'My name's Shaun. I'm from England.'

We shake hands. 'I'm Beau.'

'Beau, I've got a favour to ask you.'

'What is it?' he asks, shifting closer.

'My girlfriend over there,' I say, pointing at Kelly. 'Well, she thinks you're someone who said something to her at The Works. She's scared of you. Will you come and say hello to her?'

'Girlfriend! I thought you were hitting on me!' We both laugh. 'Let's go!'

'Thanks.' I take him to Kelly.

'Honey, I've never seen you before in my life,' he says.

Realising her mistake, Kelly apologises and hugs the man. They share club stories, discuss DJ preferences. Carson joins us and we dance to a foot-stomping mix by Pete Salaz.

The sun rises and the music stops, but Kelly keeps dancing with her eyes shut, oblivious to the fact that Chupa is over. Half of the partyers leave. The rest watch Kelly sliding this way and that as if on skates.

Squatting against a wall next to Poppy, I say, 'You want to tell her it's time to go or should I?'

'Let me do it,' he says, as if it's an honour. He approaches Kelly and taps her on the shoulder. 'Chupa ended ages ago.'

Kelly opens her eyes. Applause takes her by surprise. 'What? What?' She smiles. 'You know how it is – the music just takes you away.'

CHAPTER 17

EARLY 1995, MY fourth year as a stockbroker, and I'm summoned to see the boss.

'Sit down, Shaun,' Nick says, sat in a big black leather chair.

Shit, he's onto me for doing meth in the office.

'I've got something important to tell you.'

'What?' I ask, breaking into a cold sweat.

Nick puts on a serious air. 'You have the messiest desk in the office, but whatever you're doing is working, and I mean working phenomenally, so I don't want you to change a thing.'

Where's this leading?

'Your commissions are so high, I'm offering you a back office.'

My relief morphs into joy. 'Thanks, Nick, but aren't they all taken?'

'I'm going to move someone back to the quads whose production is nowhere near as high as yours. You can have his office.'

With an office I can expand and knock Max off the top-producer spot. 'Sounds great, Nick. I'm thinking of hiring a secretary, if that's OK with you.'

'Anyone in mind?'

'Yes, Tina Pace. She's English. She works at the George & Dragon. She's intelligent and I'm sure my clients will love her accent.'

'Good idea.'

Feeling prized, I float out of Nick's office on a high.

With an office and secretary, my commission soars.

A few months later, at the 6 a.m. meeting, Nick, wielding a whiteboard duster, shows no mercy to the proudest moments of Max's career. The rookies shift in their seats and flaunt their delight as Nick replaces Max's $27,250 gross production in one month with my $57,000, and Max's $10,000 gross production in one day with my $17,000. While Nick showers me with praise and demands everyone emulate my work ethic, I pretend to be modest. Max remains expressionless.

My production rises into autumn, increasing my excitement about the Christmas party, where Nick doles out the annual awards. Max always wins the grand prize for top producer, receiving it with an air of superiority that sends most of us home praying for his downfall.

The event is at the Pointe Tapatio Cliffs Resort. When it's time to announce the prizes, Nick gets on the dais and casts a stern eye over the tables of brokers, wives and girlfriends to hush the drunken chatter. He awards a few prizes, token gestures that mean nothing except to the recipients. Only one prize matters: the top producer. Radiating authority, Nick opens the final envelope. The room hushes. Unsure what Max has produced for the year, I don't know if I've beaten him.

'This year's top producer is a rhino whose annual gross commission came in at more than half a million dollars.' Pausing to create suspense, Nick looks from left to right.

The brokers ping-pong their eyes from Max to me, some smirking at Max's let's-get-it-over-with expression. My ability to project calmness crumbles. My body quakes. My head trembles and my teeth chatter.

'This year's award goes to Shaun Attwood. Shaun, come and get your prize and certificate.'

Yes! Squeezing Kelly's hand, I smile at her. The lights dim. The techno theme tune for the Phoenix Suns blasts. I bounce from my seat and bask in the applause. I try to walk but get mobbed by brokers, cheering, leaping around like drunken monkeys, yelling 'Sir Shaun' and 'Lord Attwood' – ecstatic that I've ousted Max. I high-five my way to the dais, revelling in the fuss.

'Speech-speech-speech-speech . . .' the audience yells.

'I'm no good at speeches,' I say, provoking laughter. 'I'd like to, er, thank Nick for providing a stable work environment, and, er, to thank Tina for putting up with me, and for being the best secretary in the world. But to be, er, honest, I think any of you can do what I did. It's just a matter of putting the hours in, of staying on the phone even when you'd rather be out doing other things, of cold-calling and keeping your pipeline full of sales leads. I started out at Kruger Financial, where the brokers burnt their clients by loading them up with penny stocks. Here at Goldstein, we've got access to money managers, we can buy the tech stocks they're buying and make money for our clients. We've got everything we need to succeed at Goldstein – so let's be rhinos!' The applause shakes the chandeliers. Struggling to return to my seat, I fear the barrage of pats on the back is going to cause spinal damage.

My income is so high I buy a three-bedroom house in North Phoenix, on a street still under construction, and a 1978 Silver Anniversary Edition Corvette for Kelly, to match her bracelets.

CHAPTER 18

IT'S 1996 AND I'm at Phoenix airport to pick Wild Man up. He wanders into the arrivals lounge, spots me, drops his luggage and opens his arms. Giddy, I rush to him. He lifts me off my feet and crushes my chest, deflating the air from me like a balloon. I brace for him to drop me, but he swings me around, faster and faster, sending my legs out like helicopter propellers. The passers-by I almost kick frown. Wild Man's gaze – combined with an eyebrow caterpillaring up to a sinister angle – scares them away. He's bigger than ever, his face meaner, harder – which I put down to prison.

In our home town, Wild Man knocked out a man rumoured to have a thousand hits of Ecstasy. Finding no drugs, Wild Man bought a kebab with three pounds the man had dropped, earning him a conviction for street robbery. Despite his cousin Hammy's warning – *You might want Peter to do well in America, but remember: the leopard does not change its spots, or in Wild Man's case his red dots* – I'm full of ideas for Wild Man, such as launching him as a wrestler. He'll be on TV, famous, not in prison. I'll fulfil the promise made on the Thinking Tree of using my wealth to guarantee my best friend a good life.

On the road from the airport, our conversation flows as if there has been no absence.

'I got off the fucking plane and thought I'd walked into a microwave,' Wild Man says, raising his sports shirt over his face to mop up sweat.

'It's like that most of the time,' I say.

Wild Man points at the desert. 'Is that a massive fucking cactus or what?'

'It is, la'.'

'Pull over, la'. I've never seen a fucking cactus before.'

Caught up in Wild Man's enthusiasm, I park by a saguaro.

Wild Man jumps out and studies the state flower of Arizona. 'It's pretty fucking cool, isn't it?'

'Some guy shot one once and it fell and killed him. It's illegal to shoot them now, but you still see all the bullet holes.'

Walking back to the car, I say, 'Peter, do you still see the red dots?'

'They don't just go away, do they? It's not like chickenpox. They're still randomly here and there.'

I house him a block north of my office, walking distance from the George & Dragon pub, where we celebrate his arrival.

A few weeks later, Kelly and I stop by Wild Man's house at night. I knock on the door. Four Mexicans answer.

'Where's Peter at?' I ask.

They stare, nonplussed.

'Where's Peter at?' I ask louder.

They confer in Spanish.

'Pizza?' one asks.

'Not pizza. Peter!'

'We no order pizza.'

'Not pizza! Where's Peter? He lives here. Peter! Peter!' I yell, convinced he's been abducted.

Handguns emerge from their clothes, shutting me up fast.

Praying I don't get shot, I stammer, 'Kelly, let's walk slowly back to the car.'

'Let's,' Kelly says.

I back-pedal, my heartbeat accelerating, sweat glands pumping. Wild Man swaggers over the street.

'What the fuck's going on in your house, la'?' I ask. 'We almost got shot!'

'Who the hell are these guys?' Kelly asks.

'Oh, don't worry about them,' Wild Man says nonchalantly. 'Come and meet them.'

I arch my eyebrows at Kelly. She shakes her head.

'Come on. They aren't gonna shoot you if you're with me.'

Against my better judgement, I follow Wild Man.

'This one's Luis,' Wild Man says. 'He's a coke dealer from Colombia, and these are his workers from Mexico.'

Smiling thinly, Luis nods. The guns are gone, but I'm still trembling. The Mexicans disappear inside.

'They like to move around a lot, so I've rented my place to them. They're letting me stay in their old place across the street. I'll move back in when they're done here in a few weeks.'

'Rented it out!' I say.

'They're paying me in crack. They can't believe how big a rock I can do in one hit. It's amazing. It goes *sizzle-sizzle*, and thirty seconds later *heart-attack heart-attack . . .*'

'Peter, I do drugs, but smoking crack with armed Latino dealers! And you've only been here two weeks! Jesus Christ!' I fear police trouble and losing my friend again.

'You'd better be careful, Peter,' Kelly says. 'People do some weird shit on crack. I used to date some guy who started doing it and it fucked his world up, so I left him. Crack can make people with good lives and serious money lose everything. I had a friend who was a doctor who had mad, mad money, and he literally went to where he had nothing – lost his house, car, job, his practice and medical licence, to the point where he was living on the streets of Houston.'

'I'll take it easy on the crack,' Wild Man says, without conviction.

'Yeah, right,' I say. 'How're you ever going to get a job if you're doing all these drugs? And why didn't you tell us you were moving them in? They could have shot us!'

'No need to trip out, Shaun. They're good people. Luis even wants to invest in the stock market with you. He's a drug lord with a lot of money.'

Wild Man ridicules the wrestling idea. I urge him to get a job and to try to live a normal life. He suggests becoming an airport porter. I help him fill out the application, list myself as a reference and buy him a bottle of Goldenseal to disguise the drugs in his system so that he'll pass the urine test – but he still tests positive for multiple substances. Disappointed, frustrated, convinced he'll get into trouble without work, I start doubting my ability to help him settle in America.

A few weeks later, Aunty Ann calls my office: 'Shaun, have you seen today's headline news?'

'No. Why?'

'They just showed Peter's place with yellow tape around it. Someone's been shot dead.'

Worried about Wild Man, I almost drop the phone. 'You're kidding.'

'No. You'd better get up there.'

'Thanks. I'm on my way.'

I speed to Wild Man's in record time. Shocked by what I see – a crowd pressing against yellow tape, TV crews, what looks like a dead body on the doorstep, police everywhere – I panic because I have drugs in the car and drive off. Back at my desk, I replay the scene in my mind, concerned my friend may be dead.

Hours later, too agitated to work, I return. To my relief, the people and the dead body are gone. I park and get out. I approach the house apprehensively, my eyes lingering on the bloodstains on the doorstep, my stomach muscles clenched as if I'm anticipating a punch. My tension spikes as I push the door open and step inside. I'm greeted by the refrigerator Wild Man dragged from the kitchen and leaves open in an attempt to cool the room down, a white void buzzing like the insides of a robot, bare other than for a bottle of King Cobra Premium Malt Liquor. Hearing voices, I look to my right. On the sofa is Wild Man – I feel instant relief – sat upright like a pupil in a headmaster's office, his customary fearless look gone, replaced by a stunned expression. The man looming over him is asking questions with an air of authority, his large, intense eyes enveloped by black circles as if he's sleep deprived. His gaze freezes me. He introduces himself as a homicide detective.

'I'm Shaun, Peter's friend.'

'The landlord says you rent this place for Peter, is that correct?'

Intimidated by his deep voice and stern tone, I say, 'Yes, I'm a stockbroker. I work down the street. He's here on vacation. I put him by the English pub on Central Avenue, the George & Dragon, so he can hang out with other Brits.'

'Where do you work?'

'Goldstein & Associates.'

As he scribbles on a notepad, I offer him my business card. Scrutinising it, he says, 'Thanks. What's your home address?'

After answering, I ask, 'What's all this about?'

'That's what I'm trying to determine. It seems a man shot himself dead with his own gun.'

My mouth opens.

'A visitor here was demonstrating his gun to Peter and he shot himself in the head.'

Flabbergasted, I re-examine Wild Man's face, which is stuck on shock as if his expression froze at the moment he witnessed the shooting; it's a look that'll probably take a long time to thaw out.

After answering more questions, I say, 'In your line of work, you must see some horrendous things. What's the worst stuff you've ever investigated?'

'You know about the female joggers going missing with their heads showing up in Salt River?'

'It's been all over the news.'

'What the news didn't tell you was how we caught the serial killer's DNA.'

'What do you mean?' I ask.

'He was decapitating the victims, and having sex with the heads so violently that when he ejaculated, his semen entered their skulls so deeply that the river didn't wash all of it out.'

A shiver runs through me.

'Sick bastard,' Wild Man says. 'Some sick fuckers around here, aren't there? I've only been here a few months, and I've just seen a suicide, and now you're telling me there's a guy running round shagging skulls?'

After the detective leaves, I say, 'Good to see you're alive, la'.'

'Speak up, la'. I can't hear properly. Them guns are totally loud.'

'What the hell happened?'

'The guy killed himself.'

'That's insane!'

'I was up for days on crack and tweak, and he came over in the middle of the night with his bird, looking for the Mexicans. I sent his bird over the street so she could get drugs. He stayed here. I see he's got a gun. I told him there's no guns in England and would he mind showing it me. He lets me hold it and I ask him to show me how to shoot it. He takes it back, says, "The safety's on. This is how we do it in America," pulls the trigger, and it goes off – *bam!* It hits him in the head and he falls out the doorway. So he's on my step with a chunk of his head blown off. Totally fucking dead.'

Wild Man has nightmares about the shooting and asks to be moved. I house him in an apartment in North Phoenix, but within days he puts the head of a roommate, a bouncer with long, curly blond hair, through a wall. Disappointed, I drive there.

Wild Man gets in my car. 'All of us are getting evicted because of the fight. This Madison I live with is pretty cool. She's moving in with her boyfriend in Tempe in some apartment complex and it's got three bedrooms. She said her boyfriend's behind on the rent so, if you can fix the rent situation, I'll be able to live there.'

An apartment will work out cheaper than a hotel. Tempe's a college town. Can't be much crack there. 'I can stop the cheque I used to pay for this apartment and use that money to set you up in Tempe, so I won't be out of pocket on this mess. But you've got to stop causing chaos. I've not got endless money for this, Peter.'

After Wild Man moves in, I discover that the complex turns into a big party every weekend. Students roam around smoking pot, drinking beer. Wild Man invites everyone he meets to party at his place. Acid Joey supplies us Ecstasy. So many people show up that Acid Joey can't get enough Ecstasy for us to party on – something must be done.

CHAPTER 19

'**I CAN'T GET** you hundreds of X from local dealers,' Acid Joey says in my office one evening after the boss has left. 'They just don't have that many, but I know where they're getting them from.'

'Where?' I ask, eager to buy bulk.

'LA.'

'From who?' asks Hector Clark, the stockbroker I've grown closest to since losing Matt. Nearly every day, we eat fish 'n' chips and shoot pool at the George & Dragon. Almost twice my size, African American Hector appears to have no neck, but he has a soft-spoken way about him.

'Sol, some surfer dude who throws raves.'

'No way! I know him!' I say.

'You do?' Hector says.

'I'll never forget that name. He's a guy in Cali who talked shit to Kelly and I ended up grabbing his balls.'

'What?' Acid Joey says, squinting.

'It's a long story,' I say. 'We went to see Sven Väth play at some sushi house. We got invited to an after-party and Sol was there, off his head on meth, talking all kinds of shit to everyone. At first it was funny, but then he said something rude to Kelly and this other girl we were with, and Kelly said, "Get this asshole away from me. He's getting on my nerves." So I'm like, fuck it, I'm high and feeling just as crazy, so the next time he talked shit to the girls we were with, I grabbed his balls. I thought he would throw a punch, but he just stared at me as if he couldn't believe it. I'll never forget his massive fucked-up evil meth eyes. So there's just four of us from Phoenix versus this house full of LA people who we barely know, and Kelly pulls out her Derringer, points it at the ceiling and is like, "Fuck you, motherfuckers! LA can kiss my ass! We don't care who you are!"

I didn't want us to get killed, so we took off in a hurry while they were stunned.'

'If you and Sol are enemies, how're we gonna bypass the local dealers?' Hector asks.

'Well, get this. Months later, I go to some other Cali rave to watch Moby and we run into Sol. He's got a big entourage with him, and I'm thinking all hell's going to break loose and I'm going to get beat up, but he comes up to me and shakes my hand. He says he was on meth last time he saw me, meth brings out the devil in him and he apologised for insulting us. So we made friends.'

'What if we go out there and he tries to pull a fast one 'cause you grabbed his balls?' Hector asks.

'My gut tells me he won't. But if you and Wild Man are with me, then what's he going to do?'

'He might have half of LA with him,' Hector says.

'What do you think, Joey?' I ask.

'If you want to step on the local dealers, you must go directly through Sol.'

'I take it you have his number?' I ask.

'No, but I can get it.'

'How much X should I buy and what should I pay?' I ask.

'If I buy fifty,' Acid Joey says, 'I get charged twenty dollars each; for a hundred, eighteen. My dealer must be getting them from Sol for fifteen or less. It'll probably come down if you buy five hundred to one thousand.'

'One thousand!' Hector says. 'What are we going to do with a thousand?'

'They'll be gone in no time,' I say. 'Me, you and Wild Man are doing almost ten each on the weekends. But maybe I should just buy five hundred in case he does try to rip me off.'

'Plus, I can sell some for you,' Acid Joey says, 'and you can use that profit to offset what you eat.'

Excited by the prospect of a new business venture, I say, 'If there was a stock I could buy at fifteen and sell all day at twenty-five, I'd be all over it. Making money off Ecstasy sounds easy. Let's give it a try.'

'There's something else I want to ask you,' Acid Joey says, his voice low, serious.

'What?'

'I'm gonna throw a rave and I need an investor.'

Has the door to throwing raves opened? The skin on my forearms tingles and I grow more excited – as if a prophecy is being fulfilled. 'How much?'

'Two thou to start, to get the flyers printed up.'

Something in his tone bothers me. 'Have you got a business plan, Joey?'

'No. I'm gonna throw it with some raver kid outta Texas. He's got it all figured out.'

'Where at?'

'The Icehouse.'

'Good location,' Hector says.

Two thou is insignificant even if he loses it. Give him a chance. 'When do you need the money by?'

'As soon as possible.'

'All right, I'll give it you at the weekend. I trust you, Joey.'

Two carloads of us, including Wild Man's cousin Hammy – here on holiday, finally reuniting the three of us for the first time since the days of the Thinking Tree – drive to Sol's house in West Hollywood. Annoyingly, he isn't home at the prearranged time. From a vantage point on a side street, we sit in our cars, waiting, our tension and frustration rising. Hours later, Sol shows up, carrying a surfboard.

'I'll go in now,' I say to Wild Man. 'If I'm not back out in fifteen minutes, come and rescue me.'

'I'd like to wrap that fucking surfboard around his head,' Wild Man says, 'seeing as he's kept us waiting this fucking long. Why don't I just kick his door down and take his shit?'

'That's not good business,' I say.

'It's not good business him keeping us waiting out here for two hours either!'

'If you rob him, then who're we going to go through?' Turning to Hammy, I say, 'Keep the Wild Man under control, would you?'

'That's like trying to keep a bull from a red rag,' Hammy says. 'I'll do my best.'

I tell Hector and Acid Joey to stay put in Hector's car, and I knock on Sol's door.

'Come in,' Sol says.

'I've been here a while.' Entering his house, not knowing what I'm getting into, I brace for someone to jump out and rob me.

'I lost track of time,' he says with indifference, irking me right away. 'I have your five hundred Mitsubishis. I'll be right back.' He goes into another room. Half-expecting him to reappear with a gun, I relax when he brings a Ziploc bag with more pills than I've ever seen.

'How much MDMA's in them?' I ask, feasting my eyes on the quantity.

'One hundred and twenty-five milligrams. From Holland. I don't sell any Made-in-America bunk. Besides, I'm told you can afford a lot more than five hundred. I'm sick of Arizona ravers coming to my house and buying a hundred here and there. I'd rather sell bulk to one person. It'd be safer for all of us. And the product will be good, like these.'

'Can I taste one?' I ask.

'Taste one?'

'I always chew them. They have a distinct taste,' I say, studying his face, rugged and tanned.

'Want a chaser?'

'Water, please.'

I unzip the bag and examine a pill. More dirty white than beige. Speckled like a bird's egg. A press of three diamonds: the Mitsubishi logo. Chewing it, I recognise the sharp chemical taste of MDMA.

'I can't believe you chew those things.'

'It's a good pill. Here's seven gees. If you want me to buy more, I expect a much better price next time.'

'I'll count the bills while you count the pills.'

CHAPTER 20

AT PHOENIX AIRPORT, Kelly's appearance stuns my parents.

'You have such a pretty face, with cheekbones to die for,' Mum says.

'Exotic looking. Just like a model,' Dad says.

'I just love those silver bangles,' Mum says.

'I can see where Shaun gets his kindness from,' Kelly says, beaming.

'And at least we can have a proper conversation with Kelly,' Mum says, referring to Sumiko.

'You haven't seen the bite mark yet,' I say, pointing at a permanent scar left by Sumiko's teeth on my arm.

'Oh my God!' Mum says. 'We had no idea she was that crazy!'

'That's one hell of a scar,' Dad says. 'She must have been really hungry.'

'Had she run out of kimchi?' Mum asks.

We laugh.

'Have you heard from her?' Mum asks.

'Not since the divorce went through.'

My parents settle into my home, oblivious to my drug activity, convinced the strange hours I keep are due to stockbroking.

In the living room one evening, I put a movie on. Halfway through, there's a knock on the door. I pause the video, walk to the peephole and see a group of unfamiliar faces, grungy drug-user types, staring angrily. *Ba-dum-ba-dum-ba-dum* goes my heart.

Oh shit. Something's going down. Not now with my parents here! How can I shield them from this? 'It's OK. I'm going to have to talk to these people. Keep the movie going.' As my parents refocus on the TV, I rush to a closet where I store a shotgun purchased for home protection. Pointing the gun down, trembling, I open the door. 'What do you want?'

Noticing the weapon, they step back.

'We're looking for Acid Joey,' says a man with long hair, beady eyes and a pockmarked face.

'You've come to the wrong place. Acid Joey doesn't live here,' I say, hoping they'll leave.

'He owes us money,' he says, his tone insistent. 'We know he comes here.'

Raising my voice, I say, 'I don't know how you know he comes here, but he owes me money, too. Two thousand dollars I gave him for a party, which he hasn't been able to pay back.'

'He took money off us to take to San Fran for LSD and we haven't heard from him since.'

'I don't know anything about that,' I say. 'Look, I can't help you. I've got visitors here right now. Please don't come back.' I slam the door in their faces and watch them slink away.

My parents spot me holding the shotgun. *Oh shit! They're going to figure out I'm drug dealing!*

'Oh my God!' Mum says.

'What the hell's going on, Shaun?' Dad asks.

'Just some kids looking for a friend of mine,' I say. 'I don't know who they are and you can't take any chances in America. They could have been robbers with guns. That's why I took the shotgun. I really didn't need it. It's all resolved now and they left without a problem.'

My parents remain alarmed. They don't mention the incident again, so I assume they believe my explanation. Attempting to assuage their stress and alleviate my guilt, I arrange for them to stay at the Red Rock Lodge in Sedona for a weekend. The rest of their trip goes smoothly and the incident seems forgotten.

CHAPTER 21

TWO COLLEGE GIRLS – Ecstasy first-timers – are sharing a bubble bath in Wild Man's tub, half-Spanish Emily rubbing Kimberley's freckly-pale shoulders, no one bothering them.

In Wild Man's bedroom, people are lying all over the carpet as if a yoga class is in progress. I find a space and assume corpse pose. I smile at Wild Man on the bed, grinning contentedly, his eyebrows relaxed, bobbing his head, rocking his big frame to the beat of a Markus Schulz trance mix on the radio – *Sugar daddy, set me free, Sugar daddy, come for me . . .* – as if warming up to dance.

'Where did you meet Kimberley at, Wild Man?' I ask.

'At 7-Eleven tonight. She'd lost her cat and her boyfriend, so I said, "Things could be worse," and invited her over.'

The window rattling attracts our attention. A figure in black leaps through the frame. 'Everyone's loving the X. I've got two thousand dollars for the hundred you gave me. Can I get a hundred more?'

'Acid Joey!' I say. 'Welcome to our little E party. Go take a look in the bathroom.'

'What's in there?' he asks, frowning.

'Just go look, Joey,' Wild Man says.

The happy Buddha sat cross-legged against the wall, called Hector, chimes in with, 'You'll like it.'

Acid Joey doesn't walk like most humans. Above nimble footsteps, his mass moves smoothly, effortlessly, cartoon-like. He opens the bathroom door. '*Wow!*' he says, his eyes widening.

'Who're you?' Kimberley asks.

'It's Acid Joey,' Wild Man says.

'His dancing is legendary,' Hector says.

'Would you like to get in the tub with us?' Emily asks.

'Er . . . not right now,' Acid Joey says coyly.

'They only just met!' I say.

'That's how good this X is,' Hector says.

'I've never felt this good before in my entire life,' Emily says.

'Can I have another Mitsu, Shaun? I'll pay for one this time,' Kimberley says.

'Not yet. You're high enough. Let it coast. I'll take care of you when you start to come down.'

Acid Joey glides back into the bedroom. 'Shaun, can you front me another hundred?'

'I only brought enough for us to party on. Stay and party with us, Joey. I'll give you ten for free if you stay here and take them all with us tonight.'

'That's tempting. Er, OK.'

Word travels fast about the pills. All kinds show up. Ravers. Street-gang members. Native American transsexuals. Drug dealers. Stockbrokers. Students. Russian mobsters. Exotic dancers. Each room packs with people on Ecstasy, talking as if they've known each other for ever. Hugging me, they lavish praise on my pills. Basking in the attention – the most I've ever had in my life – I feel like a rock star. *This is way more fun than stockbroking.*

A couple arrive: Chantelle, a petite mixed-race dancer, her light-brown skin covered in scars from S&M; her boyfriend, Todd, a bouncer, wearing a black SECURITY T-shirt, drunk, loud, not on the same wavelength as the rest of us. Todd demands free Ecstasy from Acid Joey, who looks at me for help.

I turn to Wild Man, whose cocked eyebrow means he's formulating a way of handling the situation, and nothing more needs to be said. He smiles at Acid Joey as if to say he's been waiting all night for something like this to happen. Wild Man rises off the bed and yells, 'Watch this!' With a Taser a student traded for Ecstasy, Wild Man electroshocks his arm. The crackling draws everyone's attention. 'Anyone want to Taser me?' he asks, staring at Chantelle, challenging her.

'I will!' Chantelle snatches the Taser. The whites of her eyes widen as she shocks Wild Man's arm.

Todd, no longer bothering Acid Joey, watches with a smug, proud air.

Wild Man giggles as if his toes are getting tickled. 'Thank you. It's orgasmic.'

Chantelle stops the Taser and ogles the damage: a darkening

section of skin giving off a smell likely to upset vegetarians. Her lips quiver.

'How on earth can you enjoy that?' I ask, shaking my head.

'It makes my muscles spasm really quick. It's a nice feeling when you're high. I like the uncontrollable pain after the Taser's been on my body for at least a minute.'

'You're demented!' I say.

'That's nothing.' Chantelle leans towards Wild Man and whispers so Todd can't hear, 'How about you Taser my pussy?'

'I will,' Wild Man says.

'Are you serious?' I ask.

'Hell, yeah, I'm fucking serious!' Chantelle says.

'What about him?' I ask, nodding at her boyfriend, who's harassing Acid Joey again.

'Go and tell him to make you spaghetti bolognese,' Wild Man says.

In a husky voice, Chantelle issues the command. Todd swaggers off. We listen to him banging pots and pans around and barking orders at students to locate things such as the can opener.

I close the door. 'Listen up, everyone! Wild Man's going to Taser Chantelle's vagina, and she wants us all to watch.'

The room hushes. Looks of disbelief are exchanged.

Chantelle juts her chin and furrows her brow, squashing the scepticism. Exuding pride as if performing the grand finale at a circus, she squats. She raises her skirt: no underwear. Wild Man presses the button and the Taser buzzes like a cicada. He admires the tiny blue bolts of electricity. Chantelle places her left hand at the top of her womanhood, stretches the skin back and nods at Wild Man. He brings the Taser down. We gasp as the bolts dance up and down her vulva. She doesn't flinch. We shriek and shake for her. Worried about Todd returning, I wonder how long she'll last. Chantelle moans, sways, flutters her eyelashes, presses her eyes shut, springs them open wider and shuts them again, running through a repertoire of theatrical expressions. After a minute or so, Wild Man stops the Taser. Chantelle opens her eyes and stares as if returning from another world. She smiles.

'Let's have a round of applause for Chantelle!' I say.

Chantelle stands and bows. The room erupts with noise. She takes Wild Man aside. After they chat for a while, Chantelle approaches me. 'I really like Wild Man. He said I can move in here with him. I'm going back to my boyfriend's so I can collect my clothes.'

'Won't your boyfriend freak out? Do you want Hector and Wild Man to go with you?'

Before she can answer, the door opens. Todd enters, proudly bearing spaghetti bolognese on a tray. 'Eat this and we'll go home.'

Wild Man steps in front of Todd, one eyebrow half-cocked, the other horizontal, his eyes gleaming with mischief. 'There's been a change of plan. She's staying here with me, and we'd appreciate spaghetti bolognese every Wednesday.' He snatches the tray and starts to eat, calmly, nodding his head, taking his time to chew, savouring the taste.

All eyes turn to Todd. Stunned, his face tenses. He looks at Chantelle.

She says, 'That's right. I'm moving in with him.'

He glares at Wild Man. 'Him?'

'Yeah, me!' Above eyes radiating a desire for things to escalate, Wild Man's half-cocked eyebrow leaps to an extremity. His nostrils flare so wide the sides of his nose cave in. Veins pulse from his forehead like dangerous thoughts revealing themselves.

Todd's tough expression collapses.

'This is really nice,' Wild Man says, smiling. 'I like the big meatballs. I can tell you put a lot of work into it. I could get used to this.'

Todd turns and walks out. Leaving the apartment, he slams the door. The chatter resumes.

'Shaun, I need you!' Kimberley yells from the bathroom.

'What is it?' I rush in but stop, shocked and amused, when I see Kimberley on the toilet, naked, surrounded by three females.

'I can't pee. I feel like I want to pee, but nothing will come out.'

'How many Mitsues have you munched?'

'Three.'

'How did you get two more?'

'Acid Joey.'

'I told you not to take any more! You're so high, you're in the no-pee zone. It's perfectly normal. Let's get you off the toilet. Try thinking about something else. I know, let's go to 7-Eleven and buy ice creams and popsicles and drinks for everyone.'

'Ice cream!' Kimberley says.

'That's exactly what I need right now,' Emily says.

'Let's go!'

The women get dressed. Exiting the apartment is like entering another planet with an atmosphere that feels like a cross between air and warm water; it caresses my skin, tickling every pore. Passers-by smile as if they want to join in with us.

'My knees are going out,' Kimberley says, stumbling.

'Let's all link arms so no one falls down,' I say.

'I feel so good,' Emily says. 'Everything . . . like . . . just breathing . . . feels great.'

We enter 7-Eleven, falling over each other, all propped-open pupils and permanent smiles.

'Where's the party at?' the clerk asks.

I give him directions. We return, laden with refreshments, to Acid Joey trying to justify his dislike of frogs and birds in a range of bizarre voices mixed with animal sounds, the partyers laughing hard, most of them delighting in disagreeing with him. A few hours later, the clerk arrives in his 7-Eleven shirt and we steal his Ecstasy virginity.

When everyone leaves, I count the cash. Hundreds of pills were sold at $25 and $20 depending on the quantity. I start to reconsider my job. *I can make money as fast as in the stock market but without the grind, plus I get to have fun all night long with beautiful women.*

A month later, on a Sunday afternoon, too high to drive, I call Kelly for a ride. Increasingly neglecting her to party with Wild Man, I anticipate getting told off. She's studying to be a realtor and no longer does drugs. Stewing in guilt, I await her arrival. When she parks, I rush outside and get in the car, embarrassed by my drooping eyelids and sore, bloodshot eyes – the results of two days with no sleep. 'Er, thanks for coming to get me.'

Kelly revs the Corvette and takes off. 'Good to see you're still alive. Don't you think I worry about you?'

'I know you do,' I say, slumped in the seat. 'I'm so sorry. You know how it is when you get high. Hours roll into hours, days into days. I know I'm fucking up, but at least I'm still going to work.'

'Now!' Kelly says. 'But who's to say how long that's gonna last, you know? Getting fucked up like this every weekend is bullshit.'

'You're right,' I say, hiding my eyes behind sunglasses. 'I need to chill. But don't you think if I'm holding a job down, I've not got a problem?'

'Right! 'Cause you think you're a *functioning drug addict*. Whatever! You're greedy, too. With your addictive personality, I just don't want to think how this might end.'

Is she talking about our relationship, my job, my life? 'What do you mean how this might end?'

'Look at you, you go out all weekend and don't even give me a call. Now I have to come and pick you up. I'm only here 'cause I don't want you to wreck into anybody else on the road. You need to take a long look in the mirror to see what you're doing to yourself, dude. I don't know how much longer I can deal with this for.'

CHAPTER 22

IN A SMART dark-blue uniform, a young policeman marches into a party near Wild Man's. 'I could smell marijuana from outside. Nobody move! Nobody leave!' He reaches for his radio.

I freeze. *We're all fucked.*

We gaze in disbelief, except for G Dog, a tall Mexican American, more Italian-looking than Hispanic, with long black hair and prison tattoos on his arms. G Dog pulls out a gun and points it at the policeman. 'Fuck that! You don't fucking move! The only one who's not leaving here is you, motherfucker! Everyone else get the fuck outta here!'

The policeman throws his hands up. Colour drains from his face.

I join the stampede for the door. The partyers scatter into the night. Hector and I sprint to an apartment he shares with one of my Ecstasy dealers, Fish. I follow him inside and pace in the living room, worried about losing my job. 'There's no way that cop will remember all of us. There were way too many people there.'

'That G Dog's got balls,' Hector says, wearing a ripped T-shirt. After weeks of getting high on meth with Wild Man, Hector was fired for throwing a computer at our boss.

My breathing starts to slow – until sirens wail all over the complex. A figure scales the back wall, drops onto the porch and pounds on the French window.

'It's G Dog!' says Fish, a tall man with a goatee, long, scraggy hair, small hazel eyes, a hooked nose and a gap between his front teeth. Fish slides the window open.

G Dog leaps inside. 'Shut that quick and draw the blinds. If the cops knock, no one answer.'

'What did you do to the cop?' Hector asks.

'Nothing. I just scared the shit outta him. I told him I'd shoot his ass if he comes after me. Fucking rookie.'

'Holy shit!' Fish says. 'If the cops knock my door down, I'm fucked with all the drugs I've got in here.'

'Chill,' G Dog says. 'They have no fucking clue where I am.'

'Take no notice of Fish, G Dog,' Hector says. 'You can stay here as long as you want.'

The sirens and my heartbeat grow louder.

'They can't bust in here without a warrant, and they can't just break into every apartment in Tempe.'

I find G Dog's confident tone reassuring. A helicopter's spotlight lashes the French window. We rush to the far side of the room. Fish turns the TV off. We listen in silence as radio noises envelop the building. Boots approach the door. *Knock-knock-knock.*

Oh, Jesus! Seized by the urge to rush to the toilet and flush my drugs but too afraid to move in case the police hear me, I freeze. Radio code and barking surround us. Lights flash into our windows. I brace for the door to get smashed down. The police dogs sniff around for a few minutes and move on.

For an hour, we debate safe places to hide G Dog. He ends up staying the night at my house. The next day, he thanks me and says that from now on not only does he have my back, so do his people.

A few days later, Fish calls my office: 'I've gotta situation. Can you and Hector and Wild Man come over right now?'

The urgency in his voice alarms me. 'I don't know where Hector and Wild Man are. I thought they were with you.'

'I can't leave my apartment. Can you come over?'

'I'll come right over. Why can't you leave?'

'I don't want to say on the phone. You'll see when you get here. I need you to bring whoever you can to deal with the situation.'

I make an excuse to leave work, and speed to Wild Man's. His roommates say he's with Luis the Colombian, collecting crack debts in Phoenix. I rush to Fish's.

Fish answers the door, eyes wild, face pinched. 'Come in, quick.'

Behind him, his girlfriend is sobbing. *Has she been assaulted?* A noise erupts from the living room – an electrical crackle that sends a shiver across my skin and raises the hairs on my arms. *What am I getting into?* The noise stops. Starts again.

'Go through,' Fish says, implying he wants me to see what's going on rather than explain it.

As I walk down the hallway, the sense of threat grows more palpable with each step, until it's almost pushing me back. I enter the room and stop. Shocked. Unable to continue.

On the carpet: a naked man, hogtied, gagged, his hair in a stiff rockabilly quiff, his eyes streaming tears, a group of Mexicans stood over him, two wielding cattle prods. Giving orders is Carlos, the oldest, a friend of G Dog. He says something in Spanish. As the cattle prods descend, Carlos tilts his head to get a better look, smiles and runs long fingers through a majestic mass of swept-back silver hair. The man shrieks, his eyes jolt open as if witnessing his own execution, urine spurts onto the carpet. His body moves back and forth like a rocking horse, shaking his quiff. I'm used to taking drugs, partying, selling Ecstasy, but this terrifies me. I want to leave, but I've only just arrived. *How can I go without upsetting Carlos and ending up like the man on the floor?* Noticing me, Carlos smiles like an uncle acknowledging the arrival of a favourite nephew. Sensing he wants me to stay to enjoy the festivities, I nod back, too shook up to smile. *Got to get the hell out of here!* I'm baffled by how calm they are, how casual, displaying no anger towards the man, not even raising their voices, going about the business of torture with an air of pride and professionalism.

Fish answers the question on my mind: 'I caught him in here. He came over earlier and bought some tweak. He must have watched my apartment and waited until I left, but I forgot my pager and came back and caught him in here trying to rob your drugs and theirs. I called you guys and these guys, and these guys got here first.'

Relieved I wasn't first, I ask, 'Who is he?'

'Some college kid. Carlos is gonna take him somewhere. Carlos already called his roommates and told them if they want him back alive they'd better come up with five grand. We're gonna split the cash.'

'What if the roommates don't pay?' I ask, not wanting to imagine what they might do.

'They said they're gonna pay. They're getting it together right now.'

'What if they call the police and send them over here?'

'They won't. They're all on drugs, and they know he's a burglar caught in the act. He'd be the one going to jail. They don't want police trouble.'

The more Fish talks, the more bad outcomes I foresee, the more I want to leave. Panic sets in. The man has done wrong, but I don't have the stomach to watch him suffer. Overwhelmed, I muster a deep voice to disguise my fear: 'Carlos, looks like you guys have got the situation under control. I've got to get back to work.'

'*Adios, señor.*' Carlos combines a salute with a welcome-to-the-family smile.

Images of the naked man haunt me all the way back to the stockbrokerage.

CHAPTER 23

ONE SUNDAY EVENING, I leave Wild Man's, my pockets stuffed with drugs and cash. Twelve hours later, Tempe police smash the door down. Inside, there isn't much of anything left, as Wild Man's sold most of the appliances and furniture for drugs. The walls are coated in foam from a fire extinguisher he went berserk with. The holes in the walls are from head-butting contests between him and Hector. The air-conditioning system is leaking toxic sludge because Wild Man stuffed garbage up there, set fire to it and watched little blue flames of plastic drop, emitting a zzzzzz sound that soothed his red dots. Wild Man isn't home, so Emily – who's fallen out with Wild Man – directs the cops to Hector's apartment.

The police surround Hector's. Through a megaphone, they threaten to raid unless Wild Man comes out. To avoid more people getting busted and the police finding Fish's drug stash, Wild Man surrenders himself. He's arrested for thousands of dollars of property damage. At the station, an officer introduces himself to Wild Man as Detective Reid and offers to set him free if he would be so kind as to provide the name of his Ecstasy supplier. In a boastful tone, Detective Reid says he knows the supplier is another Englishman and asks Wild Man if it's his cousin. Wild Man tells Detective Reid to go fuck himself and refuses to answer any questions.

Bonding Wild Man out of jail for $2,000 barely affects my cash flow from drug sales. He moves to Chantelle's father's unit in the projects – a neighbourhood rife with crackheads, pimps and prostitutes. I dread his return to crack.

Days later, the receptionist at work buzzes my phone. 'Can you come here, Shaun? You've got visitors up front. We've never had visitors quite like these before.'

I hasten to the reception. Shocked, I find Wild Man on the couch next to an African American in a purple suit, a matching top hat with a big feather, a shiny black shirt, black-and-white golf shoes, a cane and countless gold rings and chains. *Thank God no clients are here!* I glance at my boss's office. He's on the phone with his back turned. *Phew!*

'Let's go downstairs,' I say, ushering them out.

In the elevator, Wild Man says, 'I need a hundred dollars to get a gun.'

'For what?' I ask, reluctant to reward him for bringing a pimp to the stockbrokerage.

'Protection. I'm the only white bloke walking around the projects with a black girl and it's making all the black guys jealous. They keep yelling I've got jungle fever. I'm telling them to fuck off and leave us alone, but they're saying they're gonna kill me.'

Here we go again. Another story to get money for crack, probably from this guy. 'A hundred dollars!'

'Tell him,' Wild Man says. 'Shaun, this is Raymond.'

'Hello, Raymond.' We shake hands.

'Wassup, Shaun? Look, I can pick him up a Saturday-night special for a C-note – know what I'm saying? – a throwaway,' Raymond says, offering to get a hot gun for a hundred dollars.

'I already got a gun off G Dog,' Wild Man says. 'A .22, but I ended up selling it to the blacks for crack and now they're trying to kill me with it.'

'Let me get this straight: you got a gun and sold it for crack to the guys you think are out to kill you? Every time you do crack, things get totally out of control, Peter. Here's twenty dollars. You can't just be showing up at the office like this. You'll get me in trouble.' I send them packing.

Back at work, the receptionist asks, 'Is Peter smoking crack, Shaun?'

'How can you tell?'

'Just the pimp and the huge bags under his eyes.'

A few hours later, Wild Man calls: 'They shot at me. I told you this would happen. They tried to kill me. G Dog knows I'm in danger. He's bringing one of those guns with holes in the barrel. A MAC-11, I think.'

'How do you get into such drama?' I ask.

'They kept on saying I've got jungle fever, so I went and fought the biggest one. I knocked his arse out outside a garage. Then one of them, basically, he started yelling at me, telling me I wasn't, er, treating Chantelle right. I told him to go fuck himself and he shot at me but missed. The daft bastard.'

'You need to stay away from crack and guns!'

Days later, I'm walking to the parking lot when a figure steps from behind a bush. Expecting to be mugged, I jump. It's Wild Man, topless and tiger-striped with bleeding scratches from the belly up. 'Now what happened?' I ask, dismayed.

'We had a fight and her dad locked me out. I've walked for miles. I didn't want to come to your work because I've got no top and all these scratches. I've been behind this bush waiting for you for hours. Take me to my old house and I'll see if I can get clothes from the Mexicans.'

'And then what?'

'I can't live in the projects no more. The housing inspector is kicking me out for being a disturbance.'

'The most dangerous neighbourhood in Phoenix and you're getting kicked out for disturbing it. What on earth did you do?'

'I told you they kept yelling jungle fever at me!'

'That doesn't explain why they're kicking *you* out!'

'All right, all right, la'. One of them pulled a deuce-deuce on me, the .22 I'd sold them, so I called G Dog. He brought me an AR-15 assault rifle and he had a MAC-11. We went round the garage, jumped out of his car with the guns and all the locals shit themselves and proceeded to run away, and –'

'And the next thing you know, you're getting kicked out!' I yell, waving my arms in frustration. 'Who'da *thunk* it, la'? Unbelievable. How do you manage to disrupt everywhere you go?'

'I don't know, la'.'

'Well, I do!' I say, exasperated. 'Why don't you try and behave yourself for once in your life? You're running out of places to stay. Hammy was right: we should lock you in a cage and poke you with sticks!'

'I think I should move into Acid Joey's because he lost that money you gave him for that rave. I'm pretty certain he used it to pay a drug debt. If you let people owe you money like that and do nothing about it, you're not going to have any left.'

'Good point. But what about Acid Joey's roommates?'

'They'll have to deal with it. I'd rather be back in a nice place in Tempe, where all the college girls are and everyone's partying.'

'OK. We'll tell Joey you're moving in. Anything to get you away from crack. I'm going to ask G Dog not to bring you any more guns.'

Within days of Wild Man's arrival, Acid Joey and his roommates flee. I start hosting parties there and my Ecstasy sales soar. Within weeks, the apartment manager posts an eviction notice.

One Sunday afternoon, Acid Joey shows up, anxious.

'What's the matter, Joey?' I ask, hugging him.

'Some thug called Gangsta Dan threatened to rob your shit from me.'

On the sofa, Wild Man's ears prick up and he extracts his tongue from Chantelle's mouth.

'Who?' G Dog asks, rising from the sofa.

Wild Man gets up, grinning as if keen to harm someone. He hugs Acid Joey. 'Gangsta fucking Dan!' Wild Man's belly-laugh resounds through the building. 'I'll handle this, la'. Take me to him, Joey.'

'Hold on a minute,' I say. 'Let's get some info, shall we?'

'Yeah, Wild Man, slow down, homey!' G Dog says.

'Who's Gangsta Dan, Joey?' I ask.

'Some thug from Philly. He's been setting up fake drug deals with ravers and robbing their shit at gunpoint.'

'What's this fool look like?' G Dog asks.

'I don't give a fuck what he looks like! Take me over there right now!' Cracking his knuckles, Wild Man looms over Acid Joey as if he's about to hurt him.

'Goddam, Peter!' G Dog says.

'Chill, Wild Man,' I say.

'He's a squat dude with a missing thumb,' Acid Joey says. 'He's staying here, in the next building.'

'Here! He's my neighbour!' Wild Man grins as if he's won a prize.

'Gangsta Dan robbed a load of vials of Special K,' Acid Joey says. 'He's all K'd out right now and doesn't know what's going on. Now would be a good time for Wild Man to go over there.'

'What's his apartment number?' Wild Man asks.

'How armed is he?' I say.

'I don't give a fuck if he's got a gun, I'm going over there,' Wild Man says.

'How dangerous is he, Joey?' I ask.

'He has a box of pills from the doctor, separated into days of the week,' Acid Joey says. 'He has to take certain pills each day so he doesn't kill anyone.'

'I'd better come with you,' G Dog says.

'Nah,' Wild Man says. 'I wanna talk to him on my own.'

G Dog looks hurt to be excluded.

Wild Man marches off. I sit and wait, expecting to hear gunshots and police sirens.

Fifteen minutes later, Wild Man returns. 'I've solved the housing situation. Chantelle, pack your shit up, we're moving in with Gangsta Dan. He's cooking up some Special K for us right now.'

'How did you manage that?' I ask.

'I basically told him, "I respect what you're doing, but not when you're shitting on me. You're stepping on my toes, so I want all the money back you ganked from the K dealers, and I'm moving in."'

'And he didn't pull a gun on you, la'?' I say.

'He invited me in, gave me a hug, said he'd heard a lot about me. He said he'd give me the money back he robbed from the K dealers, that I'm welcome to stay there as a guest of his, and he gave me a gun. I said, "I don't need no gun." He gave me another hug, said, "I know we're gonna be friends," and told me what he does.'

'What he does?' I say.

'He has people spotting dealers and what houses they're at. He jumps on the roof. He has this gas, puts it in the air con on the roof and all the people come running out. His homeboys put masks on, go in and rob the place.'

A month later, they get evicted from Gangsta Dan's. With a criminal record for property damage, Wild Man is unhousable. He ends up in Tempe Beach Park sleeping under a tree next to Chantelle, a Rambo knife and a baseball bat. After Wild Man smashes an extortionist – a man who was beating up' homeless people – in the neck with the bat, the gutter punks hail him as their king.

CHAPTER 24

DRIVING HOME FROM a rave, I arrive at a junction, squinting at the sun rising behind a traffic light. Half blind, convinced it's green, I keep going.

The car I hit I don't see. *Bang! Screech . . .*

The airbag detonates, punching me in the face. I see stars. My eyes water. Spinning out of control, the RX7 swerves towards a second car. Fired up on adrenalin, I drop my head, curl my shoulders in, brace for impact. *Bang! Crunch!*

The crash jolts my body. The RX7 stops in the intersection. My ears fill with a ringing sound. The heat and fumes from smouldering oil smart my eyes. *My car's wrecked. I must be hurt.* In a panic, I check my body. Nothing wrong. Struggling with the door, I manage to open it. Afraid another car might slam into mine, I bounce out as if my sneakers have springs.

Around the cars I hit, men are yelling at me. I pull my phone out and dial 911.

'What is your emergency?'

'I'm in a traffic accident on Thomas and 7th Street . . .'

Police arrive. One interviews me about the accident and issues a ticket for running a red light. He says it happens a lot when the sun is rising.

I hitch a ride on the tow truck taking the RX7 to its graveyard. *How can I be alive? Uninjured? Kelly's gonna be mad.* I enter the house, sit on the bed, wake Kelly up and explain what happened.

She gives me a hug. 'Shaun, I'm glad you're alive. Let's go to the doctor's to make sure you're OK.'

I lie down on the bed. 'Resting my back feels good. I'm disorientated. Got a headache. Other than that, I'm fine.'

Kelly rubs my back. 'Shaun, if you keep going like this, you're gonna kill yourself. And where would that leave me? I'd have to call your family and tell them you're dead. And then they'd find out you were high on drugs. How's your mom gonna feel? You need to think about them.'

'You're right, but my parents are so far away, they don't need to know about this. It would just cause them unnecessary stress.'

'This is a smack in the face. Wake up, dude! Wake up!'

Shook up by the accident, I stop taking meth. But every day I crave it, and I grow depressed. My thoughts slow down until my brain feels as if it's barely operating. At work, I have no energy. A few weeks later, I sneak into the restroom and snort meth with Carson. I immediately feel superhuman. But each withdrawal from meth wreaks havoc on me. I barely eat. Below my cheekbones, my face caves in.

My behaviour gets more erratic. In three months, I crash two rental vehicles. Enterprise Rent-A-Car bans me for life. I go out and buy an identical RX7 to the one I lost. Driving to work, I fall asleep, come off the road and crash, but only suffer wheel damage. I selfishly keep choosing drugs over Kelly, and my love for her disappears in a haze of partying. I accept that our relationship is on borrowed time.

One night, watching TV, Kelly says, 'You've got Burnt-Out Broker Syndrome 'cause of all the drugs you do. You've got yourself too involved. Everyone idolises you. Everyone worships you. Remember how the brokers used to call you "Sir Shaun" and "Lord Attwood"? You've gotta get back on track! You're making money illegally from Ecstasy now. Are you seriously gonna throw your entire stockbroking career away for drugs, dude? You've got a pretty good life if you think about it. People bust their asses to make in a year what a stockbroker makes in a month, a bad month, and you wanna fuck all that off to party. You think it's so much fun and so cool and so this and so that, but you're gonna wind up either dead or in jail. I ain't prepared to stand by and watch you do that to yourself. You're gonna lose everything. Your house, your reputation, your work, me and everything else. I thought I used to mean something to you.'

'You do,' I say, sat on the sofa next to her. 'I just don't give a shit about stockbroking any more. I think I'm gonna quit work and live off the money I've put in Hammy's name.'

'Well, you know, you do that, but how long do you think that's gonna last? With no job, you're gonna be too busy getting high, wasting your money on getting all your friends high, and pretty soon there won't be any left. What're you gonna do then? To you? To me? To us?'

'I've got money in the stock market, and I can make money selling fun to ravers!'

'Right! That's real good. You can make money selling Ecstasy. You make quite a bit of money now legally without having to worry about getting busted. Ecstasy and Ecstasy people will fuck you up. Whatever, dude! If you think you can make a living outta that, you're in for a rude awakening. You're shit's gonna get fucked up and I ain't going down with you.'

'I'm sick of putting all these hours in, getting up at 5 a.m., going to the office, having a boss, being part of the rat race.'

'Being in the rat race! Oh, so you're just gonna swim in the sewer instead, all because you wanna get high and sell Ecstasy. It was one thing when we were partying when we first met, but you're taking it to a whole new level. You're becoming the people we used to look at as pieces of shit. It's gonna hurt everybody. If you only wanna think about you, that's fine and dandy, you go ahead and see in a couple of years from now who's there to pick you up. This is not like a rave, where you go out on the weekend. If you wanna live that way full time, it will destroy you!'

'Well, it's a chance I'm prepared to take.'

'Then you fucking take that chance and see where it takes you! And what're you gonna do later? You won't ever be a broker again, and that's something you have a natural gift for, a natural talent for from when you were a fucking kid. You're gonna lose all that. If you choose that, you're not the guy I thought you were.'

I work fewer hours. My numbers on the board collapse. I let my secretary go. I try to boost my energy by taking more meth but end up paranoid and sick.

Coming down off meth, I spend hours shivering in bed. I pull extra sheets over me one minute but sweat the next and have to toss them off. My joints ache as if cancer is gnawing at my bones. My body is so tired, I want to sleep for ever, but my accelerated heartbeat and thoughts keep me awake. When I do finally drift off, I dream an invisible devil is coming to slaughter me in my bed. I wake up, thankful the dream is over, but the devil comes again and again . . . I try to force my eyes open, unsure whether

I'm dreaming or not, but they're glued shut. I can't move my body either. My eyelids open slowly as if tearing apart. I'm awake, with double vision, coated in sweat, my head hot and heavy, my heart beating like a machine gun. It takes a few seconds before I can move and see clearly. The vomit in my mouth from puking in my sleep must be laced with meth chemicals because it's burning my tonsils. Stabbing pain from ulcers on my stomach lining forces me to rub my belly. I rush to the bathroom and spit the puke out, followed by endless amounts of phlegm, my body shuddering each time the mucus makes its journey through my throat. Snot-green phlegm clots with yellow tentacles stick to the sink, resisting the water, quivering like jellyfish. Attempting to prise one off the basin, I poke it, but it grips and clings to my finger like a living thing. I try to rub it off with toilet paper, but the paper sticks to my finger, too. *Jesus, what is this stuff? It looks more like brain matter than phlegm.* It takes soap and water to scrub it off. Pain pierces my heart in a variety of places. Scared I'm on the verge of a heart attack, I hunch my shoulders, bow my head and clutch my chest. I breathe deeply in the hope of stopping the pain and stabilising my heart's erratic rhythm. *I'll never take meth again*, I tell myself, even though I know it's a lie.

In a last-ditch attempt to boost my sales and reduce my workload, I take Carson on as an assistant. I sign trade tickets authorising speculative investments in one of his accounts. The trades lose money and the client files a lawsuit. Sensing financial disaster, I move the last of my assets into Hammy's name.

With nowhere to live, Hector moves into my house. A few weeks later, I move out, separating from Kelly on friendly terms. She uses her real-estate licence to rent me a luxury condo in Hammy's name at Regency House, a high-security building fitted with laser tripwires and a guard station. *No one will rob me here. I doubt the police could even take me by surprise. From now on, I'll operate as Sean Hamilton to protect myself from anyone trying to turn me in.*

Hector telephones: 'Thanks for leaving me in the house with Kelly.'

'I needed my own space,' I say, stood on my balcony, admiring a view of Phoenix comparable to that from the stockbrokerage.

'And what else, guy?'

'What do you mean?' I ask.

'Why didn't you say something about this house being watched?'

'That's news to me. Have you seen anything suspicious up there?'

'I've got equipment.'

'Equipment?'

'Spy stuff. You should let me go over your new pad with it. You never know who's listening in on you.'

'You're welcome to stop by if you like. Why don't you stay for a few days and try to chill out! I think you're getting paranoid.'

'I'll be right over,' Hector says.

About 30 minutes later, Kelly calls: 'Hector freaked out, smashed the light in my truck and took my beeper apart because he said they had tracking devices in them.'

'Oh no!' I say.

'You should see my beeper, he like destroyed that thing.'

'Where is he?'

'On his way to yours.'

Convinced he's snapped on meth, I brace for his arrival. When I open the door, he charges in and pulls out an electronic wand. He waves it over the walls. 'There's a few areas of concern. And there's definitely a listening device in the TV.'

'But I only just moved in,' I say, hoping my relaxed voice calms him down.

'Look how long you've had the TV!'

'What should I do?'

'I'll fix it.'

I spend hours trying to soothe his paranoia but get nowhere, so I go to bed.

The next morning, I find his pager in a bucket of water and a note: *The cops are going to bust us all. I'm off to Chicago.* I shake my head, stunned, sad to lose Hector to meth.

CHAPTER 25

'**I WANT TO** hire Wild Man to kill my stepfather,' says Desirae – a tall New York Italian with long, straight dark-brown hair, a former roommate of Acid Joey's who fled after Wild Man moved in – her big hazel eyes flashing angrily.

'You shouldn't talk like that,' I say, peeling my eyes off the sides of her black underwear, emerging from low-slung jeans, arcing over her hips. 'We don't know who might hear us in this rave. Let's sit in my car so we can talk in private.'

'Let's go!'

In the RX7, I turn trance on. 'Why do you want Wild Man to kill your stepfather?'

''Cause he molested me in the swimming pool when I was a child.'

My stomach tightens. For a few seconds, I'm lost for words. 'I'm sorry to hear that.' *Talking her out of this isn't going to be as easy as I thought.*

'I've got it all figured out. They have a ranch in California. I can get Wild Man in and he can kill him and take all the money I know is hidden there, and that'll be Wild Man's payment and it'll look like a robbery and no one will suspect me.'

'What your stepfather did is sick, but I think you're going too far with this murder business. You really want him dead?'

'I fucking hate him. He's just this fat old pervert, and he even still says shit to me when I go visit them.'

'Like what?'

'Like how he wants to pay for me to get a boob job, so long as he can be the first to touch them.'

I feel queasy. *She's right. The world would be better off without this guy.* 'Jesus! That's crazy. How much money's he got anyway?'

'Tens of millions. He sold his business for stock in some huge-ass company. My mother will get his millions if he dies.'

I listen for hours, charmed by her feistiness and the fire in her eyes. She eventually calms down and discards the murder idea. While she tells me her life story, I stifle the urge to kiss her. As if reading my mind, she leans closer.

'Your eyes are so big they sparkle,' I say, blood rushing to my face, my pulse jumping.

'Is that what you tell all the girls?' she says, narrowing her brows.

'Only the ones with eyes like yours.'

She smiles.

I lean forward and kiss her.

She responds.

CHAPTER 26

FISH CALLS MY office: 'Wild Man's in jail.'

'What happened?' I ask.

'Him and Chantelle were skipping restaurants without paying. They got busted trying to leave Monty's. They were running around like Bonnie and Clyde.'

'How much is the bail?'

'No bail. They put an immigration hold on him this time.'

'He'll be deported,' I say in a sad voice. I love Wild Man like a brother, but I expected this and felt helpless to prevent it. *I tried my best to influence him, but he's a law unto himself.*

After the stock market closes, I sit in my RX7 and count dollars from Ecstasy sales. By the time I spot a woman approaching the car next to mine, it's too late for me to hide the money. Her eyes latch onto the pile of cash on my lap. *Oh no! My boss's secretary.* I drive home, dreading the repercussions.

The next day, the boss summons me to his office. I walk in, woozy.

'Take a seat, Shaun,' he says, stood up, grim-faced. 'Shaun, you've done so well over the years, but I'm not sure what's happened lately.'

'I think I've got BOBS,' I say, referring to Burnt-Out Broker Syndrome.

'You've really got to get back to basics. Back to cold-calling. Back to building up your pipeline of leads. Back to opening new accounts.'

'You're absolutely right, Nick. I know what to do. I'll get back to cold-calling.' *Yeah, right! Why work every hour God sends when I can make easy money from Ecstasy?*

'I'm going to put you back on the floor –'

Oh no! Fuck! Back with the rookies. No way!

'– in the hope you'll be motivated by everyone around you. A back office sometimes enables people to do less. They miss out on the buzz of the floor.'

'Er . . . I guess you're right, Nick,' I say, blushing, humiliated.

'Shaun, I can sense you're at a crossroads in your life right now. You can choose to go this way,' he says, pointing his right arm up, 'and do the right thing. Be a rhino. Put the work in. Get back to where you were: the top producer. Or you can go that way,' he says, pointing his left arm down, widening his eyes as if he can see the hell that leads to. 'The way of the party scene.'

She must have told him about the cash.

'If you do choose to make the party scene your full-time occupation, I think it's a road you're going to end up crashing and burning on . . .'

While I move my files to a quad, the rookies watch like piranhas scenting blood. Humiliated, I know what's on their minds: the cannibalisation of my client book. When everything is shifted, I sit embarrassed, staring at my phone, unable to cold-call.

The next day – six years into my career – I don't go to work. I plan on living off money in the stock market in Hammy's name while concentrating on increasing Ecstasy sales using the business techniques I've learnt. *I've got the contacts. I've got the cash. I've had my fill of actively trading the stock market, but I'll get back to it.*

CHAPTER 27

'GANGSTA DAN STUCK a gun in my face and kidnapped someone from my house!' Desirae yells down the phone. 'There's blood and weed all over my carpet. Can you do something about it?'

'Calm down, Desirae.' Conditioned to talking on the phone and pacing, I rise from the black leather sofa in my condo. 'What exactly happened?' *With Wild Man in jail, dealing with Gangsta Dan will be hard.*

'Remember Skinner?'

'Yeah.' Skinner's a gutter punk with a pierced face who wanted to be fronted Ecstasy, but Desirae and Acid Joey told me not to trust him.

'Gangsta Dan kidnapped him.'

'Why?'

'Skinner stole some stripper's car and gave it to some Mexicans for a debt he owed. I didn't know that when a friend took me to the stripper's house. Dan answers the door, puts a gun in my face and yells, "Where's her fucking car?" I say, "What are you talking about? Get the gun outta my fucking face!"'

'Oh no.'

'Dan says, "You got any weapons?" and I show him my little handgun, and he gives it to some Mexican and says, "Hold them hostage till I get back." I'm crying. I'm freaking out. Dan gets back and says, "You're gonna help us find Skinner." I tell him, "I don't wanna be a part of this." He says, "You became part of this when you knocked on this door." He takes us all back here. I'm shitting it, so I call my buddy Grady and tell him my life's in danger, and he shows up. My friend Pablo comes over too. I'm trying to avoid the situation, telling Dan I don't know how to get a hold of Skinner, then guess who calls?'

'Skinner.'

'Yup. Dan says, "I wanna hear whatever you say to whoever's on the phone." I'm thinking I need to get this over with. The first time I met Skinner, he's smoking crack in my bathroom. What do I care for him? Dan hears Skinner and puts his fingers to his lips. Skinner says, "Can I come over to yours?" I'm trying to tell him not to, but Dan's watching. Anyway, Skinner shows up at the door with his buddy Worm, that Special K dealer from Flagstaff. Dan hides in my loft with the stripper and the Mexican gets in my closet. Skinner comes in and sits down. I'm fucking shitting my pants. The first thing Skinner says is, "Desirae, I just didn't know what to do. I'm in debt with the Mexicans, so I had to take her car." Then – *wham!* – Superman Dan jumps off my loft with a big ol' gun – a rifle or sub-machine gun or something – and gun-butts Skinner in the head. The Mexican jumps out of the closet and kung-fu kicks Worm, knocking him out cold. They beat the shit outta Skinner. Skinner's backpack rips open and a pound of weed explodes over my carpet. I say, "Stop! Stop! Get this fucking drama outta here!" Pablo tries pushing me into the next room and calls the cops. I tell everyone Pablo called the cops. They take Skinner – blood's coming from his eyes, ears, nose, mouth, from every orifice. His bottom lip's bleeding from his three piercings. And just as they take off to the left of the house, three, four, five cop cars, sirens going, hauling ass, appear at my right. A cop says, "We've received two reports of someone possibly getting killed." I say it was me who called the cops to report a fight out here among some Mexicans. Then Pablo appears and says, "I'm the one who called the cops," which almost screwed us. But they ask some more questions and let us go.'

'That's messed up. What would you like me to do about it?'

'Tell that fucking Gangsta Dan if he ever points a gun in my face again –'

'Where's he at?'

'Acid Joey's.'

'OK, I'll handle it.'

I dial. 'Gangsta Dan?'

'What's up, English Shaun?' Dan says in a Philadelphian brogue.

'I just got a call from my girlfriend.'

'That Kelly chick?'

'No. I just started seeing Desirae.'

'Oh shit.'

'And she's pretty upset with you right now.'

'I didn't know she was with you.'

'I understand that,' I say.

'I'll talk to her if you want.'

'She's too angry right now. I just need to be able to assure her that won't happen again.'

'I wouldn't disrespect you like that, English Shaun.'

'That's all I needed to hear. And I'm sure if you left the gun you took from her with Acid Joey, she'd calm down a lot.'

'I don't have it.'

'But your Mexican partner does. Can I speak to Joey?'

'OK.'

'What's up?' Acid Joey asks.

'What's going on over there?' I say.

'Do you wanna come over?'

'Not if he's torturing Skinner.'

'He pistol-whipped him and ripped the piercings off his face. Skinner's fucked up.'

'Don't you think that might bring heat to your place?'

'Yeah, but what am I supposed to do?'

'We don't need the cops coming 'cause of Gangsta Dan and finding our X.'

'I know. What should I do?'

'I'll come right over.'

To muster bravery, I snort a line of meth. By the time I get to Acid Joey's, I'm rushing intensely and feeling capable of taking anyone on. I push the door open and stride down the hallway towards his bedroom – known as 'the Blue Room' due to the skyscape on the ceiling and its cobalt-blue walls. Next to a navy-blue bed is a battered chest of drawers containing his black clothes and a collection of preserved frogs and birds that he enjoys spooking visitors with. In the freezer is a dead cat, roadkill found by his home. Acid Joey likes to tell partyers to help themselves to ice cream and listen to them scream. His en suite bathroom is sealed off, giving rise to speculation as to what's died in there.

Faring only slightly better than the cat, frogs and birds is Skinner, panting on the floor, his curly ginger hair and freckled face caked in blood.

'Where's Gangsta Dan?' I ask.

'He took off on a mission to get sherm sticks,' Acid Joey says, referring to cigarettes dipped in PCP.

'You need a ride to a hospital or something?' I ask, shocked by the amount of blood.

'No. I'll be all right,' Skinner says between gasps.

'You sure?' I ask, convinced he needs treatment.

No answer.

'Where you from anyway?'

'Idaho.'

'Where you living now?'

'On the streets. I'm broke. Look, I need to make some money. Let me help Acid Joey move some of your X.'

Acid Joey shakes his head.

'You're homeless, you're from out of state, I barely know you, everyone's saying, "Don't trust Skinner," so why should I front you X?'

'You'll see why. Give me a hundred pills and I'll prove myself.' Above prominent cheekbones, his green eyes, bloodshot and downcast, manage to sparkle, as if he's a martyr on the verge of death, numb to pain, finding peace with the world. His ability to shine out his inner light surprises me. *He's drawing on a lot of strength to convince me to trust him.* 'I can move them faster than anyone,' he says in an endearing accent that contains the best of country and city without being either.

'I'm always willing to give someone a chance. I'll front you a hundred pills.' Adopting the tone of voice Johnny Brasi intimidated me with after I urged him to let me sit the stockbroking exam without taking the classes, I say, 'For all I know, you might leave the state. If so, that's no big deal. Just don't ever come back to Arizona. But in the long run you'll make a lot more money if you stick with me.'

Two weeks later, Skinner's Ecstasy sales exceed Acid Joey's.

Acid Joey calls my condo: 'Gangsta Dan's gonna rob Skinner.'

'How do you know?' I ask.

'If something's going down in Tempe, I know about it.'

'What should I do?'

'Someone needs to talk to Gangsta Dan.'

Worried, I call Skinner. Mari, Skinner's tough Persian-American girlfriend, answers.

'Hello.'

'What's going on with Gangsta Dan?' I ask.

'He went to California and came back with some black gangsta dudes. They came to Acid Joey's and were trying to get something from Skinner. There was like a car full of them. They were trying to get us to take them to a pawnshop. We were all gacked out, and it was really crazy. They're looking for Skinner to try and get free shit. Your shit!'

'Who are these guys?' I ask.

'Crips from LA. Skinner's terrified 'cause they know where we live.'

I hang up, call Gangsta Dan and arrange to meet him at his apartment. Carson – presently unemployed due to meth – fails to talk me out of meeting Gangsta Dan, but he agrees to come as a bodyguard. We snort meth. On the road, I joke about getting shot to hide my fear. By the time we arrive, my thoughts are racing as I rehearse what to say to Gangsta Dan. I knock, Carson behind me, packing a handgun.

The door opens. A young Crip points a sawn-off shotgun at my face. 'Who the fuck are you?'

My body stiffens as hard as ice. My stomach clenches. Blood pumps into places I've never felt it before. *Stay calm.* 'Don't shoot.' I look him straight in the face. *An inquisitive expression. No madman about to blow my head off for no reason.* I consider sprinting. *He might shoot me in the back. No backing down.*

'Who the fuck *are* you?' he asks.

'A friend of Dan's,' I say, trying to sound calm.

'There's no need for the shotgun,' Carson says.

'You shut up!' the Crip barks.

Gangsta Dan emerges – short, built like a tree trunk, with the ill-tempered face of a battle-hardened soldier. 'Put that the fuck away! It's that English Shaun dude I told you about.' He pushes the gun from my face.

'I don't give a fuck who it is!' The Crip huffs, and disappears.

'Come through to my bedroom,' Gangsta Dan says. 'That's just my roommate.'

'Nice guy,' Carson says.

'I've got my friend Carson with me,' I say.

'It's all good,' Dan says. 'What's up anyway, English Shaun?'

'I've got something to ask you, but before I do let's snort some lines of this,' I say, waving a baggie of meth.

Gangsta Dan nods and fetches a plate. I crush the drug. We snort a line each.

'I've come to ask you not to make a move on Skinner.'

'He still owes for the car.'

'You dealt with that already. Besides, I heard you and your stripper friend aren't getting along these days.'

The Crip charges in and yells in my face, 'Who the fuck are you, telling him what to do? I'll get my shotgun!'

Politeness isn't going to get me anywhere. Pushed to an extreme after having a shotgun pointed at me, and with meth warping my logic, I punch the wall. *Bam!* I head-butt it. *Bam! Bam!* My actions command their attention. Surprised and pleased, I yell, 'I thought we were all businessmen here!' Seeing stars from the impact, something dawns: *Dan has been asking me to front him Ecstasy for months. Classifying him as too dangerous, I always decline. Maybe threatening Skinner is his bargaining strategy – ditto for his roommate's shotgun routine. If that's the case, I should be able to make him happy by offering him product.* 'You know I'm getting lots of good X. I'll give you a cheap price for any hundred you can buy cash. You'll make a lot more money from that in the long run than from robbing Skinner. Besides, Skinner's working for me, and if he gets robbed Wild Man's not going to be very happy with you, Dan.'

'Wild Man's in jail,' Gangsta Dan says.

'Where he has lots of friends, and where you may very well end up some day.'

Gangsta Dan stares at the ceiling. 'What price on a hundred Eurodollars?'

'Fifteen.'

'All right, all right. I've got enough cash here for two hundred right now.'

'Cool. We're in business.' I shake his hand and we hug.

Gangsta Dan's under control, but he's too unstable for that to last. Time will eliminate him. The police will nab him, or gangsters will gun him down.

I instruct my dealers to avoid Gangsta Dan, to never front him pills, to immediately report any contact initiated by him to me. I move Skinner and Mari to a new apartment and rent two more apartments in the same complex. I house Desirae in the front building, a new headquarters for me, and in the back building I put Alice, a Native American friend of Acid Joey's who, with the help of her brother Smiley, is now my number-two Ecstasy salesperson after Skinner. If any of the apartments are threatened, the dealers, money and drugs at risk can be moved to the others. I credit Gangsta Dan with giving me the motivation to tighten my operation.

CHAPTER 28

FOLLOWING G DOG into the house of his brother, Raul, I spot a cylindrical metal tube resting like an oversized ornament on the biggest TV I've ever seen. *It can't be. Yes it is. A rocket-propelled grenade launcher. Holy shit!* Raul is gazing at a small black-and-white screen showing the comings and goings on the street outside crowded with lowriders.

'This is the English guy I want you to meet,' G Dog says.

Raul, short, plump, tilts his head back. 'Wattup, homey?' he says without smiling.

'Pleased to meet you,' I say, shaking his hand. 'I like your TV.'

'Damn, you talk funny – like an accent. I guess you *are* from England, homey. Come through to the kitchen. Meet my homies.'

Raul introduces me to a gang of gargantuan Mexican Americans, heavily tattooed, eyeing me suspiciously, stood around a table laden with slabs of crystal meth, cocaine and scales. The biggest thrusts a spoon laden with cocaine at my face. 'Snort it,' he says, his wide, alert eyes radiating danger.

Concerned, I look to G Dog for help. He nods back sternly, not having disclosed that the men are members of the New Mexican Mafia, the most powerful criminal organisation in Arizona – or that the one with the spoon is a hit man on a killing spree. Nervously, I roll a hundred-dollar bill, push a nostril flat and snort the cocaine. The hit man nods and shakes my hand. But doesn't smile. None of them smile.

'Shaun, let's go talk business.' Raul leads me to a bedroom. 'G Dog tells me you can get this Ecstasy shit, and that it's all good.'

'I can get it,' I say, gagging on the numbing aftertaste of the cocaine.

'None of us have ever done that shit. The only thing I do is smoke good weed – know what I'm saying? – hydro, kind bud. I'm having a party at the weekend, some women are coming over and we wanna check your Ecstasy out.'

The night of the party, Raul runs out of Ecstasy. I bring more. The women are in the dining room, the men in the living room, all on Ecstasy for the first time. They're actually smiling, the lethal atmosphere gone. The men keep thanking me for the Ecstasy, hugging me, crushing me, like overgrown teddy bears. Even Carlos, the torturer of the naked hog-tied man, has the innocent aura of a child.

The hit man puts me in a bear hug that lifts me off my feet. 'I'm liking this Ecstasy. My name's Big Vato.'

'I'm glad you like it,' I say.

'What about getting acid?'

'It's available in the rave scene,' I say, eager to get on his good side.

'Acid's easy to send my homies in prison. I just mail it behind the stamps.'

'I'll see what I can do.'

'What about Xanax?' he asks.

'Ravers take them to help come down off drugs,' I say.

'Do you know how easy it is to cross into Mexico with someone asleep in your car, take them out into the desert and shoot them?' Big Vato asks.

'Er . . . no,' I say, fear creeping into my voice.

'Take no notice,' Raul says. 'Vato's just clowning. He doesn't care where he shoots them. Shaun, let's go into the bedroom.'

'OK,' I say.

'Those pills you gave me are good shit. People be wanting more. I might have to make this a regular thing.'

'No problem.'

'I also brought you here to give you a heads-up.'

'What is it?'

'Two fools out of Apache Junction been asking about you.'

'Who?' I ask, surprised.

'One's just outta prison. They jack drug dealers. They'll straight shoot your ass, and take your shit. They got some Ecstasy from your friends in Tempe.'

Intimidated by his knowledge of my affairs, I say, 'There was a guy from Apache Junction who said his partner had just got out of prison. A bit of a loudmouth.'

'That's the younger one. I just made a situation go away for you by telling them we have your back.'

'I see.'

'G Dog tells me you and your people looked out for him when he pulled a gun on that cop. We appreciate that, so now we'll look out for you,' Raul says, pointing at me.

'I really appreciate that.'

'If we're gonna be doing business together, I need to run a few things down to you.'

'OK.'

'If I page you, call me only from a payphone. If I answer, I'll tell you if you can come over or not. That's all I'll say. We don't talk any business on the phone. Ever!'

'I understand.'

'And another thing. The cops have been pulling over people leaving my house lately. If you get pulled over and they ask why you were here, just tell them you're looking for my brother. If they wanna search your car, you don't have to let them. And if they do bust you with drugs coming from here, don't fucking say anything to them. Ask for a lawyer.'

'OK, but, er, who do you use for a lawyer?'

'Alan Simpson, but he's real expensive, homey.'

The warning from Raul, and the police showing up at Mari and Skinner's apartment as part of a 'kidnapping investigation', convince me it's time to relocate the hub I've sold Ecstasy from for the last six months. I put a down payment on an apartment for Mari and Skinner and rent a big three-bedroom house at The Lakes in Ahwatukee for Desirae and me.

CHAPTER 29

'IT FEELS LIKE your hands are melting into my back,' I say to Aiden – an Irishman I met at the George & Dragon – on his massage table at my home.

'I specialise in shiatsu.'

'It feels really bloody good on E,' I say, my eyeballs rolling up.

'Who're you getting your E off these days?' Aiden asks.

'I've been going through LA,' I say, groaning, relaxed, almost falling asleep.

'That's funny. I've got a mate from Manchester in LA and he sells E. I thought you might want to meet him.'

Suddenly alert, I ask, 'Who is he?'

'Mike Hotwheelz. An artist and DJ. He's in his forties. Dead intelligent. He was working for Tony Wilson when raving began in Manchester and was part of LA's early rave scene. You'll get along great with him.'

Hotwheelz sounds ideal. 'This is bloody good timing, Aiden. I've got two connects in LA, but one keeps trying to jack the price up and keeps me waiting for hours every time I go out there, and the other's a bit hit and miss. Sometimes he doesn't have the pills ready and he has to call around.'

'There'll be no bullshit if you're dealing directly with another Englishman.'

Desirae and I drive to LA. Pulsing trance guides us to a narrow house.

'Nice tunes,' I say, ringing the bell.

'You and your fluffy-ass trance!' Desirae says.

A man answers the door wearing tartan bondage trousers and a tight black T-shirt with 3-D blinking eyes on it.

'Are you Mike Hotwheelz or Johnny Rotten?' I ask.

He smiles. 'Hotwheelz. Come in, mate.'

'Pleased to meet you, mate,' I say, shaking his hand. 'This is my girlfriend, Desirae.'

'Hi, Mike.' Desirae enters first. 'Holy shit! This is incredible!'

'*Wow!* Your house is a toyland!' I say.

There's no furniture in the living room – just toys. The centrepiece is a landscaped slot-car track looping through a multicoloured plastic city: town-hall buildings, a church, highways, bridges, palm trees, bushes, balloons, flags, people, trains, cars, a zeppelin scudding over on a yellow string. On the wall beyond the track: a golden swan, a bust of an African woman, the head of a boy puppet, a framed painting of sperm swimming away from an eyeball.

'Check this out.' Hotwheelz raises the roof of a model building with a sign reading 'THE HOTWHEELZ HOTEL' and a spring-loaded couple make love.

Laughing hard, I stoop under an arch of draperies – golden, heavy-velvet, tasselled with bell-shaped pom-poms – that belong in a Parisian brothel from another era. The wall art intensifies in the next room: a horned skull with plastic angel wings at ear level, a cow's-head mask, Christ on the cross, a teddy bear, a Cowardly Lion mask, a skeleton's hand dangling from a mirror. A couple sat on a leopard-skin sofa are snorting lines of white powder – refined crystal meth called glass – off a plate.

'This is Frankie Bones and his girlfriend,' Hotwheelz says.

'Pleased to meet you,' I say. 'I've listened to your tunes since raving began.'

'You're *the* Frankie Bones,' Desirae says. '*Wow!*'

'Not another Englishman,' Frankie Bones says, shaking my hand.

Desirae and I sit down. ''Fraid so, and from quite close to where Mike's from.' My instincts tell me to trust Hotwheelz, but having only just met him, and being in the drug business, I must be careful. 'Where in Manchester are you from, Mike?'

'Chorlton, South Manchester. Not very ghetto,' Mike says, stood over turntables.

'I'm from Widnes.'

'So you're not a Scouser, you're a Woollyback.'

I laugh. 'I went to Liverpool Uni, and clubs like The State and Quadrant Park in Liverpool, but I did most of my raving in Manchester. The Thunderdome was my favourite.'

'Fucking hell! That sketchy joint on Oldham Road! I remember all those dodgy-looking fuckers from Salford.'

'That's where I took my first E,' I say. 'When the Dome shut down, I was a regular at Konspiracy. I only went to The Haçienda a few times. I heard you were involved with Tony Wilson.'

'Yeah, I worked at Granada with him on a couple of shows, and we hung out a lot at The Haçienda.'

'How come The Haçienda got shut down?'

'Gang warfare broke out and they were losing too much money. Under the licensing laws everything was supposed to shut at 2 a.m. Of course, we're all E'd off our tits around that time, courtesy of the Happy Mondays. Anyway, there were few places you could go after the club shut. One was a snooker hall around the corner that wasn't very E-conducive and the other was in the opposite direction, a little West Indian club, which was cool, but the Rastas in there were like, "What the fuck are these kids on?" They saw the money to be made from Ecstasy and shortly thereafter Rastas, and I mean Jamaican rude boys with big hats and canes with big fuck-off silver tops on, started strolling in The Haçienda like they owned the place, thinking, *Fuck me, we've gotta get into this rave shit for the money.* Shortly after that, the whole thing started kicking off with the white boys from Salford, the Cheetham Hill Mob and the Moss Side Crew, the West Indians in the south. It went downhill fast. A doorman got shot.'

Proper old school. Frankie Bones in his house. All this knowledge. He's for real. 'It must have been fun in the early days.'

'Oh, yeah, we'd go to little warehouse parties, and the cops would show up and some big Rasta would shout, "Babylon!" and we'd get out as fast as possible. This was back in '87, '88. Then in '89 I moved to London. I missed all the Manchester scene after that. I did a few Orbital raves, and a great one in King's Cross run by Zodiac Mindwarp, who did all the visuals. The entrance was in the shunting yards through a hole in the fence. Some geezer with a Rottweiler was holding open a plank of wood so you could clamber in. The best thing was they had five or six different areas where music was playing. One was a shed and everyone in there had painted their faces with luminescent zinc paint. So under the black lights their faces were all trippy, tribal, like a scene outta *Tron*. Another area was a big warehouse with huge great fires and crazy-ass metal sculptures. My favourite was the cheapest and lowest tech of the lot. The techno stage had one strobe light on all night, with a hundred people dancing all tranced out and a bunch probably twitching away on the floor having epileptic fits. The strobe never changed sequence or anything. It was fucking brilliant!'

'So how did you end up in LA?'

'I was a graphic designer in London, earning good money, but I broke up with my wife and moved to America.'

I tell him my story, and about the problems with my Ecstasy suppliers. 'Can you get E on a regular basis?'

'Usually, and as many as you want.'

'Thousands or tens of thousands?' I ask, expecting him to bulk.

'For ten thou, I'd need plenty of notice, and I'd have to put a special order in,' he says in a confident tone.

'I'm constantly running out of E, and looking to increase the size of my purchases.'

'Well, here's your thousand Mitsubishis. See how these go and let me know if you need more.'

Trusting him, I don't ask to taste a pill. I pay and leave thinking, *It'll be much safer doing business with an Englishman.*

CHAPTER 30

'WHY DON'T WE throw our own raves?' Skinner asks at one of the weekend board meetings I hold in the Blue Room.

'Acid Joey tried that and look what happened,' I say, generating a few laughs. I still want to bring the English rave scene to Phoenix, but Acid Joey's loss raised my guard. *Who can I trust with my money to get the job done?*

'To be able to throw a party and make money you have to be business-minded,' says Pablo, a skinny philosophy undergraduate from Spain dressed in bright colours.

'What? Like you?' I say, testing him.

'I can do it,' Pablo says.

'So can I.' Skinner sounds more confident. 'Have I steered you wrong so far, big brother?'

'With me by his side, Skinner won't lose your money,' Mari says.

I don't doubt it. Mari's proving to be Skinner's backbone. 'What are you proposing?'

'The most successful parties are the ones catering to the breakbeat crowd,' Skinner says.

'I hate breaks,' I say.

'You suck,' Desirae says. 'It's all about Simply Jeff!'

'If I throw a party, I want to bring DJs from Europe, so the ravers can hear the DJs I grew up on: Sasha, Carl Cox –'

'But look how much they cost to fly out!' Pablo says.

'If you want a breakbeat headliner, I want some house and trance,' I say.

'We can get local DJs to spin that for free,' Skinner says. 'Breakbeat's the crowd-puller right now.'

'How much will I need to put up?' I ask.

'A party costs between twenty and thirty thou,' Pablo says. 'But you only need to put up half of that up front.'

'If that,' Skinner says. 'With five grand, I can get flyers printed up and put deposits down. Ticket sales will raise more cash right away, and we can use the door money to pay the balance of a lot of stuff on the night of the party. We can also use our own security.'

'Our own security?' I ask.

'We'll just buy security T-shirts,' Skinner says, 'and throw them on Acid Joey and some other big dudes.'

'I don't think so!' says Cody, a friend of Desirae whose clean-cut looks, cropped blond hair and preppy clothing make him seem out of place in the Blue Room. 'Security has to be licensed and bonded, otherwise the cops shut the party down.'

'How do you know that?' I ask.

'I work as a security guard.' Cody dips his hand in his pocket. 'Here's my licence.'

'So when the cops or fire department do a walk-through,' Skinner says, 'Cody can flash them his licence.'

'Cody, you just became the head of my security team,' I say.

'Why, thanks. And I thought you didn't even like me.'

'Cody, I like you, but you're quirky. You're the only one of us who stays sober, so I can't think of a better man for the job. There's also something I'd like to talk to you about after this.'

'Having our own security opens up all kinds of possibilities,' Skinner says.

'Like what?' I ask.

'If our security bust anyone selling X, then that X goes to the house and the house resells it,' Skinner says.

'I like the sound of that. If you can keep the cost of the party down to twenty thou, I'll put the money up. The way I see it, two thousand ravers will show up, and at twenty a head that's forty thou.'

'But a quarter of them won't pay to get in,' Pablo says. 'They'll be friends of the DJs and everyone involved in throwing the party, on the VIP list and all that. I know this because I help Swell throw parties.' Swell, the first rave store in Arizona, organises most of the local events.

'All right, if fifteen hundred pay to get in, that's thirty thou. That gives me a good ten-grand margin of safety,' I say.

'Plus we'll sell them water all night,' Skinner says.

'OK, here's the deal: I'm putting Skinner and Mari in charge of the money. Anyone who wants to work security can see Cody.

Pablo, can you help with the booking contacts you've made through Swell? Can everyone else help promote the event? OK, Cody, let's go talk.'

Cody follows me into another bedroom. 'What's up, Shaun?'

'I've got too much going on to be driving back and forth to LA picking Ecstasy up. You've got a car. You don't look like a druggie. Are you interested?'

'Sure. How much will I get paid?'

'Five hundred a trip to pick up anywhere from one to five thousand pills.'

'What if I get caught?'

'Don't say anything to the cops,' I say, drawing on Raul's advice. 'Exercise your right to remain silent. I'll get you an attorney. If you do a good job, it'll be a regular thing. I'm also looking for someone to rent an apartment as a safe house to store drugs at. Somewhere no one will know about, so if anything goes down with the rest of us the cops will never find it.'

'Let me check into that. When do you want me to go on my first run?'

'This weekend. What we'll do is use your car one week, my Corolla the next,' I say, referring to a car purchased in Hammy's name, 'and if you feel these cars are getting noticed by highway patrol, I'll buy new ones. Even if you do get pulled over, we've got fake Coke cans to put pills in. I don't see the cops doing anything worse than giving you a speeding ticket. Most police dogs can't sniff Ecstasy, except for specially trained beagles. But they can all smell weed, so never, ever travel with weed or transport anyone with it. Do you have a radar detector?'

'No.'

'Get one. Here's two hundred. What do you know about guns?' I ask.

'Why?'

'I'm clueless about them. We don't have guns in England. It's nothing like the Wild West. I bought a gun when I was a stockbroker –'

'What type?'

'A Lorcin.'

Shaking his head, Cody laughs.

'What's so funny?'

'They're cheap pieces of shit. Lorcins are more likely to jam on you than fire. What you need is a Glock. That's what the cops use.'

'I'll buy a Glock, then.'

'If I'm going to be doing these missions for you, can you get me a Glock, too?'

'Yes. Will you train me to shoot it?' I ask.

'Why don't we go to concealed-weapons permit classes? There's a place on the west side run by cops with a firing range. They'll train us and we'll be able to legally carry a gun hidden in our clothes.'

'Let's do it,' I say, shaking his hand.

With a neighbour's daughter behind our house in
Widnes, Cheshire, 1977.

Enjoying family time with my father, Derick, and
grandfather Frederick, in 1984, when I was a shy student,
before I first took Ecstasy.

Larking around with Aunt Mo, who's treating me to dinner, in 1987, four years before I moved to live with her in Arizona.

With Kelly, who's wearing 150 bracelets on each arm, in 1995. I 'married' her during a sunset blood ritual in a forest.

My feisty Italian-American ex-girlfriend Desirae, ready to rave in 1996.

Losing control on Ecstasy, GHB and crystal meth, with DJ Mike Hotwheelz at a friend's house in Tempe, Arizona, 1997.

Marital bliss. With Amy in the Icehouse, Phoenix, Arizona, 2000. I'm wearing a floppy hat to disguise myself from undercover cops and Detective Reid.

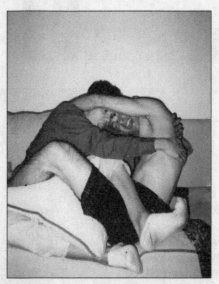

On Ecstasy, hugging my friend
Jake, in 2000.

With Amy, my proud parents and my sister, Karen, in Tucson, Arizona, 2000. I'm struggling to stay off drugs for a few weeks to be a good host.

Partying with Acid Joey (centre), who's gripping me as Ecstasy fizzes on my tongue, 2000.

Chilling with Superstar DJ Keoki – featured in the film
Party Monster – who regularly played at my raves, 2000.

Heading for a rave in a limo with Cody Bates and the Wild
Ones in 2000. After drinking a bottle of GHB, Wild Man
is semi-conscious. The limo driver called the cops on us
and it took six of them to carry Wild Man out.

Meltdown, 2000.

Adorable Claudia, my guardian angel, with Build-A-Bear Floppy, in Scottsdale, Arizona, 2002.

With Wild Man on his sofa in Widnes, Cheshire, 2012.

Sharing my story with young people at Glyn School in
Surrey, to put them off getting involved in
drugs and crime, 2012.

CHAPTER 31

MARI AND SKINNER call our first rave Clowning. To promote it, we stick flyers on cars parked at raves. I go on the nightclub circuit holding hands with my friend Karma, a partially blind albino whose pinkish eyes, long white hair and ghostly appearance attract mass attention. While I tell people about Clowning, Karma massages my shoulders.

Acid Joey shuffles into the next rave dressed as a Catholic priest. He positions himself on a platform and opens the Bible as if about to deliver a sermon. He tears pages out and sets them on fire. A near riot breaks out between the devout and atheists.

'Put it out!'

'You can't do that!'

'He can do whatever he wants! This is a free country!'

'Sacrilege! You'll burn in hell!'

'Bullshit, Christians!'

'God will strike you dead!'

'Who believes in that crap?'

Acid Joey showers the people pushing and shoving and arguing with holy water and Clowning flyers.

The date of the party approaches, but we have no venue. Concerned about losing my investment, I urge Mari and Skinner to find a location fast. Mari drives all over town, on a painstaking search, and settles on a warehouse in West Phoenix, owned by the Mexican Mafia, adjacent to a furniture showroom.

On the way to the party, I pray for plenty to show up. I'm greeted at the door by Cody, and a worried Skinner, who says the fire department have threatened to stop the party from opening if they find any safety issues and that Mari is escorting them around the premises. I put my sunglasses on to disguise my dilated pupils. We wait, frowning, hoping no hazards are found. The firemen emerge, with Mari charming them. They ask about security. Cody, sober, well spoken, states he's in charge and flashes them his licence. I expect them to study it, to find fault, but they only glance and turn back to Mari. She answers a few more questions, makes them laugh, and they leave.

The doors open at nine. Few ravers arrive. Mari and Skinner check tickets and take payment, surrounded by security. Cody positions bouncers inside to prevent the occupation of the furniture showroom. From nine to ten, hardly anyone shows up. *What a disaster!* I pace by the entrance, embarrassed, shrinking away from anyone trying to talk to me.

Grady – a tall stoner with a shaved head, a goatee and a flat boxer's nose – offers me a bottle cap of clear liquid: GHB.

'Grady, what the fuck do you think you're doing introducing Shaun to new drugs?' Desirae yells, scowling.

'How will it make me feel?' I ask.

'A little bit like X, but it doesn't last as long,' Grady says.

My inner wolves howl, *Take it, take it, take it . . .* 'Fuck it! If it's anything like X, I'll do it.'

'Like you don't have a big enough drug problem!' Desirae says, shaking her head.

As I drink the GHB, a salty-chemical bitter taste explodes in my mouth. I almost retch. They laugh at my puckered face. *It was a set-up.*

'Here, drink this quick,' Desirae says, handing me orange juice.

I snatch it, and glug half the bottle but can still taste the sickly GHB chemicals coating my tongue. Fifteen minutes later, euphoria hits. I feel drunk but lively. Breathing never felt so good: I can taste air. I attune to my surroundings with heightened, animal-like sensitivity. My jaw juts. Walking, I bounce with a new-found strength. *I am a wolf.*

Ravers arrive in droves. By midnight, the building is packed, the queue snaking around the plaza. I marvel at the success. My workforce is delighted.

With no smoke machine, we improvise. Skinner and Grady walk around with plastic bags full of hundreds of joints, giving away Mexican dirt weed. The ravers exhale so much smoke a cloud materialises on the dance floor, expanding slowly like fog. An ecosystem forms. Ravers chug water and sweat it out dancing. Vapour rises from the ravers; condensation forms on the ceiling and drops fall like rain. The marijuana cloud continues to expand, filling the room with the smell of burnt herbs with a hint of skunk musk, eventually engulfing more than 2,000 people. Robust beats shake the building like thunder, and in the cloud the strobe flashes like lightning, illuminating body parts, heads bobbing, arms waving, hands drawing circles with glow sticks, legs stomping in baggy jeans.

Ravers sneak around a barrier to nestle into the sofas in the showroom. High on Ecstasy, they rub their bodies against the material like cats in heat. I laugh. On Ecstasy myself, I want to join them but can't risk upsetting the owners of the building. I tell security to escort them back to the main room. But every time the sofas go unguarded, they're reoccupied.

I'm heady on the atmosphere – until the cops arrive. *Oh shit!* I put my shades on and watch from a safe distance as Mari stalls them at the door. The stink of weed is enough for them to stop the party, never mind all the ravers on Ecstasy, their eyes bulging unnaturally as if a chemistry experiment on the masses is under way. I imagine the cops calling backup, ravers getting searched, arrested, hauled into vans . . .

Patiently, Mari listens to the cops, who say the party is in violation of a sound ordinance. *Phew!* The sound is lowered and they leave.

Upstairs in a VIP area overlooking the dance floor, high on Ecstasy, electrified by the success of our effort, I admire my friends, glowing with purpose and triumph. Every so often, my bouncers introduce me to strangers who want to thank English Shaun for the party and the quality of the Ecstasy. At first, I'm taken aback by the reverence with which they treat me, but I begin to revel in the attention lavished by beautiful women competing to hug me, asking endless questions, and men greeting me with wide-eyed awe, impressed by my rising notoriety.

Around dawn, Cody asks, 'What do you want security to do about the girl dancing naked on the speaker?'

'That's a sign of a good party, right?' I say, my jaw quivering and my head being massaged by Jake, a soft-spoken Mexican American with kind brown eyes. 'Who is she anyway?'

'Some chick from New York with a pierced pussy and a big mouth.'

'Why don't you bring her up here so we can meet her?'

'I'll be right back.'

My closest party friends – 'The Circus' – are sprawled on the floor, massaging each other, when Cody brings in the naked woman. Short. Big brown eyes. Hair in a pixie cut. A ten-gauge barbell in her clitoris. 'This is Sally.'

'Pleased to meet you, Sally. I'm English Shaun.' I stand and give her a hug.

'*Grrrrrrrrr,*' Sally says, running her eyes up and down Alice, still my number-two Ecstasy salesperson. 'You're so pretty. Exotic. That lip piercing's hot.' She sits down and kisses Alice's full, enticing lips.

'Give her a Mitsubishi on me,' I say to Alice.

'I already took five Mitsues,' Sally says. 'Your pills are good.'

'You're not going to feel one more very much, then,' I say. 'Alice, give Sally another five.'

'Thank you,' Sally says.

'Take a few more Mitsues and we'll massage you,' Alice says.

Sally *grrrr*s as Jake rubs lotion on her.

Skinner arrives, his eyes radiating joy below a tangle of sweat-compressed hair.

'Come join us, little brother!' I say, waving him over, delighted Skinner is thriving, really feeling a bond with him. 'Well done tonight!'

'No worries, big brother.' Skinner rests his head on my shoulder and hugs me tightly in a brotherly way.

CHAPTER 32

MARI AND SKINNER pick a swingers club for our next rave. Pablo brings Hotwheelz – the headliner – from the airport to my house and heads over to the venue. Hotwheelz snorts glass, I sip GHB and we set off. I'm speeding along Loop 202 when the GHB – a depressant at high doses – knocks me out in the fast lane.

I hear Hotwheelz yelling, 'Shaun, wake the fuck up!' Leaning over me, he's steering the car in the middle lane. 'You nearly fucking killed us!'

Realising the car's changed lanes shocks me awake. But my head lolls forward like a baby's. I almost nod off. 'You'd better drive. That jibber juice hit me too quick. I'm all fucked up.' I pull onto the shoulder, outraged by my stupidity.

At the club, Hotwheelz parks amid a crowd of agitated ravers.

Pablo runs to my car. 'The owner's cancelled the party!'

'Why?' The crisis lifts the GHB fog from my brain.

'We don't know yet,' Pablo says. 'He's adopted the keep-the-doors-locked-and-hope-everyone-goes-away strategy. But it's not working. More ravers are arriving and they're getting angry.'

'If he doesn't open the club, the thousands I've spent will go down the drain!' I shake my head.

Mari and Skinner rush over. 'I've worked for months promoting this party,' Skinner says. 'If this fool thinks everyone's going home, he must be smoking crack. I've been waiting to get the word from you to shoot the door open.' He pulls his gun out.

'Give me that gun.' I grab it and place it in the glove compartment. 'If you shoot the door open, that'll just bring the cops. What's that going to achieve?'

'Actually, he would have shot the door down already if it wasn't for me,' Mari says.

'Thanks for keeping him in check, Mari,' I say. 'Let's hold off on any drastic action for now.'

Skinner storms off. Repeated requests to negotiate with the owner fail.

Fifteen minutes later, Skinner returns. 'If you don't give me my gun back, I'll get a gun off someone else and shoot the fucking door open.'

'Little brother, chill out,' I say.

Mari shakes her head.

An Italian club-kid couple – short with big eyes and smiley faces – whom I've arranged to meet show up. I explain my predicament.

'Primo's real good at negotiating things,' Marcello says. 'He stays real calm. Do you want him to talk to the owner on your behalf?'

'Yes,' I say.

The bouncers allow Primo in. The crowd swells at the entrance, threatening to riot. The situation is on the verge of igniting when Primo emerges. The bouncers leave the doors open.

'The club is open! Everyone come inside!'

We cheer and fill the small, dark venue. Mostly ravers. Some swingers. My friends settle on sofas adjacent to the DJ booth. Hotwheelz mans the turntables. His trance elevates my mood. A hippy arrives with a gallon of GHB in a brown moonshine bottle. I sip some and take Ecstasy.

'I've got a gallon of jibber juice!' I say. 'Anyone who wants a cap, come and help yourselves.'

'I want some!'

'Me!'

'Can I try it?'

'If you've never done it before, just take a small capful,' I say. 'This shit will knock you on your arse fast if you take too much. When it hits you and you're feeling great and have the urge to drink more, don't come back for more because you'll OD.'

The ravers know their GHB tolerances, but the swingers don't. They drink some, feel great and demand more. Disregarding my warning, they keep sipping it.

An hour after the arrival of the GHB, some women undress. Sally, Alice and their new glitter girlfriend Lexi start a female orgy on the dance floor. The mesmerised men – me included – don't interfere. We cheer as Sally reels in a stranger, sits her down, hikes her skirt up, pulls her G-string aside and licks the region like a cat at a bowl of milk.

Two hours after the arrival of the GHB, people start collapsing.

'Holy shit!' I say. 'It looks like the Grim Reaper's walked through here.'

Cody, Acid Joey and I rush around checking eyes, pulses and that people are breathing. Some are conscious, eyes glazed, expressions confused, others twitching as if subject to electric shocks, a few unconscious and snoring.

'What should we do?' Cody asks.

'Too much GHB puts me in a deep sleep,' I say, 'but I wake up fine. These people need to be watched to make sure there's no complications. They'll be fine if they sleep it off.'

A bouncer with a thin face, thick specs and a pterodactyl's nest of ginger hair rushes around, yelling, 'Oh my God! They're dying! They're all dying! Someone call 911! Jesus Christ! They're all dying!'

'Where's this lunatic come from?' I ask.

Cody shrugs.

'How do you know they're dying?' croaks a voice from the crowd.

'Listen to me! I'm a licensed paramedic! I can tell by their pupil dilation that they're dying!' Waving his hands, he yells, 'Good God, has anyone called 911 yet?'

The partyers jeer as if about to stone him.

'If we don't call 911 and they die, we'll all be held responsible!' he yells, shaking his nest of hair. 'For Christ's sake, someone call 911!'

The owner of the club emerges. 'They're not dying,' he says in the tone of a man regretting opening his club. 'They've just drunk too much GHB. They're in deep sleep. They need to be left alone. If anyone dials 911, I could lose my licence and the club could be shut down.'

'Don't listen to him!' the bouncer yells. 'I'm a licensed paramedic and I'm telling you they're dying! For God's sake, someone give me a cellphone before they all die!' he says, offering his palms as if expecting phones to rain down upon him.

The owner whispers in the ear of the largest bouncer. He and another security guard drag the renegade away, yelling and flailing. When the bouncers reappear, they pick the bodies up and arrange them side by side in a back room. Periodically, we check their vital signs and that none have vomited in their mouths. Eventually, they all resurrect and claim to feel well rested.

After the rave, Sally – waving a whip out of a car window – leads a convoy of bisexual women to Acid Joey's. Word travels fast about the lesbian antics, drawing male spectators from far and wide; they tour the house and leave with their expressions transformed, as if they can't believe their eyes.

I arrive home on Sunday afternoon shocked to see my clothes on the lawn. *Desirae!* Immersed in work helping handicapped people, Desirae has toned her partying down in recent months, and I've ignored her warnings about my lifestyle.

'Jesus, Desirae!' I yell, entering the living room. 'You went and chose all my best clothes! All my Diesel stuff!'

Desirae marches towards me, pointing. 'I'm sick of you staying out all weekend, doing all kinds of drugs! You're gonna kill yourself, Shaun!'

'It's not like you don't do drugs either!' I say.

'I smoke weed! I'm not the one passing out on GHB!' she yells, brow clenched, spit flying at my face. 'I can't take it any more. I'm moving out!'

'Desirae, we've been together for over a year now. I love you! I thought you loved me,' I say, shocked, devastated.

'I do, but since we met your drug intake has increased. You might have quit meth, but look at all the other drugs you're doing. Look at how much your dealing has increased. Everyone in the scene knows who English Shaun the Ecstasy dealer is. You're getting too big. I don't wanna be around when the cops come.'

I want to spend all day convincing her to stay with me, but she storms out. My thoughts go in a million different directions, as if my brain is melting down. I sob. Like a fool, I use her departure as an excuse to go on a diet of drugs and no food. A few days later, Alice finds me wasting away, heartbroken, and takes me to a house where she performs a Native American healing ritual with chanting, incense, smoke and ash. Jake and Sally move in, force me to sober up and eat, and nurse me back to health. We talk endlessly about the problems in our lives and pledge to help each other in times of crisis.

CHAPTER 33

'HELL, NO! WE won't go!' thousands of ravers chant at the cops outside of Swell's Musik 98 party. We mill around, disappointed, in a massive warehouse.

'Shaun, you need to get the hell out of here before the riot squad comes,' Pablo says.

Having given away more than 100 Ecstasy, and on 15 myself, I try to speak but end up sucking my lips.

'Quick. Let's bail in Keoki's limo,' Hotwheelz says, seizing my arm.

'Er . . . yeah,' I say.

I run with Hotwheelz. The thrill of escaping in a limo intensifies my buzz. The car weaves around a battalion of cops lined up in riot gear, about to storm the rave.

Superstar DJ Keoki is at the back of the limo, legs akimbo in black leather trousers, wearing pointy boots and sunglasses bordering on snowboarding goggles, his square, chiselled face and broad bronze chest tattooed tribally, lending him the look of an Aztec warrior. '*Fe fi fo fum, I smell the blood of an Englishman*,' he says, imitating the voice of a giant.

'Two Englishmen, actually,' Hotwheelz says. 'Keoki, this is my mate Shaun. When he's not this fucked up, he throws raves.'

'How do you do?' Keoki leans forward to shake my hand.

I try to assemble a reply. 'I'm . . . er . . .' I inhale loudly, relaxing into a smile.

'He took fifteen hits of E,' Hotwheelz says. 'My Dollar Signs.'

'Fifteen! Can people do that many and survive?' says a thin man with the air of a boffin, his squinty eyes scanning me through narrow oblong glasses.

'There's gotta be a certain level of toxicity going on there,' Hotwheelz says.

'You . . . can't OD . . . on happiness,' I say.

'He looks exceedingly euphoric to me,' Keoki says. 'What about getting crystal meth around here?'

'Shaun and his friends can get just about anything in Phoenix,' Hotwheelz says.

'Can they now?' Keoki says. 'Nice shades, Shaun.'

'Kieselsteins.' I hand them to Keoki.

'How much?' he asks.

'A thou,' I say.

'Sharp. *Hmmm*, I'll have to get me some of these. My, what big eyes you've got,' he says, handing them back.

My response floats out: 'Thanks.'

'He's breathing funny,' the thin man says. 'We'd better get him to a hospital.'

'Hospital or after-party, Shaun?' Keoki says with a smile borrowed from the Devil. 'Or would you like me to flip a coin?'

'After-party . . . always,' I say.

'Will Keoki be safe there?' asks a man with olive skin, twice the size of Keoki. 'I'm Patrick, his bodyguard.'

'Shaun has his own security team,' Hotwheelz says.

'There you have it, Patrick,' Keoki says.

We head to a one-storey four-bedroom house where Jaxson, one of my biggest bouncers, lives. Excited ravers are waiting for Hotwheelz and Keoki to arrive. We enter to cheering, whistles blowing, air horns sounding – attention that raises my high – and Sally dancing, wearing only body glitter. The living room is a mini-rave. Strobe machines firing beams. A black box breathing out fog. We hug our way through the crowd, over a carpet littered with deflated balloons. In the back yard, ravers are queuing for N20 canisters, anxious to fill balloons with laughing gas for a quick high. Keoki gets on the turntables. The house fills and we have to turn people away.

'You wanna cap of X for free?' asks a large unfamiliar man.

A competitor with a good product or a scam artist? 'What you got?' I ask.

He offers me a size 00 gelatin capsule packed with powder. *Scam artist.* One dose of Ecstasy is 100 to 125 milligrams of 3,4-Methylenedioxymethamphetamine, a fraction of a 00 capsule – such a small amount that I advise my dealers never to sell Ecstasy in 00 capsules because customers complain they're getting shorted because of the empty space.

'What's in it?' I ask.

'It's pure.'

'Pure MDMA?'

'Yeah.'

'Mind if I taste it?'

'Go ahead,' he says, smiling.

Ravers and some of my bouncers gather around. I twist the capsule open, pour powder onto my palm, lick it and hold it on my tongue. The chemical taste is sharp and unfamiliar. No hint of MDMA. 'It doesn't taste right. I reckon it's bunk.'

Jaxson – with spiky black hair and biceps bulging from a 'SECURITY' T-shirt – steps up to the man like a wall. 'You need to leave,' he says in a husky voice.

The man disappears fast.

'The thing is, I took one of his capsules,' Jaxson says.

'Glad I didn't,' says Big Jed, a bodybuilder with long permed hair. 'But a bunch of people did.'

'I took one,' Sally says. 'If this messes me up, I'll fucking beat that guy's ass into next year.'

'The powder in those horse pills smelled like angel dust,' says my friend The Prophet, handsome with short brown hair and a New York accent. 'That's why I took one.'

'Prophet, you're a crazy bastard!' Sally says.

'Never trust a 00 cap full of that much powder,' I say. 'He probably crushed up a bunch of pharmaceuticals. Whoever wants good X, come and see me for a free Dollar Sign.'

A hippy arrives with GHB. We drink capfuls. The Prophet puts some in the freezer to make popsicles.

Worm, gangly and Gothic-looking, with each fingernail polished a different colour, enters the kitchen to cook ketamine, pestered by ravers craving the veterinary anaesthetic. When it's ready, Jaxson allows a select group into his bedroom to partake. Worm goes to work arranging a small pile of powder into rows of white lines on a baby-blue plate, his forehead crinkled, his stare focused, like an engineer operating on a circuit board. The rest of us watch greedily. He raises his face and smiles to acknowledge that the ritual of dispensation is about to begin, increasing the hunger in our eyes. He exhales loudly, lodges a piece of a straw into his right nostril, leans forward and snorts a line.

'Good burn,' he whispers. 'Who's next for the kitty cat?'

Like hatchlings spotting the approach of their mother with a worm, all of our mouths open at once.

'I am,' Skinner says.

'Me!' I say.

'Over here!' Alice says.

'Me!' Acid Joey says.

'Me first,' Sally says, snatching the plate.

'Sally, you don't suit the name Sally,' I say. 'You're too wild. I'm hereby renaming you Sallywack. You know, like scallywag.'

'She is a Sallywack!' Alice says, eyeing the plate, eager to sacrifice her faculties after peddling Ecstasy all night.

Sallywack snorts a line, *grrr*s and kisses Alice. 'I, Sallywack, do hereby declare I'm going to fuck Alice's brains out later on. I even brought a strap-on.'

We laugh. Round and round the plate goes, everyone keeping an eye on how much is being snorted and calculating if there will be anything left by the time the plate returns – a kind of musical chairs for eyes. The plate empties. We groan. Worm leaves to cook more.

When the ketamine hits, I close my eyes and curl into a ball on the floor. The music – a Plastikman CD, a futuristic jumble of sounds – divides into components that connect to different parts of my brain. The conversation and music fade in and out, blend together and mix with my thoughts. I try to speak but don't know whether sentences are coming out or I'm just hearing my own voice inside my head. Attempting to force words out, I forget what I want to say. The confusion scares me one second, delights me the next. The feeling of someone massaging my neck rouses my eyes open. 'That's great. Thanks, Alice.'

'You looked like you were in a K-hole,' Alice says, smiling.

'I was. You brought me back to earth.'

She kisses me, and I suck her lip piercing.

Three batches later, we're all sedated and hallucinating.

Big Jed starts drawing triangles in the air. 'Everyone follow me, for I am the navigator and, being the navigator, I'll take you to where you need to be, for I am the navigator, so follow me . . .'

Anchored to the floor, bathing in the vibration of our laughter, I sway.

Our reaction encourages Big Jed. 'Follow me, for I am the navigator, taking you exactly where you need to be on the Special

K superhighway today, so follow me, for I am the navigator . . .'

Listening to him with my eyes closed, I imagine the house is a spaceship with Big Jed's muscle-bound physique at the helm, rising through a sky spattered with stars, streaking past planets – until the ketamine wears off. I struggle to stand up and shuffle out. In each of the four bedrooms, ravers are focused on a different drug.

'This is the pot-smokers' room!' Grady yells. 'Get back to your E and K room and your cheesy-ass fucking trance!'

I pinch my nose. 'This room stinks!' I end up in the living room, delighted by Hotwheelz blending the Batman theme tune into a mix. Everyone cheers. I join the ravers jumping and leaping as if on a bouncy castle.

The Prophet appears, yelling through a bullhorn. 'The GHB popsicles are ready.'

I join the stampede for the kitchen.

By the time the sun rises, each room contains at least one unconscious person on a bed or the carpet.

'Shaun, Sallywack's in the bathroom crying, talking to a bar of soap!' Alice says. 'C'mon! We gotta help her!'

I follow Alice to Sallywack, naked in an empty tub, a faraway look in her eyes, not responding to the ravers trying to snap her out of it.

'It's those horse pills,' I say. 'Alice, why don't you take her to your pad and look after her? I'll see if Cody will drive you home.'

The next casualty is Jaxson. I find him in his closet, shuffling hangers back and forth, mumbling softly.

'What're you looking for, Jaxson?' I ask.

His response is a blend of baby babble and smoker's cough.

'Forget about Jaxson,' Pablo says, grabbing my arm. 'You need to see what's going on outside.'

'What?' I ask.

'Follow me.'

I rush after Pablo. On the roof of the neighbour's one-storey house is a raver I barely know, a 40-ish peroxide blond in bright-red trousers.

'The police are on the way. Get down off my house!' yells an old man.

Oh shit! Tempe cops. Detective Reid . . . I tremble.

'He took one of those capsules,' Pablo says.

'We've got to evacuate,' I say, sobering up to take command. 'Let's move everyone to Acid Joey's. If the cops use this as probable cause to come in, they'll see all the people passed out on GHB and do a full search.'

'I'll get everyone who came in an SUV to park in the alley behind Jaxson's,' Pablo says, 'and we'll have security load the people who're passed out into the SUVs and unload them at Acid Joey's.'

The evacuation starts immediately. From the living room, I watch the police arrive. One car. Two cops. The man on the roof jumps onto a fence and climbs down. On the lawn, on all fours, he casually sniffs the air like an animal and moves to the edge of the garden nearest the cop car.

The officers get out and appraise him chewing a flower. The man swivels his head and sniffs and chews another flower.

'Lie down and put your hands behind your back!' an officer yells.

Nibbling on petals, the man frowns as if vexed by the intrusion. Cautiously, the other officer approaches the man. He stops chewing, raises his head and moos, a deep, protracted moo that sounds like a warning.

The nearest officer stops and draws his gun. 'Don't moo at me, mister!'

The man moos again. Even louder.

'I told you once not to moo at me, mister!' The officer moves forward as if to capture the man.

The man moos again, bolts on all fours, jumps onto the fence and disappears out of view.

'He's on the roof again. The cops are calling backup,' Pablo says.

'Whoever's left needs to leave right now,' I say. 'Keoki, would you like to drive my car?'

With the cops distracted by the mooing man, Keoki and I rush to my car. More cops arrive and park. With several cars leaving the after-party, Keoki pulls away. The cops eye us suspiciously. I brace for them to stop us. A parked cop car screeches off, pulls a U-turn and comes after us, lights and siren on.

'Fuck, dude!' Keoki says.

'We've got no drugs on us,' I say. 'What can they do?'

The cop pulls over the car behind us. I'm relieved – but upset. 'Fuck! One of my dealers, Fish, is in that car with over a hundred X. Hopefully the cops won't do a full search. Let's get the fuck out of here.'

From Acid Joey's, I call Jaxson. 'Did the cops let Fish go?'

'They're still searching the car, tearing it apart. They've got everyone in handcuffs in the back of cop cars.'

'Aw, shit!' I say, shutting my eyes. I grit my teeth. 'That's fucked up. Spread the word they need to keep quiet and I'm bonding them out right away.' *Don't want anyone snitching.* 'They've all got clean records, so if anyone gets charged it'll be a first offence, a slap on the wrist, probably probation.'

On Sunday night, I learn Fish was charged for the Ecstasy, but none of the others. I post his bond and take G Dog to his apartment the next day.

'What happened?' I ask, sat in his living room.

'They kept me in there, saying I was in very serious trouble, asking me all kinds of questions. I exercised my right to remain silent.'

'Good man!' I say.

'You sure about that?' G Dog asks. 'You know what happens to snitches.'

'I didn't tell them shit!' Fish says, offended.

'I believe you,' I say. 'Did they ask you about me?'

'They asked who I got the pills off. They asked if it was some English guy.'

'Did they mention any names?' I ask.

'No. The head dude gave me a card with his number on. He said to call him when I'm ready to talk to them. It'll save me a prison sentence.'

'That's just the cops trying to bullshit your ass,' G Dog says.

'You got the card?' I ask.

'Yeah, lemme go get it.' Fish fetches the card.

I read it. 'Fucking hell!' I say, shaking my head, a creepy feeling rising up my spine. 'This is the guy who was behind Wild Man's arrest! Who is this Detective fucking Reid anyway?'

'I dunno,' Fish says.

'Sounds like he's got a hard-on for the English,' G Dog says.

I take Fish to see Ray, an attorney who saved one of my associates from a similar situation. I pay Ray $5,000. He gets the charges dropped because the police didn't have probable cause to search the car, hence the fruit of their search, the Ecstasy, is inadmissible as evidence. News of our victory spreads. To motivate my dealers not to cooperate with the cops, I announce they're all covered by legal benefits: an attorney and bail money. More ravers request to work for me.

A few months later, Tempe police raid Jaxson's house. My friends are asked the same questions over and over, one in particular: 'What can you tell us about the guy with the English accent?' The man asking the question: Detective Reid.

CHAPTER 34

IN THE BLUE Room, four of my bouncers are stood over a man on the carpet with his hands tied behind his back, Calvin, a stocky raver with long blond dreadlocks, wearing a black T-shirt and green combat trousers.

'Stealing Joey's wallet while he was in jail was a fucked-up thing to do,' Jaxson says. Acid Joey, berserk on Special K and in a car chase with Pablo, crashed and got arrested.

'I never took his wallet,' Calvin says.

'Then what the fuck happened?' Jaxson yells.

'My roommate caught Calvin stealing shit from here while the cops had me,' Acid Joey says. 'My wallet's still missing.'

'We reckon he came here,' I say, 'saw no one was home, stole the wallet, then got greedy and came back for more.'

The front door bursts open and clangs against the wall. Mari charges down the hallway, scowling, wearing a beanie, a wife-beater and baggy shorts, her right arm outstretched, pointing a gun, Skinner behind her, also pointing a gun, his frown almost as severe as Mari's. They stop at Calvin and take aim at his face, which scrunches like a plastic bag.

'Who the fuck are you?' Mari snarls.

'A friend of Joey's,' Calvin whimpers.

'What kind of motherfucking friend are you?' Mari says, shaking the gun. 'You steal all your friends' shit? I'm pregnant and I was about to eat, motherfucker, before I got the call to come here.' She puts the gun to his temple. 'It's 'cause of you I'm angry and hungry!'

I'm stunned, yet convinced that if anyone can get the truth out of Calvin it's Mari. No one in the room will actually shoot Calvin over a few hundred dollars, as I've instructed them only to scare him.

'Chill out, Mari,' Skinner says.

'I know you stole his wallet!' Mari says. 'Give him his motherfucking wallet back!'

'Mari!' Skinner says.

'Fuck you, Skinner! Who is this fucking guy anyway?' Mari puts her gun to the tip of Calvin's nose.

Fear flickers across Calvin's watery eyes as he stares at the barrel as if it's the last thing he'll ever see.

'I'll tell you who you are: you're a fucking joke!' Mari yells.

'How do we know for sure he took it?' Skinner asks.

'Worm saw him come and go earlier,' Acid Joey says.

'Some fucking friend!' Mari says.

'Chill, Mari,' Jaxson says. 'We'll take care of this. You're pregnant. You shouldn't even be here.'

'Shut the fuck up!' Mari yells. 'Someone called me to come down here, right? Well, I'm here, and I'm gonna take care of this shit!'

'Mari, chill, for the baby's sake,' Skinner says.

'Chill!' Mari swings her arm, and points the gun at Skinner, her face red, on fire. 'You're the one who interrupted my fucking dinner for me to come over here and help you guys deal with this dumb-ass fucked-up loser!'

'What're you doing, Mari?' Skinner points his gun at Mari.

With the guns off his head, Calvin's expression relaxes a bit. But as he watches Mari and Skinner, terror returns to his eyes.

'And what the fuck do you care about our baby? You're always telling me you hope the baby will just fall out of me and die. Your only concern is money and your drug addiction! Nobody is gonna talk shit to me today and get away with it!'

Mari's and Skinner's scowls intensify.

'Hey, let's not turn on each other,' I say. 'We're trying to find out if this guy has the wallet. Let's not point guns at each other, shall we?'

'Of course he fucking took the wallet!' Mari swings her gun back to Calvin.

Calvin – with an expression hinting at an imminent heart attack – says, 'OK. Enough. I threw it on the freeway.'

'What the fuck!' Jaxson yells at Calvin.

'*Uh uh!*' Mari says. 'You'd better get your ass over to that freeway and find that, bitch.' She moves her handgun up and down Calvin's face. 'Look, motherfucker, you fucked up my meal. You'd better find Acid Joey's wallet and bring it back, or there's a lotta people you're gonna have to answer to – including me!' Panting furiously, she circles his face with the gun – forehead, temples, chin – as if deciding where to shoot him.

Skinner puts his gun behind Calvin's ear.

'How can you consider yourself Joey's friend if you could just walk in his fucking house and take his shit?' Mari asks.

'I don't know. I'm so sorry,' Calvin says, crying.

'You have no idea how sorry you're gonna be if you don't find that fucking wallet!' Mari yells.

Assuming Calvin will never find it, I put him on a repayment programme. He pays the debt in full.

CHAPTER 35

'**I'M GONNA INTRODUCE** you to someone you're gonna fall in love with,' says Salt, a Chinese striptease dancer I'm cuddling at a rave in the Icehouse, a large warehouse in downtown Phoenix.

'Who?' I ask.

'My friend Amy. She lives in Tucson. I'll bring her to the Icehouse next week.'

'What's she like?'

'She's a U of A student. Looks like Denise Richards –'

'Ooh, *Wild Things*.'

'Yeah. She's intelligent, and she's got a perfect butt.'

'OK, enough, enough. You've got me all excited.'

The next weekend, I exit the Icehouse for fresh air and eavesdrop on a conversation between Fish and what looks like a Texas beauty queen turned glitter girl. She's wearing a blue silk top with spaghetti straps and dark-blue tight trousers, spandex at the top, boot cut at the bottom, her hair curled and pinned above a face adorned with sparkly make-up. Fanning out from big, green, dreamy eyes, her fake eyelashes flutter invitingly. The sight of her raises my blood pressure.

'I can't feel this X,' she says. 'I got sold bunk shit!'

'How long ago did you take it?' Fish asks.

'Over an hour.'

'It should have worked by now. Who did you get it from?'

'It's a cap of pure MDMA from English Shaun.'

Waiting to enter the conversation at the perfect moment and about to laugh, I bite down. I ponder how to win her over.

'English Shaun actually sold it to you, did he?' Fish asks.

'No, but the guy I got it off told me it was from English Shaun.'

Fish laughs and I join in.

She turns towards me, frowning. 'What's so funny?'

'Hello,' I say, smiling. 'I'm English Shaun.'

She puts her hands on her hips. 'Well, thanks a lot for selling bunk shit!'

Taken aback, I say, 'I'm sorry you got ripped off, but if we've never met before, how can I possibly have sold you bunk shit? My friends are only selling Mitsubishis tonight. We keep the pure MDMA for our after-parties.'

'But the guy said he got it off you! He swore it was from English Shaun, blah, blah, blah.'

'That's his sales pitch. Did you see him get it off me?'

'Well, no,' she says, her voice calming down.

'You're lucky he didn't put PCP in it and mess you up, which is what happened to a bunch of my friends recently.'

'What am I supposed to do now?' she asks in the tone of a child in distress.

'Have a Mitsu on me,' I say, handing her a pill.

'I take a lot of X. Is one going to be enough?'

'You're *delightfully* hardcore. I guess I'd best give you two, then.'

Salt joins us. 'Amy, I've been looking all over for you.'

'*No way!*' I say. '*This* is the famous Amy?'

'You'd better believe it!' Salt says.

'Amy, do you mind if I ask you something personal?' I say.

'Ask away.'

'Is it true that you have the perfect butt?'

'Salt!' Amy yelps.

'Amy, don't act shy,' Salt says. 'Anyway, our ride wants to go back to Tucson.'

'I want to stay,' Amy says.

'How're you gonna get home?' Salt asks.

'I'll run her home,' I say, winking at Salt.

'Fine by me.' Amy turns to Salt for approval.

'You'll be safe in Shaun's hands. I'm outta here.' Salt hugs and kisses Amy. The sight of their tongues intertwining heats up my loins.

'So what do you do at the U of A anyway?' I ask.

'Chemical engineering.'

'Does that mean you have the knowledge to manufacture illegal drugs?'

'Not yet. But I'll sure find out.'

'You might come in handy,' I say, high on her smile.

We sit on the kerb, chatting at length, ignoring the party. My dealers emerge to talk shop. I get rid of them fast, giving her my full attention, hoping she'll want to see me again. When the rave ends, we set off for Tucson.

Cruising along the freeway in the RX7, I say, 'I love the blood-red sky at this time of the morning.'

'Have you seen it when the mountains look like they're on fire when the sun's rising behind them?' Amy says. 'It's so beautiful.'

'Where you from originally?' I ask. 'Have you always lived in the desert?'

'It's kind of like a strange story, you know. Do you mean where I was born or where, like, my family's from?'

'Both.'

'I was born in Saudi Arabia.'

'What?'

'My parents were teachers at an American international school overseas, and we lived in Saudi Arabia and Kwajalein –'

'Where the bloody hell's Kwajalein?'

'The Marshall Islands. They're literally a couple of dots in the South Pacific. Then after that we lived in Côte d'Ivoire.'

'You're truly an international person,' I reply, impressed.

She giggles proudly.

'How come you came back to America?' I ask.

'I guess 'cause my parents decided to move back here . . . and . . . er . . . they got a divorce, and I'm still indefinitely stuck here.' Amy pouts, distracting my gaze from the road, tempting me to kiss her, stirring my blood. She directs me to her mother's home, a mansion on a hilltop.

'I guess it's time to say goodnight, then?' I say, sad to part ways.

'Yes, English Shaun. Thanks for the great X. I'm still rolling.' She squares her face to mine and challenges me with her eyes.

Kiss her! Get stuck in! What you waiting for?

I lean forward.

She doesn't flinch.

I look at her lips and her eyes.

She looks at mine.

I smile. Tilt my head. Open my mouth.

She puts her tongue in.

I tingle all over.

I drive to Phoenix singing in my seat.

*

At the next rave, I introduce Amy to my inner circle. 'Here's Sallywack. They call her Turbo Dyke.' I hug Sally.

'I like girls too,' Amy says.

'I noticed,' I say.

'*Grrrrrrrrrrrrrrrrr,*' Sallywack says, running her eyes over Amy.

Amy giggles. They French kiss. Partyers stop to watch. They chatter for a bit.

Later, Sallywack takes me aside. 'Shaun, this bitch is fucking fake.'

Jealousy. 'Sallywack, all creatures must flourish in our garden. There's good and bad in everyone, and I try to concentrate on the good.'

'I bet I can fuck her before you can.'

'Now, now, Sallywack, be nice. Amy's come all the way from Tucson to see me.'

In an outdoor area, alone with Amy, I say, 'You kissing Sallywack was so sexy. How long have you been into girls?'

'Oh, gosh, OK, er . . . it's, well, actually only one girl so far. Her name's Lisa.'

'How did that come about?' I ask.

'She's a dancer at Starbutts. Oh, by the way, I also dance at Starbutts. I decided to work there 'cause I went there with my fake ID and fell in love with Lisa from the moment I saw her. So I literally became a stripper just so I could spend time with her.'

'Wow! You're a real go-getter. And you guys, like, got together?' I ask, hoping for details.

'One thing led to another. She ended up giving me X and taking advantage of me while her boyfriend was out of town doing a porn shoot.'

'One thing led to another. What do you mean by that?'

'She had one of those silver-bullet vibrator things. I'm up for trying anything . . .'

Laughing, I feel my erection press against my jeans.

I whisk Amy off to an after-party. I leave her alone while I collect money from my dealers, but when I return she's sat on the carpet surrounded by admirers, one massaging her neck. *Jesus! Where'd they all come from? I only let her out of my sight for a few minutes.* I sit next to Amy. To get rid of the masseur, I pick her up and drop her on my lap. Hours later, boisterous on GHB, I hug my friends goodbye, throw Amy over my shoulder and head for the door.

'No, don't go!' Sallywack yells.

'We're getting a room at the Mesa Hilton,' I say.

Sallywack yells, 'Amy, you don't know what you're getting into!'

Amy's cackle makes it clear she likes getting carried off by a wild Englishman.

In a room, we drink GHB. Semi-conscious, we wobble taking each other's clothes off. Admiring her rear, I decide to leave the lights on. I pick her up and throw her on the bed. When she stops bouncing, I kiss her all over, impassioned by her shrieks and groans. Although it's all I can think about, I postpone getting on top of her until she demands it. High on GHB, we kiss forcefully, frantically, but keep passing out during sex and having to wake each other up. Heavenly chaos. Hours later, relaxing in bed, Amy reveals she did lesbian Internet porn with her girlfriend Lisa, who played a striptease dancer in a recent Hollywood hit comedy.

Driving Amy home, I jokingly say, 'Why don't we fly to Vegas and get married next weekend?'

'I'd love to go to Vegas! You'd really take me there?'

'Of course,' I say, smiling.

'Wow. I've never been. I really want to see the Siegfried & Roy show.'

'How come?'

'Because I love the tigers, and it's just so incredible. My mom always told me to see it. Where will we stay up there?'

'How about the Luxor? I really like the pyramid.'

'That's perfect. I love Egypt 'cause it's so close to Saudi.'

After we sober up, we decide against getting married but still go to Vegas.

CHAPTER 36

BY 1998, I'VE mediated disputes between factions in the rave scene and incorporated them into my organisation. I host a crime-family dinner at a steakhouse each month, attended by the heads of each faction. Each head has a separate sales force – mostly college students with no previous convictions, all covered by legal benefits and briefed on how to deal with the cops.

But as 1998 progresses, a new breed of Ecstasy dealer disrupts my monopoly. They're mostly jocks with tanned bodies bulked up on steroids, their hair buzzed at the sides and slicked back or spiked on top, the type of people more associated with Gold's Gym or Venice Beach than the rave scene. They penetrate my parties and proliferate. They invade Scottsdale nightclubs such as Axis/Radius and use them as strongholds for their operations.

Despite my extensive contacts, I have no success finding out who they're working for. My only clue is their pills, not the beige or white presses from Amsterdam but coloured pills manufactured domestically and peddled in major US cities, often cut with other ingredients. With so many locals working for me, I'm confident of getting to the bottom of things.

Amy is asked by a girlfriend to introduce me to the girl's boyfriend, Spaniard. Because he sounds like one of the new breed of Ecstasy dealers, I agree. I take one of my bouncers, Rossetti, a tall, strong local with a moustache, always jumping around with too much energy.

In the parking lot at Heart 5, a bar in Tucson, I drink a cap of GHB to make me fearless. 'Rossetti, while I talk to Spaniard, make sure you're always somewhere you can pull your gun in case they try to kidnap me. I'm not going to start any shit, but who knows how big a crew he's with or what might happen.'

'No problem. If they try anything, I'll open up on the motherfuckers.'

Inside, I kiss Amy at the bar. 'Can I have some G, too?' she asks.

I take her to the car to sip GHB, go back inside and order drinks.

Minutes later, a six-and-a-half-foot man with dark spiky hair and biceps as broad as my neck taps me on the shoulder. 'I'm Mark, Spaniard's partner. He wants to see you in the VIP area.'

Intimidated, I look at Amy as if to say, *What the hell have you got me into?*

'They're not going to start any trouble,' Amy says confidently. 'It's OK. I know them. You'll be fine.'

'OK, Mark.' I shake his hand and follow him.

'Glad you came, English Shaun,' says Spaniard, a well-groomed Hispanic. 'Mark, clear that sofa so we can all sit down.'

'You need to move so we can sit down!' Mark yells.

The people on the sofa jump up. To the side of us, Rossetti slips into the VIP area.

As I sit down between the two of them, the GHB jolts my brain, making me playful and crazy. Just like my grandfather Fred used to do to me, I squeeze their legs above the knee. 'So what's this all about?'

They're taken aback for a few seconds, until Spaniard laughs and says in a friendly voice, 'Look, we know you're doing your own thing. You've got a lotta people working for you. As do we. It would be best if we worked together rather than be enemies.'

'What're you proposing?' I ask, nearly always capable of negotiating business, no matter how high I am.

'We're getting a lotta pills, and we figure we can give you a better price than what you're paying.'

'You don't know what I'm paying. I'm familiar with your pills, and I don't think the quality is there. I'm getting European pills. None of the coloured pills you guys are getting.'

'Who the fuck do you think you are, talking shit about our pills?' Mark yells.

Because of the GHB, Mark seems like a dinosaur with a little brain and doesn't scare me.

'Hey, Mark, calm down,' Spaniard says.

'Do you have any idea who Jimmy Moran is?' Mark asks, fuming.

'No,' I say.

'Sammy "The Bull" Gravano,' Mark says. 'That's who we work for. One call to him and we can have you taken out to the desert.'

I know about Sammy the Bull from the news. He had been the underboss of the Gambino crime family, run by John Gotti, aka 'the Teflon Don', so called because no charges ever stuck to him. In 1991, Sammy the Bull became the highest-ranking member of the Mafia to turn FBI informant. He confessed to murdering 19 people and helped put the Teflon Don in prison for life. The Feds dropped the murder charges and gave Gravano a five-year sentence for racketeering. Time served, he ended up with a new identity, living in Tempe under the Witness Protection Program. He was soon recognised and even gave media interviews. He told Howard Blum, who interviewed him for *Vanity Fair*:

They send a hit team down, I'll kill them. They better not miss, because even if they get me, there will still be a lot of body bags going back to New York. I'm not afraid. I don't have it in me. I'm too detached maybe. If it happens, fuck it. A bullet in the head is pretty quick. You go like *that*! It's better than cancer. I'm not meeting you in Montana on some fuckin' farm. I'm not sitting here like some jerk-off with a phony beard. I'll tell you something else: I'm a fuckin' pro. If someone comes to my house, I got a few little surprises for them. Even if they win, there might be surprises.

Jesus! My life's turning into a mobster movie. That's a heavyweight name – but still, looking at these guys in their shiny leopard-print shirts, I bet they don't have as much power in Arizona as my associates in the New Mexican Mafia. I glance at Rossetti. The look on his face says, *Should I shoot that lunkhead or what?* Almost imperceptibly, I shake my head.

'There's no need to say all that,' Spaniard says. 'Forgive Mark, Shaun. He gets upset real easy. He's a bit of a hothead.'

'I have no problems with you guys, but I really don't care who you work for. You just moved in. Over the years, I've made friends with a lot of locals,' I say, insinuating my connection with the New Mexican Mafia.

'I hear you,' Spaniard says, implying he knows of the relationship. 'But what if we can get you a better price on pills, would you be interested?'

'I appreciate the offer, guys, but no thanks. And here's why: before you guys moved into Ecstasy, the police pretty much ignored us. Now your runners are going around bragging they're the biggest Ecstasy barons in the world. That's brought considerable heat to the scene. And I'm not saying this to put you guys down, but to give you a heads-up on what's happening. Every weekend at the raves, we've got undercover cops and vehicles hanging around. We've got undercover vehicles taping who's going in and out of the raves, driving through the parking lots taping licence plates. It's no coincidence that the police moved in shortly after you guys. It's not each other's crews we need to beware of, it's the cops.'

'What about your security team?' Spaniard asks.

'What about it?'

'Will our runners have problems with your security guys jacking their pills?'

'I don't want to start a war with you guys. If my security grab someone and we find out they're part of your crew, we'll let them go. Ecstasy's so hard to get and the demand so high, there's enough of a market for us to coexist. But if I tell my security not to jack your runners, I don't expect any problems from you guys for my runners in the Scottsdale scene.'

'Sounds like a good agreement.' Spaniard shakes my hand.

Back in the bar, I'm shocked to find Amy unconscious on a sofa from drinking too much GHB. Rossetti and I carry her out like a corpse.

Resting Amy on the passenger seat, Rossetti asks, 'What went down?'

'Finally found out who they work for,' I say.

'Who?'

'Sammy "The Bull" Gravano.'

'Holy shit!' Rossetti frowns. 'Those Italian Mafia dudes don't fuck around!'

'They tried to sell me pills. I don't trust them or their pills, so I said no.'

'Do you think that'll start a war?' Rossetti asks, his eyes wide.

'Maybe not right away, but sooner or later it very well could, yes.'

CHAPTER 37

'I WANNA THROW the biggest rave ever seen in Arizona,' says Josh – a short student with pimples whose brow and features are set too close together, as if his face was slightly crushed at birth – sat next to Acid Joey in the Blue Room.

'What're you proposing, Josh?' I ask, studying his body language.

'I threw a party on Halloween,' Josh says, his eyes lighting up. 'Look how many people showed up! Imagine how many people will show up on New Year's Eve.'

'I agree. New Year's Eve makes good business sense. But just 'cause you've had one success, doesn't guarantee another. Ravers here are fickle. How much are you looking for?'

'A hundred gees.'

My laughter rips the confidence off his face. 'I admire you have big goals, Josh, but if you spend that much on an Arizona party, there's no way any of us will make any money. You'll get two or three thousand to show up. This isn't LA. You need to downscale your business plan.' *Either his expectations are unrealistic or he's highballing me, hoping for a lesser sum.*

'It won't just be an Arizona party,' Josh says, regaining his enthusiasm. 'We'll advertise it in LA and the neighbouring states. It'll be like a rave festival. We'll have a campsite. There's gonna be five stages and over a hundred DJs. The headliners are gonna be Chris Liberator and Dave the Drummer, and they cost ten grand to come out.'

'How much are tickets going to be?'

'Thirty dollars, plus five to park, plus water sales.'

30 x 1,000, 2,000, 3,000 . . . = $30,000, $60,000, $90,000 . . .
'What's the location?'

'A cowboy ranch an hour or so north of Phoenix.'

'What police jurisdiction?'

'Just some bumpkin local cops. We make a donation, they leave us alone.'

'I like the sound of that. You understand for me to invest in this you'll be obligated to use my security team?'

'I've explained all that to him,' Acid Joey says. 'It's the first requirement of the Bank of England.'

'All right,' I say. 'If two thousand show up at thirty a head, that's sixty grand, so the most I'm willing to invest is fifty thou. The gate money should cover that.'

'What if you invest that and I find some other investors to put in the balance?'

'I have a problem with that,' I say, furrowing my brow. 'In the stock market that's called diluting someone's investment. If you run the bills up to a hundred grand, how will I get my investment back if only a few thousand ravers pay to get in? There'll be nothing left over. My advice to you is to halve the party in size. You don't need a hundred DJs. Take my money and make the most of it.'

'But I'm convinced I can get five to ten thousand people if I get all these DJs booked.'

'You saw how many people showed up for his last party,' Acid Joey says.

'If you want to get other investors, then I'm going to have to add some conditions to protect my capital. As people come into the party, I want half of the door money as it comes in. That means you can only use half the door money to pay debts that you owe on the night, DJs and stuff. The other half goes to me. Then if you go over budget and there's not enough money to pay everyone on the night, that's your problem, not mine.'

'That's fine. I just don't see that happening,' Josh says.

'Well, if it does, just bear in mind, reneging on what we've agreed to today is going to carry some serious consequences.'

'He knows,' Acid Joey says.

I ask Marcello and Primo, the club-kid couple, to help promote the party, keep an eye on Josh, keep the costs down and, on the night, secure half of the take. A few months before the party, the headliners complain they haven't received their deposits or flight tickets. I FedEx them cash, but concerns remain about Josh.

The day of the party, ravers from all over the Southwest pitch tents at the ranch. Hotwheelz flies to Phoenix with 4,000 hits of

Ecstasy, Teletubbies stamped on them. Hoping to offset any loss on the party with profit from Ecstasy, I send my sales force early to solicit the campers.

I no longer risk going to parties when they start. My workers – dealers, bouncers, scouts – operate as my eyes, and inform me of any threats: undercover cops, drug rivals, loose cannons such as Gangsta Dan. The reports from the party are positive. Attendance is high. Everyone's having a great time. Cash is building up fast from Ecstasy sales. Although pleased, I hear nothing from Josh, Marcello or Primo, which worries me a bit. *They're probably way too busy to touch base. Everything's running smoothly. It'll be an easy night.*

Around 11 p.m. and in high spirits, Hotwheelz and I set off from a Scottsdale Hilton villa in a limo full of glitter girls. The limo shoots up the freeway and wobbles over a dirt road to the ranch. Near the entrance, I spot Primo amid a swarm of ravers, and thousands more in bright clothes spread across the ranch. *Yes!* Excitement charges through me.

I put the window down. 'Primo!'

He turns to me, his expression haggard, defeated.

Oh no!

'Where've you been?' Primo asks, his face twitching, eyes darting. 'We've been fighting people off all night who've been trying to get your money. As soon as you get the money off Marcello, we're out of here. It's fucking chaos. It's Josh's fault.'

'How so? Look at all these people! I've never seen so many at an Arizona rave.'

'There's probably over five thousand, but somehow Josh still owes a bunch.'

My excitement collapses. *It's not going to be an easy night.* My mind speeds up to take charge. 'That's crazy.' I tell the limo driver to keep going. We bob and jerk over the desert like a boat in a storm until he baulks at going any further.

Hotwheelz picks up a crate of records and sets off for a stage. I follow, eager to find Cody. Hotwheelz puts his records down and starts dancing. A raver whirls towards Hotwheelz, and cracks him in the jaw – *thwack!* – knocking him onto the dirt. The raver pulses on his feet like a boxer, his eyes going in and out of focus, shrieking, cackling. Hotwheelz leaps up and kicks, but the raver runs away.

I hurry to Hotwheelz. 'You all right?'

'What a wanker!' Hotwheelz says.

'There's never any violence at raves,' I say. 'I don't know what's going on. That guy looked mental.'

Hotwheelz strokes his jaw, checking for damage.

Acid Joey and more bouncers circle Hotwheelz. 'What happened?'

'Some wanker just came up behind me and whacked me here.' Hotwheelz taps his chin.

'What did he look like?' Acid Joey asks.

'A fucking curly-haired bloke cackling like a hyena. I don't know what the fuck that was all about.'

'Don't worry, we'll find him,' Acid Joey says.

Unfortunately, the raver punches a girl in view of the ranchers who own the land, patrolling on horseback, packing shotguns.

'You don't treat *gurls* like that round here,' a rancher drawls.

Another swings a rope. 'We'll hand him over to the sheriff.'

They lasso and hogtie the raver and drag him out of sight. Acid Joey checks on the girl.

Cody appears with Marcello and a sports bag full of cash: half the gate money.

'You don't know what we went through to hold onto that money. Me and Primo are leaving you to deal with Josh's mess.' Marcello disappears.

'What's going on, Cody?' I ask.

'Josh's people are all camped out at the ranch house. They used the other half of the gate money to pay down their debts, but they still owe a bunch of people. DJs and their managers are complaining. Josh's people are telling them that we're holding onto all the money. He's blaming you.'

Anger heats my face up. 'Josh agreed to give me half the money. If we've secured that money, that's our money. How's Ecstasy sales?'

'The Teletubbies are long gone.'

'Bloody hell!' I say, smiling.

'We're down to selling caps of pure MDMA, and they've nearly all gone, too.'

'What's the deal with Sammy the Bull's crew?'

'Some of his dealers are here, but they're keeping a low profile. I've got about thirty on security. The Bull's crew are wary of us.'

'Good.'

'There's a rumour that Josh took money off them, too, for this party.'

'Doesn't surprise me.'

'Like you requested, the Ecstasy money's all in Amy's old car. It's been coming in too fast to count. The car's just full of money. I've got security watching it at all times.'

'Take me to it. That's going to be my headquarters.'

Robbers, undercover cops and other threats would look for me and the loot in the VIP area, not in a rust bucket, disguised by darkness, surrounded by hundreds of cars. No pills are in Amy's car. My remaining inventory is spread out between dealers and safe houses. If I'm arrested in a car full of cash, I'll claim it's legally earned gate proceeds. I open the door and step onto a carpet of money. I count bills, seal each thousand in an envelope and stack the envelopes in a sports bag. Every so often, one of my dealers makes a deposit.

Hotwheelz gets in, shivering. 'Turn the fucking heating on full blast, for Christ's sake. I'm freezing my nuts off here.'

I laugh.

'I thought this was a desert rave,' Hotwheelz says. 'What the fuck! I wasn't expecting to wrap up like Nanook of the North.'

'How's your face?'

'My jaw's fucking killing. Got any painkillers or Xanax?'

'I'll sort something out.'

Cody rushes over. 'Josh freaked out and he's closing the party down. He told the Skiddle guys to turn the sound off and dismantle the stages. They've turned the sound off at one stage already.'

My eyes widen as if I've heard a declaration of war. 'I'll deal with the little bastard! If he thinks he's sending all these ravers home peaking on drugs, he's out of his mind. Grab some security and let's talk to Skiddle.' I snort a line of glass with Hotwheelz. The nasal burn sends shock waves through my skull.

We discover men in black T-shirts unplugging the sound, ravers booing and complaining.

'Who's in charge?' I ask.

'I am,' says a stocky man with a shaved head, about ten years older than me, moving equipment.

'The party's not over. What're you doing?' I ask.

He puts his hard face up to mine. 'Who the fuck are you?'

What a dickhead!

My bouncers watch in disbelief, darkness disguising their weapons.

'English Shaun. I paid for this party.'

The man turns his back and resumes packing equipment. 'You're him, are you? Well, Josh told us to turn the sound off, pack up and go home. The party's over. I guess a lotta people didn't get paid.'

Sensing my bouncers are about to lynch the man, I shake my head at them. 'Maybe they didn't, but you got paid in full. Twenty-five thousand dollars of *my money!*'

'That's not our problem, is it? It's between you and Josh.'

Give him a last chance. 'So you're telling me you're going to pull the plug and send all these ravers on the roads while they're sky high, putting their lives at risk, after you've been paid in full to provide your services till the party ends?'

'I'm just following orders.'

'Look, you took my money and you're under a legal obligation to fulfil your contract, which states you provide your services until the party's over.'

'I don't know,' he says, fiddling with equipment.

'I'm trying to be civilised with you,' I say, exasperated.

He ignores me. *He wants to call it a day, go home, get the six-hour drive to LA over with and get to bed. Four hours' work for a full day's pay. It doesn't get better than that. Easy money.*

I hear the time bomb that is my security team ticking. *Should I give them the nod?* A shooting star sprints across the sky, exciting me. *Tick-tock-tick-tock* . . . Upset ravers start trudging to where music is still playing. *Tick-tock-tick-tock* . . . I nod at my bouncers.

'Fuck this guy!' Grady steps forward waving an Uzi. 'If these guys are gonna fuck us over, how about we just shoot the shit outta their equipment?'

The metallic clicking of bullets chambering stops the man. My bouncers point their weapons at him. Moonlight gleams off the gunmetal. He lowers a box in slow motion, as if it contains explosives. He turns around, gazes at us, a realisation dawning, his life over in seconds. His body remains still, but his face contorts as if his features are trying to detach themselves to avoid getting shot. 'Er . . . I guess . . . we'd better turn the sound back on. Stop what you're doing!' he yells at his crew. 'Turn everything back on!'

His workers put their equipment down. They emerge from the darkness, see him at gunpoint and freeze.

'And you need to turn everything back on at the other stage, too!' I yell.

'Do it!' the boss says.

The workers scatter.

'And if Josh tries this shit again, don't let any of your guys turn the sound off!' I say.

'I hear you. We'll fulfil our contract.'

'You have no choice,' Grady says. 'You can't move your shit faster than we can shoot it.'

The crowd cheers the return of the music. But my tension doesn't drop. *Rave saved, but what will Josh try next?* As my mind churns out hostile thoughts about Josh, an electrical crackling noise fills my ears that sounds like cattle prods. Looking around, seeing no source of the noise, it dawns on me that I'm imagining it – as if Carlos the Torturer has set up shop in my brain.

Hotwheelz arrives, agitated. 'They won't let me on the stage at my allotted time. Some DJ's on and he won't step down.'

Thankful for an easy problem to remedy, I say, 'Cody, take some security and tell the DJ politely his time is up and to get off the stage, and if that doesn't work, well, you know what to do.'

In Amy's car, I brace for the next challenge. Dealers throw cash at me faster than I count it.

Cody arrives. 'I just came from Josh's camp. They've told the ranchers the party's over and to kick everyone off their land.'

The electrical crackling noise intensifies. 'That little bastard! When's this supposed to happen?'

'Any time. I told the ranchers not to do anything until I inform you. They're at the ranch house. What do you want me to tell them?'

My thoughts sprint. 'The same as Skiddle. The ranchers have been paid in full, too. This is a breach of contract. Tell them we just spoke to our attorney, and our attorney said they're welcome to kick us off their land right now and we're welcome to file a lawsuit first thing Monday morning. I don't think these hillbillies will appreciate the idea of some hotshot city attorney filing a lawsuit and threatening to take their land.'

'I'll do it.' Cody departs.

I stew for ten minutes. Cody returns. The ranchers are still going to evict everyone. I send Cody back with instructions to pretend to be talking to our attorney on the phone.

I seethe, punch the steering wheel, rock in my seat, kick the interior, convinced Josh has ended the party.

Cody returns, smiling. 'They've backed down. I fucking bluffed them. They're scared of legal action and the courts.'

I jump out of the car and hug him. 'Bloody good job, Cody!'

'That chickenshit bastard Josh and his crew are clearing out. They've given up trying to shut the party down.'

'Thank God! At last, I can enjoy the music.' I wander off and stop by a wall of speakers blasting Chris Liberator's mechanised beats – *vwwmf-vwwmf-vwwmf.* Mesmerised by the sight of thousands dancing to English DJs with the same blissful expression I had when I started raving, I tell myself, *You've realised a dream.*

Hours later, the sun peeps above the horizon, beginning to boil the air and bring the yellow, brown and orange of the desert alive.

I return to the car, joined by Hotwheelz. 'I've got a gig in LA. Can you have someone race me to the airport?'

'Yes. And here's twenty thou,' I say. 'The balance of what I owe you. Looks like your face is swelling up. Here's ten Xanax to help you relax. You don't want to go through the airport with all that money looking wired and like you've been in a scrap. Other than getting punched, did you have a good time?'

'Other than freezing my nuts off, the crowd loved it.'

'We are well into your trance.'

Amy and I leave in her car, awash with cash. I join a convoy of ravers heading for Phoenix. The petrol warning light comes on, so I pull into Gus's Gas Station, in the middle of nowhere, surrounded by cacti, overrun with ravers, cars everywhere, windows down, music playing, ravers dancing on the asphalt or in their seats, all grinning as if they share the same mental illness, the wind hurling tumbleweed at them, delighting them, exciting them, like children playing with nature. I wait my turn and park at a pump that looks half a century old. When I open the door, a dust devil hits the car, stealing dollars from the floor. The bills spin upwards above our heads and flutter down like butterflies.

'Oh my God! Quick, close the door!' Amy yells.

The ravers know me. They leap, jump, chase the money and hand it back. Stunned by the beauty of their spontaneity, I thank them and pump petrol: *clickety-clickety-clickety* goes the motor. After paying a hillbilly with rotten teeth, I chat to the ravers – *my people* – delighting in their stories about the night.

Josh tells his creditors that I stole his money, and I receive death threats. He disappears, rumoured to have a hit out on him by the Mexican Mafia for an unpaid debt.

CHAPTER 38

THE HIGHER CODY and Skinner advance in my organisation, the more sarcastic remarks and petty complaints Pablo makes about them. Attempting to outdo them, he flies to Amsterdam in the hope of getting low-cost Ecstasy. At a nightclub, he meets a supplier and buys a few hundred pills. He hides them in a money belt tucked into his trousers and returns to Arizona.

'You've got some balls smuggling that yourself,' I tell Pablo in the Blue Room. 'How can we get bulk over here?'

'To start, I say we mule back anywhere up to five thousand,' Pablo says, scratching a meth sore on his cheek.

'What will that get my price down to?'

'Below five dollars a pill.'

'Holy shit! That's less than half my cost!' I say, animated by greed.

'If we buy tens of thousands, the price will go down to two or three dollars a pill. Our main problem is US Customs. They treat anyone getting off a plane from Amsterdam with extreme suspicion. I seriously thought I was gonna get busted. It would be best if whoever we send flies in and out of a different European country. They can just take the train to and from Holland.'

Hotwheelz has been busted for sending drugs through the mail, so the Amsterdam plan couldn't have come at a better time. With no shortage of friends fancying a free holiday, a run of successful smuggling missions follows. We experiment with methods ranging from taping pills to the body to putting them in luggage in vitamin containers. Pablo hollows out company annual reports used for investment research, glues pills inside and FedExes them to addresses in Tempe.

CHAPTER 39

SKINNER, GRADY AND Jaxson burst into the Blue Room, where I'm sat on the carpet counting pills with G Dog and Acid Joey.

'One of my customers in Mesa,' Skinner yells, waving a handgun, 'said he's not gonna pay for his Ecstasy and to tell English Shaun to go fuck himself! I say we go over there and jack his shit!'

I spring up. The men stare at me as if awaiting orders.

'He really said that?' I ask, shaking my head.

'Yup.'

'What're we waiting for?' G Dog says, pumped up. 'Let's jack his shit.'

Burst into a house and risk getting shot. Take no action and risk looking weak – could be fatal in the drug business. Skinner hasn't steered me wrong so far. He wants me to show the others I have faith in him. The situation is so heavy, I reach for a bottle of GHB.

'How many are in the house? Are they armed?' Jaxson asks.

'Just three of them,' Skinner says.

'Even if they have guns,' Grady says, 'we'll go in so fast, they won't know what the fuck's hit them.'

'Are you sure there's no other way to get them to pay?' I ask.

'Shaun, you can't let people disrespect you like that,' G Dog says.

This was bound to happen. I can't back down. 'I'm in. Who else is going?'

Raring to go, they all say yes.

'Let's take two cars,' I say.

'How's it gonna work?' Jaxson asks.

'Some of us hold them at gunpoint while the rest take their shit out to the cars,' Skinner says.

'We've got to get in and out quick in case a neighbour calls the cops.' Hoping to numb my fear, I sip more GHB.

Skinner hands out masks. Gunmetal clicks. Grady chambers a

bullet, checks the safety and pockets the gun. The GHB hits my brain, making the plan seem appropriate in a deranged way. I give the all-clear to go.

I drive. The closer we get, the more sweat streams from my armpits, the tighter my back muscles clench, the louder my heartbeat roars in my ears. Parking, I check for cops, neighbours at windows, cars turning, helicopters . . . We don masks.

'Let's fucking do this!' Skinner says overenthusiastically.

'I don't want anyone shooting anyone,' I say. 'The guns are just to scare them with.'

'We'll scare these punks,' G Dog says.

I get out to the sound of sprinkler systems watering grass and crickets chirping. We march to the house. Grady pushes the unlocked front door open. *Good start.* Behind Skinner and Grady, I charge down the hallway. Even under the influence of GHB, I'm scared of getting shot – *maybe they know we're coming* – but I'm also gripped by a surge of excitement that puts me on autopilot and propels me towards the living room. As I enter, nervous energy explodes in my chest and shoots down my arms and legs, tingling my fingertips and toes. The three men watching *South Park* are stunned. *Yet again, Skinner has done his homework. No one's going to get hurt.*

'Unless you wanna get shot, none of you fuckers move!' Skinner yells. 'Is there anyone else in here?'

'No,' says a well-built man with long hair, holding a crystal-meth pipe, a length of glass with a sphere at the end.

Everything of value in sight – TV, stereo, PlayStation – we grab and take to the cars.

Two trips to the car are all I can take. In the hallway, I say, 'Let's get the fuck out of here before the cops come.'

'Lemme just grab more shit,' Grady says.

'Get a move on,' I say.

'None of you motherfuckers get up or call the cops or try to come after us, or we'll come back and shoot your asses!' G Dog says.

We run out, speed away.

While the rest boast and cackle, I sober up and contemplate how far my behaviour has gone from the plans I made for my life on the Thinking Tree. *The risk wasn't worth it. I'll never put myself in the firing line again.*

*

A week later, Mari charges into the Blue Room, distraught. 'I picked Skinner up from somewhere and we got followed. They got out and had guns on me and the baby.'

'Holy shit!' I say, jumping off a chair, shocked her baby was threatened, anxious over how out of control everything is getting. I hug her.

'Skinner grabbed my baby 'cause he figured they wouldn't hurt him if he was holding a baby. They literally followed us to the front door with guns. I opened the front door. They walked in the house with us. They looked at me, and one said, "Hey, Mari, I'm sorry. I don't wanna do this in front of you, but this is the only way we could get Skinner. We don't wanna bother you at all. We just want Skinner." I'm trying to get my baby from Skinner and he wouldn't give me my baby back. I'm like, "Give me the baby," and finally I convinced them to just meet up with Skinner another time. I'm like, "This is my house. This is my baby." They're like, "We're so sorry, Mari. This has nothing to do with you. He sold us thousands of dollars' worth of bunk shit." I'm like, "I totally understand you and don't blame you for being angry and wanting to get what you're owed, but this is my house." And they feel bad and are cool enough to just leave. But if my daughter hadn't been there, I don't know what woulda happened.'

Who's Skinner conned with bunk pills?

'I've done some checking around,' Mari says, 'and that house you guys jacked are selling pills for Sammy the Bull's crew.'

Did Skinner sell those guys bunk and con me into robbing them? 'That could start a fucking war. Do you think Sammy the Bull's crew was behind what just happened?'

'I don't know. Maybe. After that, I got into a fight with Skinner for being a swindling piece of shit. He's the only motherfucker I know who'd rob his own parents. You need to watch him, Shaun, he has no loyalties, even to you.'

A few days later, Mari shows up even more agitated: 'Skinner got robbed and had his teeth knocked out by Sammy the Bull's people.'

'What?' I say, rising to hug her, furious that someone hurt Skinner.

'He was over at some club in Scottsdale in some rinky-dink plaza meeting up with some people. He had a whole bunch of drugs and money on him. Some gangster dudes were over there who're selling X, the Bull's crew. It was payback for that house you guys robbed and took their TVs and all kinds of shit. They locked Skinner in the bathroom, punched his face and knocked his fucking teeth out. Skinner's dumb ass wanted to get the police involved.'

'The cops?'

'Yeah, he was gonna tell them he got robbed. They'd be like, "Why'd you get robbed? Why'd you look so skinny?" C'mon now. I had to get up off my ass at like two or three in the morning and pick his ass up. I brought him to the house and took him to the dentist the next day. But all his shit, all his money, everything was stolen.'

'Shit, how much?'

'It was a lot. At least like thirty thousand.'

'Fucking hell.'

'And before this, someone else even came to my house when I had the baby with me and I was freaking out. I called G Dog and told him, "I can't find Skinner and some fucker's outside my fucking house." G Dog came to my house, drove from Tempe, got out there in, like, not even ten minutes. With a gun in the middle of the day, G Dog was running after him and told him to get in his car. G Dog gave me a gun and I went and hid it in my house. He grabbed the guy, threw him in his car and was like, "Don't you ever come around here again or I'll kill you," you know, scaring the shit outta him. G Dog took the guy and dropped him off somewhere and the guy never came back after that.'

CHAPTER 40

SINCE THE ATTACK on Skinner, I can barely sleep. In bed, I shift from side to side. Every sound springs my eyes open out of fear the cops or Sammy the Bull's crew are coming in. During the day, I constantly peep out of the windows. I ask my friends not to tell anyone where I live or to visit me with strangers. I'm warned that Sammy the Bull has put a bounty on me and that an Arab is in town offering $10,000 for my head on a silver platter. Outside of home, being around people is unbearable. I see imaginary enemies, working for Detective Reid or Sammy the Bull, everywhere: the grocery store, petrol stations, the gym, inside vehicles.

Exhausted from living on high alert, I flee 108 miles south of Phoenix to Tucson, which I hope is out of harm's way yet close enough that I can keep a grip on my operation. In a hotel room, scouring real-estate ads, Amy and I settle on a five-bedroom million-dollar mountainside home, with a swimming pool and jacuzzi, in Sin Vacas, a private community. To view the house, we have to stop at a gate and tell the guard the address and realtor we're visiting. He calls her and, with permission, raises the gate. *Just the security I need.*

Moving into the southwestern-style one-storey home – multiple fireplaces, plush carpets, tiled floors, impressive log beams running across the ceiling – I'm thrilled to be realising the goal I set myself in 1991 of living in a massive house like the ones I admired in Paradise Valley and on Camelback Mountain. From the north, the house looks down on the city. It's nestled into the Catalina Foothills, on plenty of land, guarded by an army of saguaros, our neighbours so far away they'll never know what I'm up to.

We go on a furniture-shopping spree. A Sony plasma screen. A customised pool table in rust-coloured felt. A dining table imported from Italy. A massive bed, its thick columns stretching almost to the ceiling. A waterbed for guests. Egyptian art. We furnish the master bedroom's anteroom with a peach sofa set.

The cooler climate is a relief. In the evenings, it often rains hard and a waterfall appears behind our house as if by magic. It runs into a stream that gurgles and bubbles past our little wooden gate. Lightning sometimes bounces down the mountain, reaching out like the fingers of a hand. When it strikes our roof, it leaves a strange burning smell. During the heaviest rain, Amy demands sex on the lawn.

What we lack in human contact, animals compensate for. Leaving the house to collect mail, I encounter deer, stood still, regarding me with large eyes. Baby bobcats with leopard spots frolic on the lawn, watched over by their mother. Around dusk, bats swoop on the pool after mosquitoes. Tarantulas creep over the French windows like hairy hands. When a pack of wild pigs called javelinas come snorting at the gate, I let them in, sit down on the lawn, feed them Fruit Loops – much to Amy's horror – and recoil from the bad breath they blast through long-fanged smiles. Snakes shelter under our cars, revealing themselves when we back out. Praying mantises glide around the house like fairies. After monsoon showers, frogs rise from the ground as if resurrected from the dead and I have to fish some from the pool. Gila monsters, impressive lizards the size of small dogs, plod across the roads like dinosaurs, holding up traffic, showing off their dappled contours: vivid pink, yellow, orange, silver . . . The presence of so many animals provokes a passion in me for wildlife.

In love with Amy and surrounded by nature, I reduce my drug intake. It's been three years since I actively traded, but I have Internet access for the first time since I left my job as a broker and it reignites my enthusiasm for the stock market. I submerge myself in online investment research and order numerous company annual reports. When the reports arrive, I ignore the pictures of smiling directors and the rosy highlights and forecasts near the front. I flick straight back to the notes to the accounts and scrutinise the small print, where the dirt is hidden in incomprehensible accounting terminology. After weeks spent screening thousands of companies, I sell the stocks in Hammy's name and make aggressive investments in technology shares. My largest position: 30,000 shares of PT Pasifik Satelit Nusantara, an Indonesian satellite company, that I pick up for $5. It rockets right away, reaching more than $50 during the dot-com bubble. I convince Amy to borrow $10,000 to invest. I turn it into more than $100,000 and she buys an SUV, a white Nissan Pathfinder. I have so much at stake, I hand the running of the Ecstasy business over to Cody and spend every work day focused on the stock market.

My ex Desirae slides into heavy drug use. She gets pregnant, so her parents put her in a thousand-dollar-a-day rehab not far from my home. She invites me to visit her there. At the centre, Desirae tells me excitedly about the famous people staying there and that the waiting list is months long, making my business antennae prick up. The staff confirm business is booming. As soon as I get home, I google the rehab. It's owned by Nexthealth, trading on NASDAQ under NEXT at a dollar a share. The company has a clean balance sheet and seems undervalued, so I buy 10,000 shares. Within months, they rise to five dollars.

'Why don't we go on holiday abroad?' Amy asks, during a bath together.

My body stiffens. My first marriage ended before I became eligible for a green card. As an illegal alien, I've avoided the issue for years. *Shit! Why now?*

'What's wrong?' Amy asks.

Should I tell her? I trust her. But what if we fall out? I love her. We're going to stay together. Ha! Your relationships never last! But it feels right with her. She won't use it against me. Fuck it! Tell her. One phone call and I could get arrested. The end of everything. Just tell her. She might tell the wrong person. I love her. Must tell her.

'Shaun, what's wrong?'

'Oh, Jesus, look, I wasn't expecting you to ask that. There's . . . er . . . something I'm going to tell you, but I need to know you'll never tell anyone, as it might be used against me.'

'What is it?'

'You sure?' I ask, raising my brows.

'I promise I won't tell anyone. Of course I won't tell anyone.'

'OK, then. I'm in America illegally. I can't leave the country.'

'Are you fucking serious?'

'I came on a visitor's visa in '91 and just stayed. If I leave the country, they won't let me back in. They can even arrest me and put me in prison.'

'Can't you apply to be a citizen because you've been here for so long?'

'No. The only way I can apply for citizenship is if I get married.'

'Oh. Aha! You did propose to me already when we first met.'

Encouraged by her enthusiasm, I say, 'Let's get married, then. Las Vegas, eh?'

'What're we gonna tell our friends, family, parents?' she asks, her voice speeding up. 'Yes, I'll do it, but is it gonna be real, like really real? If I'm getting really married, I want a big wedding and a ring and –'

'It can be real for me and you and for getting-me-legalised purposes. It won't be a big wedding, just a quickie, but I'll definitely get you a big ring.'

The next day, I give Amy's best friend $10,000 to buy a ring – as she knows exactly what Amy likes – instructing her to keep quiet. I drop the subject for a while, trying to create the impression that I've lost interest. Months later, I whisk Amy off to Las Vegas to see the Siegfried & Roy show.

I take my seat in the theatre, nervous, excited, convinced marrying Amy will make us happier, stronger, and keep us together for ever, the ring in a box bulging from my trouser pocket.

The show starts. Classical music. Blue light and mist bathe the stage. Coloured laser beams fan out, rave style. Siegfried and Roy materialise in outfits with more baubles than Christmas trees.

Wait a bit before you pop the question. 'They've got great smiles and teeth,' I say, holding Amy's hand.

'Not like you snaggle-toothed Brits,' Amy laughs.

A menagerie of white lions and tigers appear on raised platforms. Siegfried and Roy cuddle them, kissing the lips of mouths big enough to bite their heads off. While robot dragons breathe flames, Roy rides a tiger through the air. The applause and music grow louder.

All right, go for it. Trembling, I dig my hand into my pocket. I extract the box, almost dropping it. I turn to Amy and show her the ring. 'Will you marry me, Amy?'

'This is so sweet,' Amy says. 'Yes, yes, I'll marry you!'

We hug, kiss, cuddle in the theatre.

In a suite at Caesars Palace, we dress in black for the ceremony: Amy, a skirt and beaded spaghetti-strap top; a pinstripe suit for me. We stop at the courthouse for a marriage certificate. We set off for the Little White Chapel, hand in hand, hurriedly, excitedly, almost breaking into skips, every male in the vicinity slowing down to admire Amy, some stopping completely, causing a logjam of tourists on the Strip, their heads swivelling, even married men, oblivious to the disbelief on their wives' faces, hypnotised by Amy, some even brushing their wives off to soak up Amy's beauty, to inhale the vanilla and cinnamon scent wafting from her bouncy blonde mane, their bodies rotating, wrenching from their wives like cells dividing, and the more they react, the more I feel as if I'm marrying a movie star.

At the chapel, I trip on the step and almost fall over. Inside smells like a funeral home: fresh flowers, candles, wood polish. The sign on the wall:

MARRIAGE MESSAGE OF THE DAY
A marriage may be made in heaven,
but the maintenance must be done on earth.

A chubby, balding minister ambushes us like a waiter in a hurry to seat diners. He rushes through the paperwork and jumps right into the ceremony, assisted by a female.

'Do you Shaun Attwood take Amy Rae Faulkner to be your lawful wedded wife, to have and to hold, from this day forward, for better, for worse, for richer, for poorer, in sickness and in health, to love and to cherish till death do you part?'

'I do,' I say, eager to get the diamond on her before my shaky hand drops it.

We giggle through the ceremony and, at the end, kiss. Gazing at her big, happy eyes, I feel so much in love with her. I thank the minister and head for the door. My wedding band slips off, clinks on the floor and rolls away so quickly I lose track of it. We get down on our hands and knees to search, joined by the minister and his assistant, but the ring has vanished as if fleeing a crime scene.

'No worries. I'll buy a ring that fits better,' I say.

At Treasure Island, we dine and guzzle two bottles of dessert wine. Through the restaurant window we watch a battle between the pirate ship *Hispaniola*, which catches aflame amid heavy cannon fire, and the British frigate ship HMS *Britannia*, which eventually sinks. On the walk back to Caesars Palace, a hobo hands me a sleazy magazine. Amy snatches and studies it.

'I've heard there are real, like, whorehouses out here,' Amy says.

'Why are you so excited about that?' I ask.

'I wanna go to one!'

'On our wedding day?' I ask, smiling.

'Why not?'

'Well, if you want to, I'm up for anything.' *I thought I had no boundaries, but Amy running wild in a brothel: wow!*

'Good. Let's call the numbers in the book then.'

Back in our room, I wait till dusk and call a brothel in Pahrump. 'I'd like to make an appointment to come over there with my wife.'

'Sorry, sir. This is a gentlemen's club only. Women aren't welcome.'

'But she's bisexual.'

'Sorry, sir. Women aren't allowed.' *Click.*

I tell Amy.

'Keep trying!' Amy says, pouting.

'Look, if I can get you into a brothel, what do you have in mind?'

'I want a woman to pleasure the both of us.'

Mercy! I redouble my efforts, but the brothels all say the same thing: no women allowed. I'm disappointed, Amy on the verge of a tantrum.

'I'm extremely distressed! It's my fucking wedding night and I want to go to a brothel!' Amy snatches the magazine. Leafing through it, she says, 'I've got a better idea. If we can't go to a brothel, why don't we just order someone to our room?'

'Good idea!'

'Here, try this escort agency.' Amy hands me the magazine.

I dial. 'Hi. We're a couple looking to be pleasured by a female. Do you offer that kind of service?' I ask, bracing for the same response as the brothels.

'I have just the girl for you. Brunette. Tall. Slender. Bisexual.'

Twenty minutes later, a woman arrives in a short red outfit and high heels. 'Can I get the money up front, please?'

'How much?' I ask.

'One hundred and fifty for the hour.'

'And you know what we want, right?' I ask, worried she might take the money and run.

No answer.

I turn to Amy. 'You'd better tell her what we want first.'

'We only just want, er, just give him a blow job and go down on me. We don't want to have sex, full-on sex, with you.'

'That's fine. It's still one hundred and fifty,' she says, her tone implying she's going to vanish if the money doesn't appear.

I pay.

'I'll go first, but I need a line of coke.' Amy tips cocaine onto a tabletop, and separates out a line with a bank card.

Watching Amy snort it, the escort's eyes light up. 'Mind if I try some?'

'No. Go ahead,' Amy says. 'It's pretty pure stuff because we live near Mexico.'

While the escort snorts two huge lines, Amy and I raise our eyebrows.

'OK. Let's do this,' Amy says.

Anticipation heats my body up.

They undress and get on the bed, Amy facing upwards, smiling at me more than the escort. The escort kisses Amy, moves her lips to Amy's breasts, belly, thighs . . . Everywhere the escort kisses, I feel my own blood rush to that region. Gripped by a desire to join in, I struggle to stay put. The escort licks Amy gently between the legs, and massages that area. Amy closes her eyes. Pants. Shudders. Gasps. Wriggles. Lets off little shrieks, stirring my blood further. By the time Amy opens her eyes, her face is blotched pink, and I've stood up without realising it, entranced, sleepwalking, about to dive into the action. 'OK, husband dearest. It's your turn.'

Yes! I abandon my clothes and jump on the bed. The escort rubs my chest and massages my thighs. Her body movements speed up as the cocaine takes effect. She kisses my belly, takes my penis in her fingers and puts it in her mouth. Whereas she treated Amy softly, she does the opposite with me. She starts bobbing her head frantically between my legs. To anchor myself, I grip the bed. She comes up for air, panting, grabs my penis with an iron-welder's grip, spits on it and slaps it against her tongue. *She's out of control on cocaine.* While she simultaneously sucks and masturbates my penis, I employ a method to prevent premature ejaculation: reciting the Pythagorean theorem: *In any right triangle – God, this feels great – the area of the square whose side is the hypotenuse – mustn't say how good this feels or Amy will get jealous – is equal to the sum of the areas of the squares whose sides meet at a right angle. Sweet Jesus! I can't hold out much longer. God give me strength . . .* 'That was . . . er . . . we'd better stop now.'

The escort jumps up. 'Mind if I have more coke?'

'Go for it,' Amy says, amused.

She shouldn't be doing any more. She's high enough.

She snorts two heaped lines, shocking us, and launches into her life story, unstoppably, allowing no pauses for us to insert even a syllable. She's from Ohio, new to the business, a proud mother. She yanks family photos from her handbag. Her parents are babysitting her children in Ohio. She's making money to support them, doing things she sometimes doesn't like. Amy and I are the coolest couple she's ever met. I feel sorry for her, but as the monologue expands, Amy's expression turns first impatient then annoyed. With spittle fermenting at the corners of her mouth, the escort finally slows down.

'It's really sad that you have to be separated from your kids like that,' I say, hoping to steer her into leaving. 'We're out here from Tucson. Newly-weds. Today, actually.'

'You're shitting me?' she says, her eyes glowing.

'I shit you not,' I say.

'You guys are off the hook, calling me out on your wedding day! Why don't you fly me back to Tucson to live with you as a kind of maid/sex slave?'

I laugh but regret it when Amy fires me a nasty look, her lips hardening, head trembling.

Embarrassed, the escort goes to the toilet.

'This is not what I wanted,' Amy whispers. 'The whole purpose of having someone you pay for sex for is they're supposed to leave.'

'What should I do?' I ask.

'Tell her she has to go.'

'It'll break her heart. You tell her.'

'Huh! OK. If you won't, I will.'

'Oh, God. I guess I better,' I say.

When the escort returns, I say, 'We're off clubbing now.'

'Where at?'

'Club Utopia,' Amy lies.

'Hey, I'd love to come with you.'

Amy rolls her eyes, grits her teeth, flutters her eyelids. I suppress laughter.

The escort's phone rings. Her boss complains she's been with us for too long, another client is waiting.

Thank God!

'I have your number from the agency,' she says. 'I'll catch up with you later.' She leaves.

'Did you enjoy that?' I ask.

'Are you kidding me? I'm never ordering a prostitute like that again!'

CHAPTER 41

A FEW MONTHS later, when it seems like my ability to make money in the stock market and the bliss of matrimony – Amy having fitted the house with an S&M room complete with a sex swing – are never going to end, I'm watching TV in the living room when a news report attracts my attention. A shoot-out at a house. Neighbours in uproar. The house looks familiar, but I can't place it. My pager beeps.

A voicemail from Cody: 'Fuzzy Zack's house got shot up. It's headline news. You'd better get your ass down here.' Fuzzy Zack deals Ecstasy for me and manufactures LSD.

I pack a bag and speed to a safe house Cody oversees in Mesa. He says Skinner tried to rob 50,000 hits of LSD from Fuzzy Zack.

'Why would our top salesman try to jack our LSD chemist?' I ask.

'Dunno. But something needs to be done about Skinner. Don't forget, he was smoking crack and eating outta dumpsters before you made him what he is today. Word on the street is he's gonna kidnap Gangsta Dan with his black gangsta crew. Revenge for Gangsta Dan ripping all the piercings off his face.'

'I thought I had everyone working together peacefully. Violence like this just attracts the cops. I'll have a word with Skinner. He always listens to me.'

'You need to have more than a word with him.'

'What do you mean?' I ask.

'This has come about 'cause you moved to T-Town.'

'A power play?'

'Don't underestimate Skinner's ambition. If it's a power play against you, I will gladly hunt him down and shoot him, and his body will never be found.'

'Cody! I appreciate the gesture, but that's not necessary,' I say, shocked that he'd murder someone for my benefit, yet feeling an uneasy sense of gratitude that he'd go that far for me.

'I was suicidal when I met you. My plan was to join the military, get access to bombs and blow myself up with the corrupt fucking politicians in Washington. Working for you has structured my life and I will always love you for that.'

'I really appreciate that, Cody. I love you, too, bro.' I hug him. 'But we don't need to be knocking anyone off. Even if he disappears without a trace, there'd be a police investigation. And we've got Mari to think about. She's helped us out a lot, and Skinner is the father of her baby. But you're right, this is way more serious than I thought. Thanks for doing the homework on this one. Now that I have a better understanding, I'm going to think it over.'

For the next few days, I can't concentrate on the stock market. *If I threaten Skinner, he might turn against me. Come after me with his south-side gangstas. If G Dog threatens him, it might get out of control. Don't want anyone getting shot. But if Skinner's resorting to guns, how do I fight fire with fire? No. We're not the New Mexican Mafia. Use diplomacy. Win him back over. Maybe it's just a cry for attention. Charm him. But then he might think I'm soft. Shit. What to do?*

Checking my portfolio online, I'm grappling with the situation when Wild Man calls: 'I need to leave England in a hurry, la'. Can you get me a ticket to America right away?'

Perfect timing. Wild Man will sort Skinner out. 'How soon?'

'Like right away right away.'

'What did you do this time?'

'I'd rather not say over the phone.'

'I hear you. It's probably just as well that I don't know. I'll do it, but what about the last time I got you a bloody ticket? I spent a small fortune and you never even got on the plane!'

'I'm getting on the plane this time. No need to worry about that, la'.'

Reassured by the conviction in his voice, I say, 'With you banned from the US, I'll have to fly you to Canada. I'll send someone to drive you across the border.'

Wild Man arrives at the Phoenix Greyhound bus station in thick English sports clothes. I drive to Skinner's, explaining the situation en route.

'Sounds like we can't trust this Skinner,' Wild Man says. 'If he did shoot Fuzzy Zack's house up, obviously we've got to give Skinner the iron fist.'

'But Skinner's my top salesman.'

'Business is business, but you can't take disrespect. If you take disrespect, it leads to anarchy. I can't wait to have a fucking word with this Skinner,' Wild Man says, clenching and unclenching his hands.

'Hold on. Listen, I just want unity restored.'

'If you've got two of your moneymakers going up against one another, at the end of the day, you're gonna lose money.'

'I still think we can win him over. He's heard loads of stories about you, like the time you put Gangsta Dan in check. I think your presence alone will scare him back in line. The other thing is, you haven't met his girlfriend, Mari, yet. She's truly loyal.' I park.

Mari answers the door, holding the baby, smiling. 'Come in.' Spotting Wild Man stiffens her expression.

'This is Wild Man,' I say. 'He just got here.'

In the living room, Skinner sees Wild Man and drops his grin; his eyebrows leap and anxiety flickers across his face, but he quickly composes himself and beams. 'Big brother!'

I hug Skinner. 'We've got an even bigger brother now.' I nod at Wild Man.

Wild Man hugs Skinner and joins me on the sofa. For about ten minutes, we entertain them with the story of how Wild Man was smuggled into America. All done, I turn to Skinner and ask in a relaxed way, as if it's an afterthought, 'What's the deal with you and Fuzzy Zack?'

'He tried to get me shot!' Skinner says, scratching his ear.

Here we go. Bullshit justification. 'How come?' I ask, faking concern. Straightening his body up, Wild Man expresses friendly curiosity.

'I put an order in for some LSD. Fuzzy Zack's being real sketchy with me, so I took an armed crew over there.'

'Why would you take an armed crew when we're all supposed to be working together?' I ask.

'Well, it's a good job I did, 'cause wait till you hear what happened.'

'I can't wait to hear this,' Wild Man says.

'We get there, and we don't know it but Fuzzy's got snipers

with AK-47s positioned at the back of the house. We try to do the deal. I ask him to show me the acid, and he asks to see the money, and next thing there's a big argument, and then, *pop-pop-pop*, guns are going off all over the place.'

'That's crazy!' I say, hoping to encourage him.

'Yeah, my homey, T, opened up with a shotgun and bullets were flying everywhere. Lucky nobody got smoked. The neighbours were lucky, too. It showed on the news how the bullets went through like three or four of Fuzzy's neighbours' houses.'

'It was on the news?' Wild Man asks.

'All over headline news the night it happened,' Mari says.

'We don't need that kind of heat,' I say, shaking my head.

'You better speak to Fuzzy, then,' Skinner says.

'We intend to,' Wild Man says, narrowing his eyes.

Skinner goes upstairs to get money from a safe.

I whisper to Mari, 'What's really going on with him?'

'To be honest, I don't know. He's been smoking a lotta sherm, staying up for days, stinking and going off on tangents. He gets all fucked up and he has to be out doing stuff, robbing, trying to mix shit into drugs, making bunk shit to sell.'

'What do I need to do to get him back in line?' I ask.

Before Mari can answer, Skinner reappears. He gives me two large Manila envelopes containing $5,000 each.

I stand up. 'Little brother.' We hug. 'Good job on such high sales.' Pointing at Skinner, I turn to Wild Man. 'This is my number-one producer right here. Top dog!'

We all smile.

'Big brother and biggest brother,' Skinner says proudly. 'I've got some inside info for you on one of your boys.'

'What?' I ask.

'Fish is selling pills for Sammy the Bull's crew.'

'No way!' I say.

'Fish!' One of Wild Man's eyebrows arches up to the danger level and stays there, quivering; the other remains fixed in place. 'You want me to deal with Fish?' he asks.

I turn to Skinner. 'You sure?'

'Yup,' Skinner says.

'Poor Fish.' Wild Man grins.

We hug them and leave.

On the road, I say to Wild Man, 'What do you reckon?'

'I don't like him. We can't trust him.'

'What did you think of his story?'

'I believe that as much as I believe Russia needs more vodka.'

'What should we do?'

'I can do him in. Make an example.'

'I think that'll make matters worse. From the look on his face, I reckon you being here is enough.'

'If you don't put him in check now, he might try other shit.'

'That's a chance I'm prepared to take.'

'What about Fish?' Wild Man asks.

'He's been acting sketchy lately. I can easily find out through other sources. If he is selling for Sammy the Bull, then he's all yours.'

I rent a hotel room for Wild Man to meet Fuzzy Zack and his roommates. I tell them what Skinner said.

'Skinner's so full of shit,' Fuzzy Zack – heavyset, bright-blue hair, big friendly eyes, ears pierced with black studs, wearing massive fluffy trousers – says. 'He came over to jack me.'

'That's what I think, too, after hearing Skinner's version,' Wild Man says, nodding.

'I only had the guys with AK-47s stationed 'cause I knew Skinner was up to something. He didn't bring any money. When I asked him for the money, T pulled out a shotgun and started blasting. That's why we opened up with the AKs. I didn't want no shoot-out in my house or to be on the news. The neighbours are angry. We're gonna have to move out now.'

Wild Man tilts his head towards me. 'I'm telling you, Shaun, we need to keep a close eye on Skinner. If he thought he could gank Fuzzy just 'cause you moved to Tucson, who knows what he'll try next? But he might start thinking differently if I break one of his fucking kneecaps.' Wild Man's belly-laugh frightens the ravers.

'There's still no need for that,' I say. 'I'll get him back in line.'

More ravers arrive and confirm that Fish is selling for Sammy the Bull. I summon Fish over and tell Wild Man he can deal with him however he likes.

Fish arrives, shoulders hunched, staring at the floor, apprehension in his voice. To put him at ease, I get him high on Ecstasy. We chat for two hours. He lightens up, settles in, just like old times. Throughout the charade, I'm braced for Wild Man to broach the subject of Sammy the Bull, afraid of what he might do but in awe of his ability.

'We're gonna get going,' Fish says, standing up to leave with two companions.

I get up and hug them, as does Wild Man.

Perhaps Wild Man's going to let them go. Deal with it another time. Maybe he wants to talk to me first.

When all three are lined up in front of the door, Wild Man leans to one side and springs up with a punch that hits them in the face one after the other – *bop-bop-bop!* – toppling them like bowling pins.

'That's what happens when you stab Shaun in the back, Fish!' Wild Man yells.

On the carpet, they wriggle and groan. Fish fingers a mouth leaking blood. One rubs a jaw, the other an eye.

'How could you go behind our back with Sammy the Bull when we've had your back for years?' Wild Man yells.

No answer.

Staring at his left hand, Wild Man growls, 'My knuckle's fucking bleeding with a tooth fucking stuck in it.'

'Fucking hell, la',' I say, shocked to see Wild Man extract a tooth from his hand.

'This is your fucking fault, Fish!' Wild Man opens the door, grabs Fish, drags him outside and throws him down the stairs. Fish tumbles, yelping, his head banging against cement and metal railing. Wild Man turns and glares at Fish's friends. As if miraculously recovered, they leap up and run. They grab Fish and haul him off.

Minutes later, the phone rings. 'This is the manager. We've had a report of a disturbance in your room.'

'I'm sorry about the noise,' I say. 'I'm about to send everyone home.' Not wanting Wild Man to get arrested on his first day back, I tell everyone to leave, except for Wild Man and my bouncer Rossetti. The danger seems to pass.

Fifteen minutes later, someone knocks on the door. Sensing trouble, I hope it's ravers. Through the peephole, I see the manager with a young Tempe police officer in a smart dark-blue uniform. *The same cop G Dog held at gunpoint!* My heart bounces. 'It's the five-oh,' I say in a low voice. 'You two go fake like you're asleep in the bedroom.' They get on the bed. I take a deep breath and open the door.

The manager and cop are staring angrily, impatiently, unsettling me further. 'Can I come in?' the cop says, sniffing for marijuana.

'I've sent everyone home. There's no need for you to come in.'

The cop gazes beyond me, surveying the room in the hope of spotting drug paraphernalia. 'If you're not gonna give me permission to come in, then I'm gonna seek permission from the manager.'

'There's no need for you to come in,' I say. 'Everyone's gone home.'

The cop turns to the manager. 'Do I have permission to go in to inspect for property damage?'

'I give you permission,' the manager says. 'We've had noise complaints.'

The cop barges in, knocking me against a wall.

Shit! He's going to find Wild Man. He'd better not run Wild Man's name.

He whips out a torch and shines it in every cranny, his eyes tracking the beam for evidence of drug use. He picks through an ashtray with the zeal of a hobo hunting down a fag end and combs through the trash. 'Was this an alcohol party or were drugs involved?'

'Alcohol party,' I say.

Smirking, he raises his eyebrows. Giving up on the front room, he opens the bedroom door.

Oh shit! Here we go.

His eyes latch onto my friends.

He's going to see how high they are and call backup.

'I thought you said you'd sent everyone home. Who are these two?'

'They were so tired, I told them they could crash here.'

He shines his torch on them.

Stay still. Stay down.

Wild Man pops his head up. 'I'm trying to sleep here. Got work in the morning. What's going on, mate?'

The accent. The big bloodshot eyes. He's a dead giveaway.

The cop contemplates Wild Man with a distracted look, as if remembering something.

Oh no!

Wild Man drops his face out of sight.

The cop disappears into the bathroom and bangs things around. He re-emerges. 'There doesn't appear to be any damage. Keep the noise down. I don't wanna come back.' He leaves with the manager, abruptly, as if he's up to something.

'What was all that about?' Rossetti asks.

'Something's up,' I say, rushing to the window. I watch them walk away and confer outside the reception. The cop gets in his car and drives away but parks down the road.

'He pretended to go and stopped,' I say. 'Pack your shit up! We're leaving.'

As we grab our things, more cop cars join the first.

'They're gonna raid the room,' Rossetti says. 'Let's get the fuck outta here!'

I leave in such a hurry, I walk into a cactus. Feeling a burning sensation, I see numerous spines stuck in my leg and blood leaking out. I drive off, taking a detour around the cops, aware that my months of researching the stock market in peace are over.

CHAPTER 42

AFTER TAKING OUR morning nakèd swim, Amy and I frolic in the pool.

'When my parents and sis get here, we need to be on our best behaviour. My crazy relationships caused them all kinds of stress in the past. Can we act normal for a few weeks?'

'Does that mean absolutely no drugs?' Amy asks, raising her brows.

"Fraid so. A break'll do us good.'

'But I love having sex on drugs,' Amy says.

'I know. Me too.'

'If you can do it, I can do it,' Amy says, splashing me.

'Together, we can do it!' I say, splashing back, making her shriek.

'Perhaps we'd better do a load of drugs before they get here?' Amy wraps her arms around my neck, clings to me and we kiss.

'Good idea. We'll party our arses off, then go cold turkey. I want to show them a good time. Let them enjoy the house. Take them fine dining.'

'We should take them to the Gold Room, the Tack Room,' Amy says, swimming away.

'And our favourite: Anthony's. I'll pretend I'm going to order one of their most expensive bottles of wine.'

While excited about the visit, I worry about my family finding clues to my other life. I love my parents and sister, but doubt I can go for weeks without drugs.

They arrive at the airport jet-lagged, but as soon as they spot us they beam. We hug in the lounge and chat on the drive home. Approaching Sin Vacas, the talk stops as they gaze at the grandeur of the houses.

I take a winding road up and down hills. 'There's our house!' I say, pointing ahead.

'The size of it!' Karen says.

Inside, they wander from room to room, gasping at the decor.

'We've seen photos of the house, but the reality is something else,' Mum says.

'So this is how the other half live,' Dad says, stroking the pool-table felt.

'Yes, Paul McCartney has a ranch along the mountain range east of us. It's where Linda died.'

'Not so sure about the art work, though,' Dad says, staring at the glamour-girl street-art painted by Hotwheelz.

'I quite like them,' Karen says.

'I took one down before you came,' I say. 'They're not too pervy, are they?'

'I can live with them,' Mum says. 'And I could get used to this lifestyle.'

They unpack their clothes and we eat. I try to relax and chat naturally over dinner. They don't notice my drug-withdrawal anxiety.

The next day, sunbathing poolside, Karen says, 'This is the life.' She gets in the pool to teach Mum to swim. 'Come on, you can do it,' Karen shouts, pulling Mum along with a float.

'This is the best way to learn,' Mum says. 'In a private pool, with no strangers looking at you. It's wonderful. I love it.'

Afterwards, we relax with Dad in the jacuzzi, chatting and laughing.

'Who wants a margarita?' Amy says, holding a tray laden with giant cocktail glasses, salt on the rim.

Everything's working out. Everyone's having fun.

Later on, I insist they watch me trade the stock market online. In the computer room, they gather around. I examine some charts and buy $25,000 worth of Starbucks, which appears to be in a strong uptrend. The investment immediately loses $500, making my stomach lurch and sweat bead on my forehead. I take a deep breath, compose myself and invest another $25,000 to average my price down. The loss increases to $1,000, and I brace to close the position out if it reaches the most I'm prepared to lose on a day trade of this size: $1,500. I start to tremble but put on a brave face. As the stock rises, my pulse falls. As it moves into a profit, my smile and mood expand. I dump it all.

'I just made two grand in fifteen minutes!' I say, flushing with excitement. *That'll convince them my wealth is legally earned.* Seeing the deception as necessary to give them peace of mind, I feel no guilt.

'What a genius I've spawned!' Dad says.

At Anthony's in the Catalinas, a fawning waiter in a dickey bow seats us at a window-side table with a view of Tucson.

'They have some good wine here, Dad. Do you fancy this one?' I say, pointing at the list, bracing for his reaction.

Dad reads the description and gasps. 'No! That can't be right.'

I chuckle.

'What?' Karen asks.

'Twenty-five thousand dollars!' Dad says.

'For one bottle?' Mum asks.

'One bottle,' Dad says.

'Bloody hell!' Karen says. 'And this is your local restaurant!'

'They only sell a few a year,' I say. 'Usually when businessmen sign contracts. I'm paying, so, Dad, pick a bottle, but not one that's five figures.'

'A cheap bottle!' Mum says.

We laugh.

Dad studies the list, and orders a bottle of Mount Veeder Cabernet Sauvignon.

The size of the diamond in Amy's ring attracts Mum's attention.

'You want to see it?' Amy says, taking it off.

'Promise you won't get married without us being there,' Mum says, trying on the ring. 'We missed your wedding to Sumiko. We don't want to miss this one.'

Hoping they don't notice, I exchange guilty glances with Amy.

'I felt sad just watching it on video,' Mum says. 'I want to be there next time.' She twiddles the ring around a finger, closing her eyes, and passes it to Karen. 'You've got to make a wish. You can guess what I wished for.'

'What a rock! It's beautiful,' Karen says, repeating Mum's ritual. She hands it back to Amy. 'We all want to be there next time.'

Having deceived them about everything – drugs, lifestyle, criminal activity – I don't see any need to disclose our marriage. Trying not to think about what I've become, I can't look Mum in the eye. I hoped to alleviate my guilt by splurging on them, but now I feel worse. *At least their holiday's going well.*

We order food and eat. Filet mignon for dad and me. Seafood

for Mum and Karen. After hiding her first-ever foie gras under lettuce leaves, Amy goes to the restroom.

'What do you think of Amy?' I ask.

'She's lovely, very pretty, and she seems like a nice person,' Mum says.

'And she's made us very welcome,' Dad says.

'She's gorgeous and she's clever, but she's very young,' Karen says.

'Is she really ready to settle down?' Mum says.

'Mum, we love each other. Isn't that what matters?'

'Don't go rushing into things,' Mum says. 'You know what you're like. Get to know her properly. It may be just infatuation, living up here like a princess, having whatever she wants. That could easily turn a young girl's head. Don't marry her till you're certain of her, certain she loves you.'

'I am certain she loves me, but I won't marry her yet,' I say, blushing.

The holiday goes well, but every day I stay sober, the louder I hear the wolves howling for me to come out and party. *Acid Joey, Alice, Sallywack . . .* Near the end of my family's stay, I break down. *GHB won't last long. It won't make my eyes all big and crazy like Ecstasy or speed.*

As my dad drives us to Mount Lemmon, I'm giddy on GHB. We hike to a remote spot, where I can't resist rolling boulders down the slope.

'Don't do that. Someone might get hurt,' Dad says.

'Stop it, Shaun,' Mum says.

'Listen to your parents,' Amy says.

But I just giggle and cackle and run ahead, rolling boulders, mesmerised by the trajectory of their fall and my own insanity.

Karen plans to meet friends in Mexico and to go diving at Cozumel before travelling around South America. Karen and Amy get along so well, Amy asks if she can accompany Karen. I agree and pay for diving lessons and equipment. Excited about the trip, they test the equipment in the pool, bobbing up and down in the water, flippers splashing. Two days after my parents leave for England, Karen and Amy fly to Cozumel.

CHAPTER 43

DURING WILD MAN'S second month at the Tucson Ramada Inn, I arrive and am shocked to see four cop cars parked by his room. In a panic, I start to drive away, but Worm opens the door and waves me over. He explains that a crack deal went bad, so Wild Man kidnapped the dealer's accomplice. The cops showed up just after Worm freed the hostage.

'Why do you go to such extremes over stupid shit?' I ask Wild Man, unwilling to express the extent of my frustration lest I provoke his anger.

'You know what it's like when you're so focused on something. I just wanted my crack. I wasn't gonna be a victim – I heard about that shit on *Jerry Springer*.'

'Tucson's too small for you, la',' I say, raising a hand to my ear. 'I hear Phoenix calling you.'

I ring Sallywack: 'Wild Man's here. I'm bringing him to Phoenix, but I don't know where to house him.'

'Bring him to my apartment. He can stay with me.'

'Sallywack, I can't do that to you! You don't understand, he's destroyed everywhere he's ever lived. He's a maniac!'

'He won't fuck around like that in my place or I'll fucking kick his fucking ass and set my fucking dogs on him.'

'OK, if you insist. I need to get him out of Tucson in a hurry. See you soon. Love you,' I say, relieved by her kindness.

'Love you, too.'

A few hours later, Sallywack answers the door, naked, flanked by two mongrels resembling pit bulls on steroids. She hugs us and we sit down in the living room. 'Wild Man can stay here as long as he wants provided he walks the dogs daily and has a word with some guys who've been giving me shit.'

'Sounds good to me, la',' Wild Man says, stroking the dogs.

'La'. What's this "la"' mean?' Sallywack asks.

'It's Liverpool slang, short for "lad",' I say. 'Like saying "mate".'

'I like your piercings,' Wild Man says. 'Do you always sit around naked?'

'Yes, la',' Sallywack says.

'Fucking hell,' Wild Man says. 'I can get used to this.'

'You like her dogs, la'?' I ask.

'I love dogs, me. I'd rather kill a human being than a dog,' Wild Man says, scratching Bella-Boo's belly. Competing for his attention, the dogs yelp, whine and smile.

'I'm going to put you in charge of his allowance, too, Sallywack. Make sure he doesn't spend any of it on crack,' I say, handing her $200.

CHAPTER 44

AMY CALLS FROM Cozumel, saying what a great time she's having with my sister. Lonely without her, I focus on the stock market. *The drug trade's too risky. If I quit now, I can sit in my big house with Amy stress free and my parents will never know about my illegal activity.* I look forward to discussing my plans with Amy. *Maybe I'll do a master's degree in finance to improve my stock-market knowledge. We'll both go to the University of Arizona.*

Amy returns from Mexico pale and nervous. I ask what's wrong, but she won't say. Eventually, she starts sobbing. 'I was raped by a Mexican.'

Devastated, I almost fall backwards. I hug her. 'Everything's going to be OK.' But as she describes what happened, I fill with fury towards the rapist. I let go of her and punch a wall, momentarily distracted by the pain. 'I'll get the bastard. Who was he?'

'Some Mexican who saw me in a bar.'

'Where was Karen? How did he get you on your own?' A thousand questions invade my mind.

'He spiked my drink. I didn't know what was going on. I woke up in some strange place.'

I hug her and we both cry.

Amy checks into a hospital as a rape victim. Upset and angry and hearing wolves howling, I revert to snorting meth. I plan a trip to Mexico with Wild Man and G Dog to try to find and kill the rapist. They agree to go, so I prepare the logistics.

I call my mum, distraught, and rant to her. My parents panic over Karen's safety, but track her down by email. Days later, Karen calls. I vent on her for not protecting Amy.

'You're wrong, Shaun,' Karen says. 'Amy wasn't raped. She disappeared from a club with one of the locals and didn't come home all night. I had a huge row with her and we barely spoke again for the rest of the trip.'

'That's not what she told me!'

'I saw her kissing him in the bar. She must have made up the rape story 'cause she's terrified I'm going to grass on her and you'll break up with her.'

Who can I believe? Why would my sister lie? My brain snaps again – the wolves howl louder than ever – and my anger swells in a new direction: at Amy.

I hang up and storm into the living room. 'I just got off the phone with Karen. She said you never got raped! What the fuck's going on, Amy?'

Amy gets off the sofa. Sniffs. Cries. 'I'm so ... so ... sorry, Shaun. I was off my head on drugs and I slept with someone.'

My heart twists. Pressure builds in my brain until it hurts and electrical crackling noises commence. 'Amy, I fucking love you! How could you do this to me? And to think, around my sister! My whole fucking family's devastated!'

'I love you, too. That's why I didn't tell you. I don't want to lose you,' she says, her expression agonised.

'It's too late for that now!'

Amy sobs so much she can't speak.

I grab a bottle of wine, smash it on the tiles, march to the bedroom, stuff clothes in a case and take off, hitting high speeds on the freeway. *Not been raving in Phoenix for months. Spending too much time in Tucson. Ignoring my friends in Tempe. I miss Acid Joey dancing, Sallywack running around naked hitting on glitter girls, Jake massaging me, Alice letting me suck her lip piercing. Can't wait to see them all, get high and numb my pain ...*

I put on a Markus Schulz trance mix and turn it up loud, hoping to drown out thoughts of Amy – but I can't stop thinking about her. Waves of sadness push me to tears. Bursts of anger make me grit my teeth and punch the dashboard. The pressure in my head feels as if a metal band is tightening around my skull, trying to split it in half. Speeding up, overtaking every car in sight, I tell myself, *Crashing might fix my pain.*

In the twilight, a mountain is visible to my side. Glancing at it, I'm consumed by a peculiar feeling. To get a better look, I slow down. For the first time ever, in my mind's eye I see my wolves close up. Light-coloured wolves – a ghostly grey that turns dark above their eyes and on the top of their backs. They're moving up a rocky slope, briskly, stealthily, with a purposeful stride and stare, their breath visible in the cool night air. Realising I'm watching them, they stop, turn their heads and gaze at me invitingly, an eerie glow in their amber eyes. They howl that they've always been with me and I'm not alone. A ticklish sensation runs down the sides of my head, across the nape of my neck, up the back of my head and around the top, like a force field. The hairs on my arms slant up so slowly I can almost feel each one rise. I'm warm inside. For over a minute, my arm hairs stand erect, the force field stays in place, tingling my skin, and tears stream.

My drug rampage in Phoenix with Wild Man lasts for weeks. While I'm away, the stock market crashes. Wealth that took years to build evaporates. When I go back to Amy, we take more drugs and have more sex than ever before, but things are no longer the same.

CHAPTER 45

WILD MAN STAYS with Sallywack for a few months until the arrival of his English girlfriend, Wild Woman – a short blonde spitfire who not only fights with Wild Man but often gets the better of him.

In their Holiday Inn room – thick with meth smoke, blinds closed, lights and TV on – I say, 'I know how Peter got the name Wild Man. How did you get Wild Woman?'

Rolling a joint on a desk, Wild Woman says in a raspy Liverpudlian accent, 'It was in a pub. I was having a night out with my friend. We were dancing, and I was massive back then. I looked over and some woman's pulling my friend by the hair, so I walked over, head-butted the daughter, put her on the floor, broke the husband's ribs with a chair and battered the woman, who ended up in a wheelchair. I got bound over to keep the peace for five years and three counts of grievous bodily harm. They called me the Wild Woman of Borneo after that.'

'You took a whole family out!' I say.

'Basically, she was causing a riot on her own,' Wild Man says, sat on the bed, nursing a meth pipe.

'How did the Wild Ones meet?'

'She's lying on the floor in some house,' Wild Man says. 'I turned to her and said, "If I smoke another one of these spliffs, I'll probably wanna shag you."'

'He didn't say that!' Wild Woman hisses, turns and punches Wild Man's arm. 'He said, "I just might get a semi hard-on if I have another pull on this, looking at the tits on you." I said, "You cheeky bastard!" He walked me to the taxi rank and a week later he was outside Top of the Town, and I was having a party back at my house, so I invited him to mine and we were never apart from that day on, except when he came to America to see you.'

When Wild Woman goes into the bathroom, Wild Man whispers, 'Let's go to a titty bar, la'.'

The bathroom door bursts open. Wild Woman emerges, hands on her hips.

'I need to go and take care of business somewhere with Shaun, love.'

'What do you mean?' Wild Woman says, scowling.

'Me and Shaun are gonna go meet some people, collect some debts and shoot pool.'

'Well, I'm fucking coming with youse then!' Wild Woman snatches her handbag.

'Love, I need to spend some time alone with Shaun!' Wild Man growls.

Wild Woman marches up to Wild Man. 'What the fuck are you two up to? You planning on going to a fucking titty bar again? Is that fucking Chantelle waiting to shag you somewhere? You dirty fucking bastard!'

'Come on, la',' Wild Man says. 'Let's get the fuck outta here.'

'Fuck you, Peter!'

'Fuck you!'

Wild Woman chases Wild Man from the room.

In the car, I say, 'You two getting hostile like that's way too stressful for me, la'.'

'That's nothing. We're always fighting. One time, she went to the kitchen, grabbed a knife and stabbed me in the belly.' Raising his top, he says, 'Look at the scar.'

'How can you have a relationship based on domestic violence?'

'It's all about the make-up sex, la'.'

I take Wild Man to Club Freedom, where Keoki is spinning. Wearing a business suit and Gothic make-up, Keoki looks up from the turntables. I remove the disguise I'm wearing to dodge undercover cops: sunglasses and a bandanna. Our eyes meet. Keoki smiles like a fiend.

Spaniard spots me, his crew dozens strong – all working for Sammy the Bull – versus the six I'm with. 'English Shaun!' Spaniard says, approaching with some large friends.

While I shake Spaniard's hand, G Dog and Wild Man flank me. My body steels for conflict. My heart speeds up.

Spaniard's partner, Mark, steps up to Wild Man, looks him up and down and says to me, 'So this is all you've got for backup, is it?' Mark shakes his head at Wild Man.

'What the fuck did you just say, you fucking tit?' Wild Man says, pointing at Mark.

'What the fuck are you guys doing in here?' Mark yells.

'Are you deaf, you fucking spaghetti-head motherfucker?!' Wild Man says, balling his fists.

'You're way out of your league,' Mark says.

'Go and fuck yourself. Me and you outside!' Wild Man yells.

'No, you listen!' Mark yells. 'We've got respect for your family, but this is our turf.'

'Let's go outside, then!' Wild Man yells.

Spaniard gets in between them. 'C'mon. Chill out, guys.'

'Yeah, come on, Wild Man, forget about it,' I say, grabbing his arm, wanting to leave fast.

'If you don't wanna go outside –' Wild Man shifts and shoves Mark.

Bracing for an explosion of violence, I say, 'Calm down, la',' my heart beating as if Wild Man's big hand is clenching and unclenching in my chest.

Spaniard pushes Mark back. Cody and G Dog grab Wild Man.

'Calm down, Wild Man,' Cody says.

'He fucking disrespected me,' Wild Man says.

Spaniard pulls Mark away from Wild Man, their eyes locked. *There's enough of them to annihilate us.* 'Hey, Spaniard, Mark started this, talking shit to Wild Man,' I say. 'We don't want any trouble. Come on, let's go.' I help drag Wild Man out, relieved to escape unscathed.

A few weeks later, I visit the Wild Ones' flat in Tempe.

Wild Woman opens the door, agitated. 'Wild Man's been arrested.'

'For what?' I ask.

'We were walking towards Mill Avenue and he slapped me across the face. A cop on a bike arrested him and took his ID. It had a woman's name on it, Candy Huff, next to his picture. He ran his name and took him but let me go.'

'Unbelievable! All the trouble it took to smuggle him in and he gets busted for acting a twat to you. Now he's had one deportation, they'll definitely put an immigration hold on him. He's also looking at prison time, because last time they banned him from the country for being a menace to society. Sorry, Wild Woman, but we might not be seeing Wild Man for a while. I'll have an attorney check into it, but don't get your hopes up.'

'Now I've got my own little place in Tempe, I'm better off without the bastard. Before he got arrested, we were shagging and he reached under the mattress, pulled out a huge knife and started stabbing the mattress between my legs. When I asked him what the fuck he was doing, he said, "I know there's a Mexican under the mattress fingering your bum while I'm trying to make love to you."'

'I don't know how he comes up with these things!'

'He'd been up for weeks on meth, Shaun. He was going mental with the mattress, saying, "Who's under it?" The mattress is on the floor. No one could get under the bed even if they wanted to. Then, before this, he was stood for two-and-a-half hours, Shaun, with a butterfly knife behind his back waiting for the Mexicans to come and kill him. Nobody was out there. I ended up opening the door, saying, "Come on in, anybody," being sarcastic, know what I mean? Then he flipped out on me for doing that!'

'If I leave you some pills, can you sell them to raise cash to pay for Wild Man's attorney?'

'I'll do my best.'

CHAPTER 46

IN BED ONE night, I say to Amy, 'For all I know, you've been using me for money the whole time we've been together.'

She winces. 'I like money just as much as you, Shaun, but I also love you,' she says, resting on her side.

'I find that hard to believe after Mexico. What were you thinking?'

'I wasn't thinking. I was so high. I got scared coming home, so I made up a story. I figured it would be better for you like that.'

'Better for me! I blew a gasket. Most of my money's gone and I don't even give a shit what happens any more. I was so happy. I tried so hard to show my family how happy we were and now they're worried sick about us. How did everything turn so ugly so fast?'

'Look, if you think I'm using you for money, how about I do something to make you more money than you've ever spent on me?' she says in a pleading tone.

'What are you on about?' I say, sitting up. 'I don't even know how much I've spent on you.'

'No one's getting caught smuggling through Mexico. What's the most Ecstasy anyone's brought in so far?'

'Twenty thousand.'

'I'll bring in more. I've got some ideas of my own, you know.'

'Like what?'

'Diving tanks. You know how many pills can fit in a diving tank? People cross into America with diving tanks all the time. I can actually go diving before I bring them over.'

'You're out of your mind! Say you get caught with pills in Mexico and end up in some Mexican prison? Think about that. You're my bloody wife! The Mexican authorities will notify the US authorities and they'll raid this house. And what about your parents? They'll want to kill me.'

'I'm going to do it, and you're not going to stop me!' she yells, raising herself to look me in the eye. 'I'll call Pablo and set it up myself. And that's another thing: if Pablo just flew over to Europe and connected with some people, don't you think I can do that? Then we can get Pablo out of the picture. He's such a fucking asshole to deal with. If he did as you told him, a lot of shit that's gone wrong would never have happened. He has you by the balls. He knows it, and takes advantage.'

'True. More pills could have been smuggled if it wasn't for him giving his word and not following through or delaying things for months. He did well going out there on his own, but now he's got attitude.'

'Look, Shaun, I do love you, and I want to earn your trust back. I'm going on the next mission and I'm going to bring thirty thousand hits.'

Amy flies to Europe. She gets pills from Pablo in Amsterdam, packs them in pillowcases and takes the train to Germany, where she meets a dealer in a nightclub and gets samples. She flies from Germany to Hermosillo with the pills in her luggage, still in pillowcases. No one stops her. Her student friends on vacation in Rocky Point pick her up in a car packed with their belongings, including diving equipment. At the border, they flirt with the guard, who waves them through. I chew the samples. All are high quality. I'm impressed by Amy and delighted with the new connection.

CHAPTER 47

WITH THE PILLS Amy smuggled beginning to restore my wealth, I'm caught off guard by reports that Wild Woman's place has been firebombed. It's almost a year since Wild Man was arrested, and by now she's selling tens of thousands of Ecstasy pills.

Concerned for her safety, I speed to her place and rush in. 'What happened?'

She's slumped on a chair, gloomy-eyed, a cut on her face. 'I was sat at the desk by the bedroom window and Grady was on the bottom of the bed. I was talking to him, weighing out stuff, and the next minute there was a loud *bang*. The firebomb skimmed past my face and blew up. Grady dragged me out and I was like, "No!" I went back and grabbed my stash. I gave it to one of my mates and she locked it in the back of her car.'

Relieved she isn't seriously injured, I'm shocked that someone had the nerve to attack one of the Wild Ones. 'Do you think it's Sammy the Bull's crew trying to run us out of Tempe?'

'No,' Wild Woman says. 'One of my dealers, Joey Crack, told me Skinner was making a bomb thing. When that went off, his was the first name that came into my head. I knew it wasn't the cops 'cause they don't raid with firebombs.'

Skinner! 'When did Joey Crack tell you that?' I ask, incredulous.

'It was about a week or two ago. He's lost the plot, hasn't he, Skinner?'

'He's smoking sherm and meth, according to Mari, but I don't think he'd go this far. You had any problems with him I don't know about?'

'No. I think his problem is that he thinks if he hurts me in some way it's like hurting you and Wild Man. 'Cause he can't hurt you two physically.'

'Mari said now you're in the scene, taking over Tempe, he's no longer getting the attention I used to give him.'

'Well, I'm selling more than him now, aren't I?' Wild Woman says, her eyes lighting up. 'Those black gangstas Skinner shot up Fuzzy Zack's house with showed up here right after the firebomb, telling me to grab my drugs and get in their car.'

It dawns on me that she's right, but my mind struggles against it. *Will Skinner strike at me next?*

'I told them to stay away from me. They kept telling me to get in their car. They wanted to take me to some strange place, an apartment in the middle of the Foothills. I was like, "I'm not getting in no fucking car with you. I don't know who you are and I don't trust you." It was just the way they turned up. It was dead sketchy. I wigged out on them and they're like, "We're not gonna hurt you. We're just gonna take you somewhere safe." I said, "I don't know who just put that through my window. You might be taking me out to the desert. Do you think I'm fucking stupid?" The other thing is, Wild Man's been calling Skinner from prison, threatening him over money he owes me. But he thinks 'cause Wild Man's in prison, nothing's gonna happen to him.'

'Let me check into this. I'm sending my immigration attorney to see Wild Man. It's been almost a year. They shouldn't be holding him this long. I just remembered something else: a few days ago, Skinner asked me if Wild Man was facing prison time in England. Does Wild Man know about the firebomb yet?'

'Yeah, it's got his red dots going. He said Skinner just dug his own grave.'

A few days later, I track Skinner down at an apartment, walk in and give him a hug. 'Viddy well, little brother.'

'Viddy well, big brother,' Skinner says.

After chitchat, I ask, 'Hey, did you hear what happened at Wild Woman's?'

'No, big brother. What happened?'

Recounting the story, I study Skinner's face. *He's either telling the truth or he's a great actor.* He suggests Sammy the Bull's people did it. I play along and leave on a friendly note, unsure how to deal with him.

In Wild Woman's apartment, I install Vince – one of my bouncers, 6 ft 4 in., with a chiselled body and a thick scar streaking down his right cheek from a machete wound. I instruct him to answer the door with a shotgun and to flaunt it to deter further attacks.

Wild Woman calls, complaining: 'Vince is making me more nervous and scared.'

'What's he doing?' I ask.

'He's supposed to be looking after me, but he keeps walking around with this big gun all the time.'

'I told him to.'

'I said to Vince, "Can you put that fucking gun away? I'm sick of looking at that gun all day." Grady's better than Vince. Grady sits all night with a gun while I sleep.'

'Vince is just following orders, but I'll tell him to chill.'

I've been testing Vince – a newcomer to my organisation – with a view to promotion. That he frightens Wild Woman – who doesn't scare easily – pleases me. *Her customers are probably terrified and any potential robbers they talk to put off.* Rewarding him with more responsibility, I give him 500 Ecstasy to sell, but he returns claiming he was robbed. After interrogating him with Wild Woman, I discuss the matter with her.

'I don't trust him,' Wild Woman says. 'There's something dead sneaky going on. Since I met him, I've thought he's trying to be something he's not, telling his tall stories and what he has and hasn't done, but it's all false. He's also up Skinner's arse. I'm convinced Skinner's sneaking around doing underhand shit with Vince, too.'

Has Skinner corrupted Vince already? 'When was he up Skinner's arse?' I ask, alarmed.

'In my flat. You're always in Tucson. I don't want Vince near me no more. I don't trust him. He's lying about the pills. When you were quizzing him, his story kept changing. He kept tripping himself up, saying it was three dudes, then it was two.'

Disappointed, I grant Vince one mistake, but advise him there'll be consequences next time. I drop the price of the 500 pills he lost to my cost and tell him he must work to repay me, starting with helping collect a debt.

While I drive to the people who owe the debt, Vince asks, 'What's the deal with these guys?'

'Primo and Marcello are into me for thirty grand. They've been getting off their heads on meth and ketamine and anything they can get their hands on. They're so spaced out, they think people are on the roof. They're mellow. It's not going to turn hostile. I just need to teach them a lesson.'

'How're you gonna get them to pay up?' he asks.

'You'll see,' I say, not expecting to get paid today, but hoping to demonstrate the meaning of consequences to Vince.

Primo and Marcello answer the door, their eyes bushbaby wide, dark bags below. 'Come in quick,' Primo whispers, swivelling his head, casting paranoid glances up and down the street. 'Did the neighbours see you?'

'You guys need to take some Xanax and chill,' I say. We walk into a living room painted gold with a red sofa, Greek statues and rave posters. I hug them and introduce Vince. 'So you guys got any money for me?'

'We got robbed!' Marcello says, pacing like a prisoner in a cell.

'By who?' I ask, frowning.

'Crackheads,' Primo says. 'They're still on the roof.'

I glance at Vince and shake my head. 'You said that days ago. How can they still be on the roof?'

'They just are!' Primo says.

'Do me a favour, Marcello. Turn the music up,' I say.

'Why?' Marcello bites his bottom lip.

Vince stares at me, confused.

'I don't want your neighbours to hear what I've got to say.'

Marcello and Primo stare at each other, terrified, as if turning the music up might kill them.

'Vince, can you turn the stereo up, please?' I ask.

Marcello and Primo's eyes follow Vince to the stereo. He raises the volume of the house music.

'So the guys who robbed you are still on the roof?' I ask, staring at the ceiling.

'Yeah,' Primo says.

'Can you point out exactly where they are on the roof?' I ask, putting my hand in my pocket.

Primo and Marcello shuffle around, whisper to each other, stare at the ceiling. They point at a section near a back corner.

'Are you sure that's the right part of the roof?' I ask, positioning myself below it.

They nod.

I pull a Glock handgun out and brace for the noise. They watch in disbelief as I aim at the ceiling. *Bang-bang-bang* . . . They all jump. Plaster sprays down.

With the shooting ringing in my ears, I say, 'I guess that takes care of the thieves on the roof. I suggest you guys sober up and have some money for me next time. Let's get out of here, Vince, in case the neighbours call the cops.'

A few days later, Mari calls: 'I've dumped Skinner and moved in with my mom.'

'What's he done now?' I ask, sat at my computer.

'I was over at Grady's apartment. I went to my car to get something. You know how the back parking lot is so dark by the train tracks?'

'Yes.'

'The next thing you know, someone comes out of the bushes with a knife at my neck.'

'What?'

'He cut my chin, and my tyres are slashed. It was Skinner.'

'You sure?'

'Yeah, it was fucking Skinner. He came up behind me and I didn't know who the fuck it was 'cause he had a mask on. My first instinct was to kick him in the nuts or elbow him in the chest. Next thing you know, he says something and I'm like, "You're fucking kidding me!" I pushed him off me. He's like, "You're fucking Shaun," and I was like, "Shaun isn't even fucking in there! He's probably in Tucson. I'm just hanging out with Jake and Grady." He's like, "Come with me now, we need to talk," and I'm like, "I don't wanna talk to you. I'm done with you." He starts yelling at me, "You fucking bitch. All you motherfuckers are gonna be sorry. I'm gonna rat you all out."'

Shook up by Skinner's antics, I resolve to stop being so sentimental about him.

CHAPTER 48

WILD WOMAN CALLS: 'Grady was minding my flat while I went shopping. When I came back to the flat, he said, "I don't want to make you worry, but you need to get outta here. I think you're gonna get robbed or raided." He said he'd seen two people walking past, looking into the flat.'

Has she been up for too long on meth? 'Take some Valium,' I say. 'Let's discuss this after you've had a good night's sleep.'

'I don't need sleep. I'm fine. I'm going on what I've been told. I trust Grady with my life. I feel dead uneasy.'

'I suggest you stay at a mate's pad, then, and let's see what happens.'

I drive to Wild Woman's the next day to see if she's OK. Her front door is off its hinges. My heartbeat accelerates. I scan the area to see if anyone's watching. I step inside, my hands trembling. Her scattered belongings look as if they've been ransacked by looters. When a figure appears in the doorway, I jump.

'The cops just left.' Grady walks in and hugs me. 'They took Wild Woman and all her shit. It's a good job you didn't arrive earlier.'

'Fuck, dude! I'll send her our attorney right away. She's in deep shit if they caught her with thousands of Ecstasy. Did they go next door?' I ask, referring to one of my safe houses.

'I don't think so,' Grady says. 'I was watching from upstairs.'

'Let's check it out.' I open next door. The bare apartment is untouched. 'That's a relief. Do you think they've still got surveillance set up around here?'

'Not now it's been raided,' he says.

'I've got a shipment of Ecstasy coming in the mail. Can you watch out for it from upstairs?'

'Yeah.'

'Whoever has the balls to retrieve it after this raid will get five hundred dollars.'

'Sweet.'

The next day, the cops release Wild Woman. I arrive to find her frying chips, the apartment tidied up.

'What happened?' I ask, sitting down on the sofa.

'After we spoke, I stayed at my mate's like you said, all night till like ten o'clock in the morning. The minute I walked in here – I'd just got right through to the back bedroom – there was a *boom-boom-boom* and they just came charging in. They'd been waiting for me and I couldn't do anything about anything. The safe was full. Thousands of pills. They cuffed me and put me on the bench outside the front door. The key to the safe was on my key ring on the couch, but they battered the safe with a hammer thing. The cop in charge was that Detective Reid who nicked Wild Man years ago –'

'Detective Reid!' The name jangles my nerves. 'Not him again! I thought we shook him off. I can't believe his name has come up again. What's he look like?'

'A proper serious hard bastard with long hair. He doesn't look like a cop. He looks like a biker, a Hell's Angel. He asked me what was in the safe. I said, "I don't know. I'm staying here 'cause I'm stranded 'cause my boyfriend's being deported. He's in immigration. Some fella who knows my boyfriend said I could stay here until I get something sorted for my plane fare home." Detective Reid came out with a big brown envelope full of LSD.

'"What are these?"

'"I don't know what they are."

'"Well these were in the safe."

'"It's not my safe."

'"Whose safe is it?"

'The key to the safe was still on my key ring and he never got it.'

'Detective Reid's not that bright then.'

'They left the bottle of ketamine, too. They thought it was Sprite. Detective Reid took me to the station, interviewed me and asked if I knew English Shaun.'

The hairs on my forearms rise. *How does he know my nickname? Someone's talked to him. Skinner?*

'I said no. He said, "Is it English Shaun's stuff?" I said, "I don't know anybody called English Shaun. I don't know anybody here. My boyfriend's been arrested and I'm just stuck." Then he said, "We know you're scared." He gave me twenty dollars for a taxi home, his card, and told me to ring him in a couple of days.'

'Shit, Wild Woman! It's a set-up. They've let you go to get to me. Pack your shit up right now. We've got to get the hell out of here! I'll pay a friend to house you. When Wild Man gets back, I'll figure out where to send you. It'll be far away from Tempe.'

Wild Man's deportation is imminent, but he's planning to return to the US as soon as he can.

Detective Reid's closing in. The Wild Ones will have to go to Mexico for their own safety. If she disappears, she can't be prosecuted and it'll stop Detective Reid using her to find me. But what about the Ecstasy shipment? With Wild Woman gone, the package might lead Detective Reid to me. With the loss from the raid, I can't afford to abandon it.

Days later, Wild Man lands in England. I make arrangements to smuggle him back. He leaves a voicemail: 'That punk Skinner tried to set fire to my woman. Tell him he's dead and I'm on my fucking way!'

A week after the raid, Grady calls. 'The flyers have landed,' he says, referring to the Ecstasy.

'Do you want to handle it for what we discussed?' I ask.

'No. The people in the apartment opposite haven't stopped looking at it. I'm too sketched out. I think if someone doesn't take it soon, someone's gonna grab it.'

I visit Jaxson, who agrees to pick it up on his motorcycle. 'I'd like you to drive around a bit to suss out if you're being followed. Then meet me at Walgreens parking lot and we'll transfer it to my SUV.'

'What if I'm followed?'

'Try and ditch them, or stash it somewhere. Just don't bring Detective Reid to me.'

Jaxson is so loyal I hate the idea of sending him on a kamikaze mission. When he leaves, my gut fills with a bad feeling. After a short wait, I get in the SUV, convinced I'm falling into a trap set by Detective Reid. I wait at Walgreens, watching every pedestrian and vehicle, sweat dampening my clothes. *Hurry up, Jaxson.* Attempting to relieve my facial tension, I pinch my bottom lip and tug it down several times. By the time Jaxson arrives with the box on the back of his bike, my mouth is dry. I watch him park at my rear. I jump out, nod at him and open the back.

'I made sure I didn't get followed.'

'Good job, man.'

He slides the box in, jumps on his bike, speeds off.

I drive slowly, not wanting to give the cops any cause to stop and search. My eyes dart from mirror to mirror and scan every vehicle. I get away scot-free, but a voice tells me, *The risks you're running are too high.*

Unable to pay my rent and the $20,000-plus in monthly bills, including payments for multiple apartments, I abandon the house at Sin Vacas. Amy and I move east along the mountain range to a three-bedroom apartment. The shock of her infidelity wears off and eventually our closeness returns. We settle back into a routine. It's a small place and I spend little money, but Amy stays with me.

CHAPTER 49

VINCE PROPOSES REPAYING his debt by picking up Ecstasy from his friend in Germany. With Amy scheduled to buy Ecstasy from her German supplier, I send Vince with her.

From home, I call Amy. She sounds uneasy but insists everything is fine. She flies to Hermosillo, intending to give her Ecstasy to students to smuggle into Arizona. Vince stays in Germany, claiming his friend needs more time to connect.

Amy calls from a hotel: 'All my luggage, including the flyers, didn't get here.'

I shudder at the prospect of Amy getting busted by the Mexican police. Assuming the Ecstasy was intercepted, I say, 'I'm pulling you the fuck out of Mexico before the cops figure out where you are. I'll call Cody right away to come and get you.'

'Chill! Chill! Let me finish what I'm saying. I spoke to the airline. They said this happens a lot in Mexico and not to worry. They've put me in a hotel. They're gonna bring my luggage here when it shows up.'

'How do you know the airline isn't setting you up for the cops?'

'It's not like that. They would have arrested me by now, wouldn't they? Bags get lost all the time in Mexico.'

'In the stock market, at the first sign of things going bad, it's best to cut your losses. I don't see how this is different.'

'Shaun. I'm all right. I'm staying until the luggage is found.'

'I don't give a shit about the pills. It's you I'm worried about. I'd abandon the mission.'

'I'm staying.'

'You've got bigger balls than me.'

'I know.'

After the call, I regret ever letting Amy smuggle pills. Unable to sleep, I use Xanax to knock myself out. For two days, I call Amy every few hours. I become increasingly worried, but she insists on staying. *The Mexican police will tip the Tucson police off and our place will be raided. I can help Amy better from Phoenix. I'll meet the attorney and have him offer a bribe for Amy's release. Whatever it takes, the money will be raised.* On the third day, I make plans with Cody to evacuate her.

Amy calls: 'The luggage is here.'

'Thank God! I miss you so much.'

'I'll be home soon,' Amy says in a sad, low voice.

'Amy, you sound more stressed out than when the luggage was missing. What's wrong?' *Has she been arrested? Are they forcing her to call?*

'Shaun, you said if I ever fucked up again and I told you the truth right away you wouldn't get mad at me,' she says, her voice faltering.

Pressure rises in my head. 'Yes, and I meant it.'

'I've fucked up again.' She starts crying. 'When we got to Germany, Vince said it would be best if we share a room to save money. We ended up getting high and sleeping together. I'm so sorry, Shaun.'

My heart rips where it was recently patched together. I breathe deeply, expanding my belly. I close my eyes. Exhale. My head throbs. Anger swells. The wolves inside me snarl. 'Fucking hell, Amy! Sleeping with Vince! What were you fucking thinking?'

'At least I told you the truth.'

'You did. It's fucked up, it's really fucked up, but you did the right thing. You've got nothing to worry about.' *Vince is dead.*

'There's more I need to tell you, 'cause I think you're in danger from some of the people working for you.'

I want to yell, vent, kick, scream, bang my head against a wall until my brains spill out, but I force myself to speak slowly, to sound calm: 'Just tell me everything you know.'

'It started out with Vince ordering room service and joking about spending your money. So I played along to hear what he'd say. The higher he got, the more he told me. Like that time you fronted him those pills and he told you they were robbed off him at gunpoint. Skinner told him to tell you that. Him and Skinner sold those pills. They used the money to invest in other drug deals.'

'What else?'

'By the end of my stay, he was telling me you're on your way down, and him and Skinner are taking over, and if I have any sense I'd leave you and join forces with them . . .'

I hang up, feeling sick, thoughts of Vince and Amy burning a hole in my mind. *I'll make an example of Vince. If I do nothing, I'm finished. I'm owed half a million in drug debts that'll never get paid. Soon everyone'll know that Vince fucked my wife, and I'll be a laughing stock. I'll be overthrown. I must act swiftly, and without Wild Man to show I have other means. G Dog's ideal. People are more scared of him than ever since the New Mexican Mafia made headline news, accused of murder for hire. I also need a second person. Jaxson is Vince's friend. If one of my key bouncers shows loyalty to me, it'll send a signal that my crew is unified. Wild Man would probably kill Vince. We'll hurt Vince, not kill him. He fucked my wife, for Christ's sake. Wants to overthrow me. I must act . . .* In a rage, I channel all of my energy into planning Vince's abduction.

I meet Jaxson and G Dog at an apartment in North Phoenix where Tulips – a Mexican American Ecstasy dealer of mine whom Vince gets along with – lives.

Inside, I tell them, 'I'm going to bring Vince here. When I say to him, "I'll take you home now," I want you guys to grab him.'

I drink GHB, snort meth, take half a Xanax and set off for the airport in a borrowed truck, a tornado of angry thoughts battering my skull, Vince at the eye of the storm. At the terminal, too furious to stand still, I stride around, rehearsing what to say, sparks going off in my brain. *Crackle. Sizzle. Zzzzzz . . .*

When Vince arrives, I muster the willpower to appear calm. 'It's good to see you, Vince.' I hug him and step back, appraising his body language, sunglasses hiding the rage in my eyes.

'You too. Sorry I couldn't get the pills,' Vince says, hanging his head remorsefully.

'It's no biggie. Amy got hers.' I force a smile. 'Maybe your friend just needs more time to set it up properly,' I say, trying to preoccupy him with the failure of the drug deal.

'I think he can do it with more time,' he says, digging a forefinger into a cheek.

'Just let me know when and I'll send you back out there.'

Walking back to the truck, I say, 'You must be really tired.'

'Yeah, I'm about ready to crash.'

'I'll drive you to Tulips' real quick, so I can count the money. Then I'll drop you off at home.'

'Why don't we just count the money at my place?' he asks, alarm creeping into his voice.

'Tempe's not safe for me these days. I'd rather do it at Tulips'.'

No response. Just palpable tension.

When I park, Vince asks, 'Who's at Tulips'?'

Calmly, without hesitation: 'Jaxson and G Dog.'

Vince turns to me, brows raised. 'G Dog. Isn't he the one whose brothers were on the news?' Vince licks a mouth corner.

I've got him this far and now the bastard isn't going to get out. 'Yeah. Mexican Mafia dudes. Crazy stuff, huh?'

'Everything's cool in here, right?' Vince asks, frowning.

He's cottoning on. If I answer incorrectly, he'll panic and refuse to go in. In a light-hearted tone I reserve for paranoids, I say, 'Of course it is. There's hardly any cops come around here. It's the safest place I've got for us to count the money.'

'And we're cool, right?'

Get back onto the failed drug deal before you lose him. 'Vince, don't think I'm mad at you because you didn't connect. You tried your best. You flew to bloody Europe for me! That's all that matters.'

'I still think my friend can hook up.'

'I think you'll pull it off, too. It's just a matter of time. Hey, what do you think about the clubs over in Europe?'

'They blow America away.'

We get out.

'I've always liked German DJs: Commander Tom, Sven Väth,' I say, smiling.

At the front door, Vince asks, 'You're sure everything's cool in here, right?'

'It's really quiet. Tulips is moving out.'

I open the door.

'Hey, what's up, Vince?' Jaxson opens his arms, their bodies slam, a steel embrace. 'How'd your trip go?'

Vince smiles. 'Had a blast but didn't come back with anything.'

'What's up, Vince?' G Dog hugs Vince.

'All right, G Dog,' Vince says in a respectful tone. 'I've heard a lot about you.' The hugging relaxes Vince. He unlocks his luggage and hands me envelopes.

'I'll count the money on the carpet,' I say.

They chat, settling Vince in. I stack the bills in piles of thousands, not taking my eyes off the money, trying not to hint at what's to come. Near the end of the count, my pulse quickens, thoughts rush, hands tremble. *Don't give yourself away! It'll be over soon.* All that remains is to total the piles of cash. *One thousand, two thousand* . . . Crackling sounds start in my skull. My counting slows – or maybe time does, I can't tell which. The crackling grows louder, as if something's igniting. I see Vince fucking Amy.

Sparks. Crackling. Wolves snarling.

Vince and Skinner planning on taking over my organisation.

Crackle. Sizzle. Zzzzzz . . .

My eyes shift to the last pile of money.

He fucked my wife and wants to overthrow me and now it's time for him to get what he deserves.

The crackling becomes continuous, as if a power cable is running through my head.

Stay calm. If he sees you now, he'll know and try to escape. Stay calm. Stay calm . . .

I finish counting. Staring at the money, I say, 'Vince, the money's all there. I'll take you home now.' I stiffen into something mechanical, inhuman.

Jaxson and G Dog grab Vince and knock him down.

'Help me! Fucking help me!' Vince yells over and over.

I spring up to help keep Vince down. He struggles, wriggles this way and that, but the crush of our bodies pins him. G Dog gags Vince with a towel. I worry about the neighbours hearing the commotion. *Maybe the cops are on the way.*

They strike Vince with Maglites, heavy metal torches. Every time he squirms away, they beat him harder and drag him back to the centre of the room. He ends up in the foetal position, blows raining down, blood streaming from his nose.

I remove my sunglasses, revealing the loathing in my eyes. In a low voice, I say, 'I want to talk to you, Vince. We're going to take the gag off. If you yell and scream, it's going to get ugly. Please don't bring that upon yourself.' I nod at G Dog.

G Dog removes the gag, slowly, cautiously, as if ready to put it back on at the slightest sound.

Emphasising each word, I ask, 'Did you fuck my wife?' I pace over Vince. Sparks. Crackling. Explosions. Howling.

Sobbing, he says, 'Please don't kill me, Shaun.' Urine darkens the crotch of his jeans.

For days, all I've thought about is hurting Vince, returning the pain I blame him for. But seeing how afraid he is, I'm losing heart.

'Shaun, please don't kill me. Please don't kill me, Shaun. Please –'

'If you tell me the truth, things will remain calm. Did you fuck my wife?'

Vince shudders.

'Answer the fucking question!' *Crackle. Sizzle. Zzzzzz . . .*

A Maglite strikes his torso. 'Yeah. But it wasn't my fault, Shaun. She came on to me.'

'Maybe she did! But even so, what the fuck were you thinking, fucking your boss's wife?' I yell.

He cries. Shivers.

'Look, Vince. Do you understand you brought this upon yourself?'

'Yes, yes. I fucked up big time. I was high. I didn't –' Shuddering, sobbing, he mumbles.

'What you did is so serious – and I'm also talking about you lying to me about those pills you said were stolen – I could have gone to G Dog's brothers over this. But I feel what's happened today cancels what you did. If you feel it doesn't, and you get the urge to go to the cops, then I'll be forced to escalate things very quickly between you and me.'

'If you go to the cops, motherfucker,' G Dog says, prodding Vince's Adam's apple with a Maglite, 'you know where you're gonna end up.'

'I ain't going to no cops,' Vince says. 'Look, Shaun, I'm sorry. I fucked up. I'll make it up to you any way I can.'

'Gag him back up and tie him to a chair,' I say.

Vince doesn't struggle.

'I ought to have done much worse to you, Vince.' I put on a baseball cap and sunglasses. 'Let's go before the cops come,' I say.

We leave briskly, wearing hats, heads bowed. We turn at a corner of the building.

A security guard appears from nowhere and tries to block us. 'What's going on in there?'

Tilting my face away from him, I mutter, 'Nothing.' I swerve around him, my footsteps and heartbeat accelerating.

The security guard rushes to the apartment we came from.

Jaxson jumps on his motorcycle and speeds away. G Dog and I scramble into the truck. Convinced the cops are coming, I drive off, my body tense, my arms as rigid as the steering column, my eyes scanning every direction. Pumped up, I'm ready to leap from the truck and run if the cops stop us – in which case the owner of the truck will report it stolen. Every approaching vehicle spikes my tension until I see it's not a cop car.

As I drive onto the freeway, G Dog says, 'Cops won't catch us now.'

I call Cody, tell him to drive by Tulips' to see what's going on and to ensure Vince gets medical treatment.

Thirty minutes later, Cody calls: 'I got up there and the place is crawling with cops. They took him out on a stretcher and put him in an ambulance.'

Shit! A stretcher. How injured is he? Will he snitch? Even if he doesn't, the cops will investigate the crime. At least word will spread to Skinner. Will Skinner back off or try something else?

G Dog asks to be dropped off at his brother's. It's night-time when we arrive. The street is blacked out, as if suffering a power cut. With light sticks, men in black uniforms are directing traffic. I see federal agents in SWAT armour swarming Raul's house, and some men, including Carlos the Torturer, in handcuffs. Two Tempe cops stare at us. I don't stop.

'Damn!' G Dog says, shaking his head. 'They were out on bail and now they're all in jail. Those motherfuckers are looking at some serious time.'

I drop G Dog off at a hotel and head home.

Later on, the day's events torment me. I take Xanax, but sleep doesn't come. My mind replays what we did to Vince. Regretting the violence, a kind of hangover sets in. I recall Carlos torturing the naked hog-tied man, and how afraid I was. *Today I acted just like Carlos. I've crossed a line.* The raid at Raul's also worries me. *What if the Feds know I'm Raul's Ecstasy supplier?* The wolves tell me. *You need to get higher than ever at the next rave to forget about all this shit.*

CHAPTER 50

IT'S PARTY TIME. *Take me higher. Never come down. Fuck Amy for moving out. Fuck Vince and Skinner. I'm still on top of my game. I'm English Shaun. Who cares if I die? Numb the pain.*

In a limo. Tons of drugs. Ecstasy. Special K. GHB. LSD. Magic mushrooms. Cocaine. Crystal meth. Glass. Valium. Xanax. Somas. Uppers. Downers. Acid Joey. G Dog. Grady. Jaxson. One of my Ecstasy dealers, Q, and his friend Billy the Hippy. Two glitter girls in sexy punk clothes who I just met today. Blonde Samantha. Native American Aubrey. *Nice contrast.* We devour drugs. *Crackle. Sizzle. Zzzzzz . . .* Mix them up. Take more. Electrical storm: *Crackle. Sizzle. Zzzzzz . . .* Glitter girls kissing, I notice. Pale skin against bronze. *Mmmm . . .*

Our chauffeur: Larry. *An open-minded motherfucker from the south side. Won't call the cops on us like the last jerk-off.* Larry parks at the Icehouse: Swell's annual Musik rave. Glitter girls out, legs first, heels and thigh-highs drawing all eyes. Black and white and outrageous attire. *The effect I hoped for.* Getting out: presenting English Shaun and his bodyguard, G Dog. I pause for attention. Stretch. Lungs fill to capacity, feasting on warm air. Jaw juts: wolf inside coming alive. Behind Kieselsteins, my eyes assess the crowd. *My people.*

Cut the queue to the door, G Dog in tow, foaming at the mouth, meth-crazed, his prison-hardened gaze probably probing for shanks.

'These are all with me!' I announce.

'English Shaun plus eight!'

My entourage hand-stamped in for free. Everyone watching. Bubbles of joy fizzing in my brain. *I'm still on top.*

Inside. The artificial world jolts G Dog's eyes. A mirrored mosaic disco ball bathes us in multicoloured light. Wall-to-wall bodies, stomping like rain-dancing Navajos. Glow sticks and strings, pockets of moving colour and light. High on more than the atmosphere, the DJ – one ear to a headphone, the other free and listening, spray bottle on hand – is working decks displayed on plain foldable tables, powered by a black snake of a cable.

Ravers flock to me. *I am on top of this world.* I open my arms, hug them, feel safe. *My people.*

G Dog shoves two ravers away.

'It's all right, G Dog,' I say.

'What a trip,' he says.

'Don't trip. These are my friends.'

'I automatically think they wanna fight. I gotta stop myself.'

'It's OK, man. You've been up for days.'

'Yeah.'

'Try varying your drugs. Take some X.' I hand him a pill. 'Relax. Tune into the music. You'll be like everyone else in no time. C'mon, let's explore, bro. This is just one room.'

Sideways, shoulders first, we slice through the crowd. We swerve around a cuddle puddle: a circle of ravers massaging each other's backs, some sniffing Vicks inhalers.

Next room. Fashion show. A stage lit pink and blue by filtered spotlights fixed to metal ladder structures. A woman struts on the runway in a tight shirt with silver flames, a jacket dangling from her elbows, blue leopard print with combed white plush drooping from the bottom, bright-pink patent vinyl trousers completing the look. Primo walks on in a white suit hand-painted with orange and green stripes and spots, his torso naked and hairless, carrying a tray with glasses and a pitcher patio set, seven-inch-thick platform heels on circus shoes, with grey vacuum cleaner tubes spiralling around his ankles. A woman in a white faux-rabbit-fur bolero crop jacket over nude breasts sashays with strength and confidence, a Betty Boop tattoo peeking out of white thong panties, curves dressing her up.

Starting to bob his head, G Dog stares, smiles.

Yes! Cheery brain bubbles. 'Welcome to my world!' But as the words come out, I'm seized by a premonition of losing my grip on the rave scene. I shudder. *What the fuck? Take more drugs. GHB.* 'C'mon, let's go back to the limo.'

With the VIPs of the drug business in my limo and free drugs being doled out, the queue to get inside is longer than the one for the rave. We squeeze in. Aubrey going down on Samantha. *Nice.*

Acid Joey snorts a line of Special K, raises himself through the moonroof and, in a demonic voice, warns that it's the end of the world.

To be as high as him! I'll get there.

'Snort some CK1,' says Q – a student with big glazed eyes peeping from under long brown hair – to our chauffeur.

'What the fuck's CK1?' Larry asks.

'Coke and ketamine,' Q says.

'Coke is boring on its own,' I say. *Crackle. Sizzle. Zzzzzz. Howl.*

Larry abandons the cabin.

Get him fucked up.

Larry joins us in the back and snorts a line.

'Larry, you might as well try some GHB, too,' I say. 'Here, drink a cap.' *I'm the devil. He will love it.*

'Might as well.' Larry sips the GHB. 'Damn. That shit tastes foul.'

'It's saltier than come,' Aubrey says.

I can't stop laughing, even though I'm drooling. *Crackle. Sizzle. Zzzzzz. Howl.* 'Chase it with this quickly.' I hand Larry a fruity drink.

Twenty minutes later, Larry tries to rise but falls. He stammers: 'Q, you guys are off the fucking hook. I'm gonna have to call out another limo driver. I'm too fucked up to drive.'

'Yes!' I yell, raising the bottle of GHB. 'Here's to toppling Larry the limo driver. I'm pleased to announce we have brought our chauffeur down to our filthy level. We truly are the scum of the earth.'

They cheer. *They still love me. Crackle. Sizzle. Zzzzzz. Howl.*

A female chauffeur arrives. Everyone transfers to her limo except for me, Samantha and Larry.

'Let's do it in the limo,' Samantha says. 'Lie down.'

'Oh, yes please.' I look at Larry, too messed-up to move.

'It's cool with me,' Larry whispers.

I sniff Samantha's neck, vigorously, as if trying to vacuum up skin flakes. Penis pushes against zipper. *Crackle. Sizzle. Zzzzzz. Howl.*

'You should stay and watch us, Larry,' Samantha says, tugging my pants off.

Samantha's tongue tickles my penis. My jaw elongates – wolf libido rising – straining the bone joint. My lower lip quivers. My eyeballs roll backwards in sync with her mouth strokes. I close my eyes. *My world will not slip away. Fuck Skinner! Fuck Vince.* 'Ooh, that's good.'

Larry gazes, body dead, eyes alive, catatonic.

Samantha stops. Coolness. My eyes lock onto her dark hold-ups and pale thighs. I yank the red G-string from under her tartan skirt. She squats. I moan – louder than usual for Larry's benefit. *I'm still on top* . . . Close my eyes. *Howl.* Lost. The tangle of legs, drugs. I leave earth. Vince. Skinner. Amy. Pain. Wet warm strokes. Up and down. My eyeballs bobbing like bottle corks on pond ripples.

Too high to climax, we ditch Larry for limo two.

Acid Joey's face is contorting, his body shifting, squirming, next to G Dog whom he's too high to recognise.

We take off for Billy the Hippy's house party. G Dog blows bubbles. Acid Joey climbs from the moonroof, threatening to leap to his death. We grab his legs, rein him in. He yells about his hatred of frogs and birds and makes jokes about dead cats in freezers.

'I have pets,' Billy the Hippy whispers to me. 'I don't want Acid Joey coming to my house in this state of mind. You have to do something, Shaun.'

'It's just high talk. I'll watch him. He's more sensible these days. He has a good job at an ISP. He's a functional, recreational drug user, just like the rest of us.'

'No. Please, Shaun, let's not take him to my house like this.'

I tap on the divide and ask the driver to take us to an apartment I rent. We stumble out. Acid Joey forward-rolls.

I love his antics!

Turned on, I usher Q, Samantha and Aubrey into a bedroom. Trance music. We wobble on the waterbed. I swig GHB and pass the bottle to Q, pushing thoughts of Vince, Amy and Skinner further away. The girls undress. My nostrils flare – wolf devouring their scent, sweat, perfume, pheromones. More GHB. Less Vince, Amy, Skinner . . . Girls kissing. GHB. *Bring out the wolf.* GHB. Girls fondling each other. *My kind of art.*

Samantha kisses Q. *Here we go.* Aubrey unbuttons my pants. *We'll do it side by side, everyone getting off on everyone else.* GHB floods my brain, washing away the *crackle, sizzle, zzzzzz, howl. Shit! Stay awake! Need speed!* Aubrey's fingers find my penis. Double vision. My head lolls back. As she puts my penis in her mouth, I pass out.

CHAPTER 51

INSIDE MY TUCSON apartment, I'm feeling sick – coming down after weeks of partying – when my friend housing Wild Woman and the newly arrived Wild Man calls, demanding I take them elsewhere because of the fighting and property damage. 'And on top of all that,' she says, 'Wild Man was trying to lure Skinner over to kill him – in *my* place!'

I need to send them to Mexico ASAP. If he kills Skinner, the cops will be all over us. I pack a bag and drive there.

Wild Woman answers. 'Wild Man said he was going to the shop, but I wouldn't be surprised if he's gone for Skinner.'

'I know. That's one of the reasons I'm here,' I say, entering the apartment.

'The red dots are telling him to kill Skinner and bury him in the desert and all that stuff. He's also saying you were trying to hook me up with Vince in the flat. He's jealous of Vince, and he thinks you and Vince have arranged to take him out to the desert too, so I can hook up with Vince. He's not slept since he got back to America. He's been doing meth every day.'

Wild Man arrives, eyeing me strangely. 'Hello, la'.'

I hug him and say in a serious tone, 'Look, la', here's why I'm here. 'Cause of Wild Woman's bust, our attorney thinks you two shouldn't be setting foot in Tempe. You'd be much safer out of Arizona. Cody's going to run you to Rocky Point. He's got money to get you a monthly rental down there.'

'I ain't going,' Wild Man says, frowning. 'I need to take care of Skinner first.'

'Mexico is the smart thing to do right now, la'. Not Skinner.'

Wild Man glares at me.

'Shaun's right,' Wild Woman says. 'I was raided. We've got to go. You've just got back in town. If you go and do something stupid to Skinner, they're gonna have you, and this time they won't just send you to England, you're gonna end up in prison for the rest of your life.'

'What if you need me to handle a situation up here?' Wild Man lights a crystal-meth pipe, inhales, expanding his chest.

'You're just a short drive away in Mexico. I'll send someone for you. It's a holiday town on the Sea of Cortez, and there's a beach, and you can rent jet skis. From now on, I want our smugglers who land at Hermosillo to be transported to Rocky Point with the pills. In Rocky Point, we'll switch the pills to somebody else, who'll cross the border. It'll be an important base of operations for our smugglers.'

Wild Man exhales a thick funnel of smoke. 'Mexico sounds all right, la', but I need to take that fucking punk Skinner out to the desert first.'

'We're not getting into the murder business,' I say. 'Wild Woman's bust's enough heat as it is.'

'I'm not getting you into the murder business,' Wild Man says. 'This is personal. He tried to set fire to my woman. It has nothing to do with business or you.'

'The Skinner business will have to wait. Cody's on his way over here.'

Cody houses the Wild Ones in Rocky Point, where cellphones don't work, so I have no way to contact them. A month later, Cody goes to pay their rent and shows up at my apartment distraught. 'The house has been bombed. All of the windows are blown out and everything inside burned. There was no sign of them. I scoured the area and came home. Do you think they pissed the locals off?'

'I don't know,' I say, worried. 'But the Wild Ones are indestructible.'

I send Tulips, who speaks Spanish, to talk to the locals. He returns with an explanation: 'The Wild Ones had a fight. Wild Man threw a coffee table into the plasterboard and cracked a gas pipe and didn't notice. They kept fighting, but they stopped to take a smoke break. The next thing, a carpet of blue flame spreads across the floor. Wild Woman was on fire, so Wild Man grabbed her and got her out of there. Dragging her out, he cracked three of her ribs, but he saved her life. They got out just as the windows were exploding – just like you see in the movies.'

If they're attracting attention in Mexico, how can I run smuggling missions through there? I'll have to risk crossing the border to talk to them in person. But if I'm stopped coming back, I'll be arrested and deported. I've got so much E coming in the next shipment, it's a chance I must take to ensure things run smoothly.

CHAPTER 52

AFTER I ARRIVE at the beachfront condo I'm renting for the Wild Ones, I tell them, 'Grady's getting forty thousand pills in Amsterdam, stashed in a computer tower by Pablo, and flying to Mexico City. From there, he's getting a bus to Rocky Point that takes a few days. His arrival here should coincide with spring break. I've got students ready to smuggle the Ecstasy into America. The end of spring break is the busiest it ever gets at the border. I've lost so much in the stock market, if this mission fails, we're all screwed.'

'You'd better hope the Federales don't jack Grady,' Wild Woman says, referring to the Mexican Federal Police.

'The Federales aren't up to speed on Ecstasy yet,' I say. 'I don't think they'll snatch Grady off the bus. We've also got to worry about Sammy the Bull's crew.'

'Plastic gangstas.' Wild Man bites the top off a beer bottle and spits it against a wall. 'They ain't shit. They hang around Taco Bells scaring little kids.'

'That's easy for you to say. They've got some massive dudes working for them, cage fighters, and the Devil Dogs,' I say, referring to a White Power gang known to bark like Dobermanns while they attack their victims. 'And there's a shitload of them. They're not to be underestimated.'

'I've built my own little crew down here,' Wild Man says.

'Who?' I ask.

'They started off as beach bums,' Wild Man says. 'They were selling fucking seashells and shit, living in huts. I gave them a few pills to sell and they moved from huts to shacks and they're really fucking happy with me, and loyal. Loyaler than dogs when you've fed them steak.'

I laugh.

'How come you didn't bring Skinner with you, la'?' Wild Man asks.

'What for, la'?'

'You know what for.'

'He's scared of you. There's no way he'll ever come down here. Anyway, forget about Skinner for now. We've got the Federales, Sammy the Bull's people and local drug-dealer robbers to worry about. We need to go out and rent multiple rooms all over town, so if anything goes wrong we can move shit around fast.'

Students invade Rocky Point for spring break. Sammy the Bull's workforce is more than 50 strong, mostly students peddling pills, guarded by jocks. They bring thousands of hits into Mexico from Arizona – the opposite of what I'm trying to achieve. But I need them to think I'm here for the same reason: to sell Ecstasy in Mexico. If they know I've got a big shipment going to Arizona, they might try to steal it, or tell robbers or cops for a piece of the action. To create the illusion I'm on a sales mission, I have dealers sell pills. Sammy the Bull's dealers are making so much money, I don't anticipate them robbing my workers for a hundred pills or so, risking a conflict that might damage their Mexican operation. The strategy exceeds my expectations. Motivated by the competition from my dealers, they redouble their sales effort, almost run out of pills and grow dizzy on success.

At the condo, I'm anxiously waiting for Grady, who has no way to contact me from the bus. When he doesn't arrive on time, I grow concerned and send Cody looking for him. I awake the next day hoping to hear news, but no one has seen him. Finally, he arrives the following afternoon, raising my spirits.

'You just pulled off the biggest mission yet,' I say, hugging Grady.

'Well done!' Wild Man raises Grady off his feet and swings him around.

Grady grins as if stoned. Wild Woman and G Dog hug Grady.

'Your job's done. Here's five gangstas.' I hand Grady $5,000 in an envelope.

Cody comes in. 'He doesn't appear to have been trailed.'

'OK.' Wanting to separate Grady from the drugs in case he was spotted and reported to the Federales, I put on a bandanna and shades, pick up a cardboard box concealing the computer tower and leave the building, accompanied by a shaven-headed American fluent in Spanish whom I'm relying on to negotiate us out of any difficulties with the locals. I put the box in the back of the SUV and get in, my vision sweeping the street for cops.

I drive, stiff, tense, hyper-aware, monitoring everything: students on both sides of the street; men in T-shirts, baggy shorts, baseball caps, sunglasses, holding bottles of Tecate beer, yelling, swaggering; women in bikinis, clutching towels and tubes of suntan lotion, sauntering, sashaying, showing off tanned limbs, drunken ones staggering; street kids pestering, promoting, joking; music blaring from every bar; cars cruising, blasting techno, tyres swirling up dust; quad bikes roaring by; a military helicopter flying low over the sea. I slow down at a junction. A warm breeze carrying the stink of fish and taco stands brushes my face. Police are directing traffic, one blowing a whistle.

On the next road: a pharmacy mobbed by students buying drugs unavailable stateside. After that, the crowds of people thin out. At the foot of a palm tree is a pack of dogs, half-starved, with mangy bald patches, circling, snarling.

Everything's going to plan. I drive down a lonely sandy road. A vehicle screeches from a side street: a white truck with a red, white and blue lightbar on its roof. It speeds up, siren wailing.

My heart high-jumps to my throat. 'He's fucking after us, isn't he?'

'He is. Don't sweat it. I'll talk to him,' my passenger says confidently.

I pull over. Two dark uniforms strut towards us.

'*¿Cómo están, señores?*' I say.

No response.

In Spanish, my passenger addresses them too fast for me to understand. Shaking his head, he says, 'They want us to get out to search us.'

'Don't they need probable cause?' I ask, on the verge of throwing up.

'Not in Mexico.'

We're fucked. I step out. My eyes seek the best direction to flee on foot. *Not quite yet, but if they open the computer tower I'll sprint. I'm disguised; they'll never know what I look like.*

The police stare into the SUV and demand we empty our pockets.

Trembling, I extract dollars, my driver's licence, a shopping receipt . . . The money sparks an idea.

My passenger empties his pockets. Unsatisfied, a cop puts his hand in a pocket, rummages and extracts a pill: Valium. My passenger's Spanish speeds up, as if he's trying to talk his way out of trouble. They cuff him.

Me next? 'Should I offer them twenty dollars to let you off?' *Ba-dum-ba-dum-ba-dum* goes my heart.

'Already did. They wouldn't take it.'

'Strange.'

'Yeah. Something's not right.'

'Reckon I should run for it?'

Before he can reply, the police drag him away to their truck.

Alone at the SUV, I'm gripped by an impulse to sprint, but I'm too frightened to move. *Run, stay, run, stay . . .*

The police shove my passenger into the cabin.

Bracing for them to arrest me and search the vehicle, I'm perplexed when they both get in the truck. The engine starts. They drive away.

I watch, trembling, my relief rising in proportion to the distance between us. I don't want to get back in the SUV. Ever. But, driven by greed for fast cash, I can't abandon the Ecstasy. I watch them turn out of sight. *Maybe it's a set-up. My passenger's in on it. They removed him to arrest me alone. Fuck it! Get the hell out of here!* I jump into the SUV and drive, half convinced I'm getting off scot-free, half convinced I'll be surrounded at any minute. Scouring the street for cop cars, I swivel my head, imagining them waiting around every corner.

I park outside a hotel, next to a car belonging to a student on my payroll. I alight, thankful I haven't been tailed. I stretch and groan with relief as my shoulders unclench. *If I've got away with this, I'll never transport drugs myself in Mexico again.* Quickly, I transfer the tower into the trunk of the student's car.

I return to the condo. I bail my passenger from jail. He says someone reported my SUV to the police with instructions to arrest me. Because of his shaved head and my disguise, the police mistook him for me. They didn't search the SUV because the Valium was all they needed to arrest the man they thought was me. The passenger called in a favour from a local with connections, and the police allowed him to be released upon receipt of the usual bribe. Why they're after me remains a mystery. *Probably out to shake down a drug dealer. I must be even more careful. I'll delegate all handling of drugs. I'll no longer drive the SUV until it's time to leave. My disguise worked and I'll maintain it.*

Sammy the Bull's dealers sell out of Ecstasy. Spaniard sends word that he wants to buy some of mine to tide them over. Trusting Spaniard, I agree, but on my terms. He sends a female student with cash to a hotel room. G Dog takes the cash to Cody in exchange for pills and returns to complete the trade. Cody brings the cash to me and I store it in fake Coca-Cola cans. This is done several times.

Towards the end of spring break, I drink some GHB and set off for a small rave in a bar Wild Man frequents, wearing a bandanna, shades and, for extra disguise, warpaint.

Outside the door, a midget panhandler with a cluster of boils like grapes on his neck smiles and says, '*¡Hola, señores!*'

'*¿Cómo estás, amigo?*' I give him a hit of Ecstasy.

He stares at the pill, perplexed.

'Eat it!' Wild Man points at his open mouth. 'It'll make you mucho happy.'

We enter a dark room lit by a strobe and lights over the bar, including neon palm trees and pink flamingos. We weave through people dancing and join our friends, clustered in a corner.

'That giant tranny with the long hair is the Black Widow,' Wild Man says, pointing at a tall transsexual in a skirt and make-up, purple lips smiling slyly. 'He lures people to hotel rooms. They wake up with their organs missing and he sells them.'

We drink, chat and relax while watching people dance: women gyrating rhythmically to the beat, lashing hair, thrusting hips, waving arms; sweaty men swerving spasmodically, some spilling beer.

Q approaches, frowning. 'Sammy the Bull's muscle boys just rolled in.'

'Who? The Devil Dogs?' Cody asks.

'Big dudes,' Q nods.

All our heads turn. We squint towards the far side of the room. Six men. Four women. No Spaniard or friendly faces.

'So much for a good night out,' Cody says.

'If we don't start any shit, they won't start any shit,' I say.

'What fun is that?' Wild Man says.

G Dog laughs.

Over the next hour, Sammy the Bull's gang stay in their corner, we in ours, but their number doubles. More and more arrive, eyes glazed as if high, drunk or both. When they swell to about 30, they start casting us dirty looks.

'Let's leave,' Cody says. 'It's gonna go off.'

'Fuck that!' Wild Man says, furrowing his brow. 'Leaving looks weak. I don't give a fuck how many wannabe spaghetti-head motherfuckers there are!' he shouts, as if talking to them not us.

'Chill, Wild Man,' Cody says.

'You're off your fucking head, you!' Wild Woman hisses.

Wild Man stomps like a bull about to charge. We hold him back. It takes minutes to calm him down.

Thirsty, I join the crowd at the bar waiting to be served.

One of the oldest from Sammy the Bull's gang swaggers up to me – stocky, short, with a round, flaky, sunburnt face. 'English Shaun!' he says in a raspy voice.

'What's up?' I ask, widening my stance.

'I'm Tom,' he says, gripping my hand. 'I've heard a lot about you.'

'Good things, I hope.'

'Was expecting you to be some big tattooed thug.'

'Doesn't sound like good things to me.'

He laughs.

I take a speed pill from my pocket, chuck it in my mouth and chew it but can't chase it as I have no drink.

'English Shaun, we're not looking to start any shit with you guys. We know you helped us out with pills. When I get back to Arizona, I'd like to sit down and talk business with you. Is there a number I can reach you at?'

The slimy bastard's trying to set me up. 'I never talk on the phone,' I croak, my mouth sandpaper dry from the speed.

Cody walks over, grabs me and escorts me back to our corner. 'There's two police vans outside.'

'*Arrr*, shit! Vans mean they're probably going to raid,' I say.

'I say we get the fuck outta here,' Cody says.

We head for the door.

Coming into the bar, one of Sammy the Bull's gang – whose neck is as wide as his head – bumps into Wild Woman.

'Watch where you're fucking going!' Wild Man yells.

'Fuck you!' the man grunts.

Wild Man launches a left fist at the man's chin. He falls. Q, Cody and G Dog push Wild Man out of the bar. A friend of the man scoops him off the floor and helps him to the rest of their gang.

'Let's fucking go!' I yell, my heart palpitating.

'Come on!' Cody shouts.

At the door, I look over my shoulder, shocked to see them mobbing after us. I rush out but skid to a halt at what I see: cops charging at me from all directions. *I'm getting arrested! I'm fucked! It's all over!* I freeze.

In dark uniforms and wielding batons, the cops push me aside and wade into the bar, which erupts into chaos.

We dash down an alley, cackling, praising the police as our saviours.

When I get back to Phoenix, there'll be retaliation from Sammy the Bull's crew.

Spring break draws to a close. It's time to smuggle the Ecstasy into Arizona with the flow of students. I inform the student I paid to smuggle the pills that she's no longer taking them. She's served her purpose by boasting about her mission, setting herself up as a target for cops and robbers – the perfect smokescreen. I switch the task to two students who have no idea why I brought them here, other than to acquire suntans.

They set off in a car cluttered with student belongings and tourist bric-a-brac. I drive behind, monitoring their progress. Approaching the border, seeing endless cars backed up, I smile. *Odds are they'll never get searched.* The tension from being stuck in traffic for two hours makes my head vibrate. *Soon we'll be across and it'll all be over.* Bouncing my legs up and down and from side to side, I fight the urge to urinate for as long as possible. When my bladder feels like it's about to haemorrhage, I relieve myself in a Gatorade bottle.

Approaching the checkpoint, I practise my American accent. 'Hi. I've been to Rocky Point. Have a nice day, now.' I have to fool the guards into thinking I'm a US citizen or I'll be arrested and deported. *They're so busy, hopefully they'll just wave me through.*

Pulling up at the barrier, I drop my window and smile. 'Hi.' Blood rushes to my face.

'Where've you been?'

'Rocky Point.'

'What's your citizenship?'

'US.' Although it's not requested, I offer my Arizona driver's licence, to create the illusion I'm American and naive about border procedures.

He glances at it and looks beyond me into the SUV. 'How long was your stay in Rocky Point?'

'Just spring break, unfortunately,' I say, smiling.

He steps back and sweeps his vision over the exterior of the SUV, spotting the University of Arizona sticker, another part of the illusion.

'OK. Continue.'

Driving into Arizona, I grin with relief – until I realise I don't know where the car with the Ecstasy is. Worried, I park at the meeting spot: a busy gas station in Lukeville. Observing the comings and goings, I tap the steering wheel.

Ten minutes later, the car arrives. *Yes! The highest-risk part is over. But where's the car with the student who thought she was bringing the Ecstasy?* I transfer the tower to my SUV.

Minutes later, the missing student shows up, claiming she was stopped and searched thoroughly.

They were tipped off. Must leave fast. She doesn't appear to have been tailed. The authorities suspect something but haven't pieced it together.

I give the students cash in envelopes, take off and set the cruise control to the speed limit.

About 20 minutes later, I spot a car at my rear, closing the gap: Native American reservation police. My body tenses. *Stay cool. He's just running your plate.* The longer he remains behind, the higher my heartbeat rises up my chest, until I can feel my pulse in my mouth. After a few long minutes, he overtakes and races ahead.

Approaching Phoenix, I'm high on the hundreds of thousands I'm going to make from Ecstasy sales – money that will restore my organisation to its former glory.

CHAPTER 53

SAMMY THE BULL and 54 of his workers, including his son Gerard Gravano, Spaniard, Mark, the Devil Dogs and even Fish, are raided. I praise the cops for eliminating my competition and restoring my monopoly. With Sammy the Bull gone, I assume the investigation of the rave scene will wind down. But instead the number of undercover cops increases. Disappointed, I console myself – *I've been outsmarting the cops for so long, I'm above the law.*

From the Mexico shipment, I front 3,000 hits to Worm in Tucson. He sells the Ecstasy and calls me from a payphone. 'I'm being followed,' he says, his voice strained.

'By who?' I ask.

'I don't know if the dudes are trying to jack me or they're five-oh.'

'What do you want to do?'

'Give you the gangstas,' he says, referring to the money.

'Don't bring the five-oh to me!'

'Dude, chill. I'm gonna drive around a bit and ditch them.'

'OK. Make sure you ditch them. Meet me at Fry's on Grant in half an hour. I'll be shopping in one of the aisles. Don't say a word to me. Act like a shopper. Drop the gangstas in my basket. If you can't ditch them, abandon meeting me.'

I page Cody to collect the cash before putting on shades and a beige floppy hat and going to Fry's. Selecting items in each aisle, I glance from side to side looking for Worm. When he doesn't show up, I trek the rear of the store, checking every aisle. Convinced something bad has happened, I hasten for the checkout. I spot Worm arriving, sweaty, grim-faced. I nod at him and go to the fruit section. I put my basket down to weigh some bananas. Worm stops next to the basket, looks around, drops an envelope and leaves.

No one follows me to my SUV. But a white van tails me on the road. Instead of going home, I drive up and down the freeway for half an hour. I arrange to meet Cody at a gas station. I give him the cash and go home – unaware I've just slipped through the net of a sting operation with $22,500 of government money. Worm had sold the pills to undercover cops.

In Phoenix, I front 5,000 pills to Q. He drives to sell them in a separate car from his runners. Upon arrival, his intuition makes him flee, but his runners are arrested with 5,000 pills. It makes headline news. Q has no way to repay.

Each disaster is a warning that the authorities are closing in, but, other than Wild Woman, none of my inner circle has been arrested. Until the cops pierce that shield, I don't believe they can get me.

Concerned about my remaining Ecstasy, I spread the pills among various people – if one gets robbed or raided, there'll still be plenty left.

A student has 5,000 in a safe when masked men enter her apartment, hold her at gunpoint and take them. I send G Dog and Fingers, a man the size of Wild Man, to retrieve the pills. They track the culprits down and attempt to lure them to another student's apartment by posing as Ecstasy dealers.

The student calls me in tears: 'Shaun, you've gotta stop them. These two have bought all kinds of torture things from the hardware store. I don't want people getting their fingers cut off in my place. I can't take violence like that.'

Not having the heart for it either, I recall G Dog and Fingers.

I reinvest most of my cash in two more smuggling missions, but both shipments get seized at the airport.

Running out of money, I advise the Wild Ones to turn themselves in to the British Embassy and return to England until my finances improve.

At night in my big bed, I feel more alone than when I rented my first small apartment in 1991. So much time has passed, I seem to exist in a different world. Back then, I hardly knew anyone but was overflowing with enthusiasm for conquering the stock market. Now, with hundreds of friends, I feel empty after years of partying. *Where has all the glamour gone?* I close my eyes and remember swanning into raves with my entourage – Acid Joey, Sallywack,

Alice, Lexi, Mari, Skinner, Cody, Jaxson, Smiley, Jake, Pablo – getting hugged and thanked all night by partyers high on my Ecstasy. *How did it get like this? All I do is hide out. From the cops. Rival criminals. Even from people I thought were my friends. Drugs have messed my world up. I'm lost.*

CHAPTER 54

HAVING REFUSED TO return to England, the Wild Ones cross into Arizona a few days before 9/11 heightens border security. In Tempe, they move in with a meth-addicted couple: DJ Sketch – bespectacled, mellow, pale-faced – who tinkers all day with computer equipment, and Boo, a chubby woman prone to crying over the goings-on in her fish tank.

Within days, Wild Woman telephones warning that Wild Man is berserk on crystal meth: 'There was just me in the house, but he was convinced that you and five Mexicans were in the bathroom waiting to stab him.'

'Bloody hell! He's not turning on me now, is he?'

'He was sitting on the couch by the window, and he kept going *shhh, shhh,* and then his eyebrow shot up. He said, "Shut up." I said, "What's wrong with you?" He said, "There's somebody in the bathroom." I said, "There's nobody in the bathroom 'cause they can't get in without walking past you 'cause the front door's there, and the back door's there, and there's no window in the bathroom." He kept going on and on: "It's Shaun." I said, "What the fuck would Shaun be doing hiding in the bathroom? C'mon, get a grip." He said, "I can hear it." I said, "If there's five men in there with guns and knives, why aren't you protecting me if you're this big tough man?" He said, "I know it's fucking Shaun." I said, "What would Shaun be doing in the bathroom?" He said, "He wants to kill me 'cause I know what's going on."'

''*Cause I know what's going on,*' I say. 'Holy shit!'

'He'd even been asleep. He said, "I'm not sketching, I've been asleep for nine hours. What's that tell you?" I said, "Exactly! You're fucking mental!" He'd just woke up. I'd knocked him out with Valium in his drink. I have to 'cause he's up for days going mental. He'll kill someone for nothing one of these days.'

'Let's hope it's not one of us.'

Word spreads that Wild Man is going to kill Skinner for firebombing Wild Woman. I urge him not to, pointing out that murdering Skinner could get him the death penalty, but he won't listen.

Mari says Skinner is working in car sales during the day but smoking crystal meth and embalming fluid at night. I try to arrange a meeting to reassure him that no harm will come to him, but he refuses to take my calls.

I call Mari: 'I'm really worried about Skinner. He left a voicemail saying the music on my pager means I'm out to kill him and he knows me and you are having sex.'

'What the hell?' Mari says. 'He's getting crazier. He was OK for a while in his apartment. Then he started freaking out on drugs one night and called me to go over there. I go over and he's calling people and leaving messages, saying, "You guys are gonna be sorry." I think he called Wild Woman or something and left a message saying he was gonna call the cops.'

My stomach tightens. 'I know he's freaking out over Wild Man, but why's he got it in for me?'

'To be honest, this is what I fucking tell him: "You're fucking in love with Shaun. You like to have Shaun's attention and Shaun isn't giving you his attention right now, so you have to act the fool." He liked being your little mate, you know, or little brother. That's what you always used to call him. Shit changed. You got so many people involved. I always remember telling you that too many people know what the fuck you guys do and you need to lay low. Too many people still know way too much shit, Shaun.'

'What about him firebombing Wild Woman's?'

'I just know he has a big problem with the Wild Ones. He's paranoid that Wild Man's gonna come and, you know, kill him, hurt him or whatever. I told him, "Whatever you did, you probably deserved it." Everything Skinner does makes it likely that someone's gonna come and beat his ass. He's so scandalous. He has no loyalty to you, the Wild Ones or anybody. He has this big thought that you and Wild Man are coming after him, that *you're* coming after him. You know, it's that tweaker shit. He gets all fucking paranoid. In the house, he would sit with all the lights out and the door fucking open with a machine gun in his hands, and he would tell me that you or Wild Man was standing out there.'

'That's insane.'

'Yeah, well, I've stopped doing drugs and I've taken a step back, and I can see I was involved in way too much. You need to think about what could happen if Skinner's gone to the cops.'

My Ecstasy business is dying. My sales force blame their inability to pay their debts on the absence of pills. Fearing a visit from Wild Man, some skip town. His best efforts to collect only put a dent in the half million I'm owed in total. DJ Spinelli can't repay $30,000, so I house the Wild Ones with him. He abandons his apartment.

Wild Man smokes so much meth he has a stroke, causing us all concern. He refuses to go to hospital. Blowing meth smoke out of one side of his mouth, drooling from the paralysed side, he says, 'People thought I used to look scary, just fucking look at me now! *Ha-ha-ha-ha-ha . . .*'

The Wild Ones fight and Wild Woman moves back to Boo's. The next morning, I find Wild Man sat on a wall outside DJ Spinelli's apartment, his clothes singed, his face coated in soot, his expression gloomy. He explains he set the apartment on fire by tampering with electrical equipment while high, almost burning himself alive as he slept.

The Wild Ones rent a house in Tempe – on the same street as Wild Woman's place that was raided by Detective Reid. I have no drugs to supply, so they run up credit with other dealers.

Within days of them moving in, Wild Woman summons me over for Sunday dinner and to relay an incident that has spooked her: 'Grady was taking me in a car to pick up five ounces of weed in Mesa off two new fellas that have come on the scene. Anyway, we got followed by a bald guy in a black Impala. He had like a ginger goatee and a really scary face. Really horrid and pale, like an inbred-Jed type person. I'd know him a mile off. As we pulled out from Farmer, his Impala pulled out behind us. I only noticed it 'cause the windows are so black; I thought it was illegal. We go down to Mill Avenue, and it follows us all the way onto the freeway. Grady said, "That car's right up my arse." He turned off into a car park at Fry's. The Impala came in behind us. He goes out. The Impala goes out. He pulled into Castle Boutique and we go in. We come out and he's waiting at the gate. We came out and he pulled out behind us. Then we went to another Fry's. I ran in and got a loaf. I come out and he's sitting there. As we came out, he ended up getting stuck behind another car. I waved goodbye to him and called Wild Man. I said, "I'm gonna be a minute, love, as some bastard in a black Impala is up my arse and he has been for the last hour." We came onto the freeway and there was roadworks, and we lost him on the freeway.'

'Would a cop be so obvious?' I ask, tucking into a plate of roast potatoes, gravy and chicken breast. 'Do you think he's a drug-dealer robber?'

'Wild Man does, but I think he's a cop. The other thing is that all our phones are clicking, and you can hear yourself echoing back. When I log onto the Internet, a little box is coming up saying, "Someone else is logged on."'

'It's been saying that on your computer?'

'Yeah. Why?'

'It's saying that on mine!'

'Fuck!' Wild Woman rasps, shaking her head. 'And my rubbish is never getting took. My wheelie bin is always outside. All the neighbours' are getting emptied but not ours.'

I was wrong about the Sammy the Bull threat being over. Most of his workers are released on bail. Tom – who asked for my number in Mexico – keeps calling Wild Man, accusing him of blowing his car up and trying to coax him to meet to settle it one-on-one.

'I'll go and twat the bastard,' Wild Man says, on his living-room sofa, smoking meth. 'He's threatening to do this and that to me.'

'Don't be daft!' I say, my eyes smarting from the fumes. 'It's fucking obvious he's working for the cops.'

'He won't listen,' Wild Woman says. 'The red dots are telling him what to do.'

'What's going on with the red dots, la'?' I ask in a gentle voice.

'The red dots have got more intense. Like a strobe light. At first, there was time for caution, but now there's no caution whatever. I used to have a millisecond to decide whether something was good or bad. Now, there's no millisecond: just do the person in.'

I consult my attorney at his law office.

'How're you doing, Ray?' I ask, shaking his hand.

'I'm good. It's you I'm worried about.'

'Why?'

'My sources at the DEA tell me it's time for you to get the hell out of Arizona.'

'Since the stock market crashed, I've not been doing much anyway.'

'You shouldn't be doing anything at all! You've had a good run. Now's the time to get out. You're an intelligent guy. You've got your whole life ahead of you. If you continue, there's only one way this is going to end.'

CHAPTER 55

'WHO'S THIS?' I say, entering an apartment I share with ADD, a tall brunette with bright-blue eyes who works for me.

The pale blonde staring back – a Scandinavian beauty whose irises are concentric circles of brown and grey and blue – is wearing tight pink trousers and a black rhinestone-studded tank top that complements her long hair.

'My friend Claudia,' ADD says, hugging me. 'Claudia, this is Shaun.'

'Hi,' Claudia says, smiling.

'Pleased to meet you, Claudia.' Embracing Claudia, I tilt my head and loudly sniff her neck, hoping to provoke a reaction. 'You smell so good.'

'Gucci Envy.'

'*Mmmm*. You should come and party with us some time.'

'I'm not a raver.'

'Not a raver! *Huh!* What the bloody hell are you doing here if you're not a raver? What music are you into?'

'Green Day.'

'Green Day!' I say, throwing my arms up, shaking my head as if losing control. 'Am I hearing right? Bloody Green Day!'

Her eyes sparkle. 'I've been in love with Billie Joe Armstrong since I was fourteen. They used to call me Punk-Rock Claudia. I can't understand techno. That *boom-boom-boom* is irritating. All everybody at raves does is get high, rub each other and look like a gang of idiots, basically.'

I burst out laughing. 'Listen, Punk-Rock Claudia, if you keep talking shit like that, I might just start to like you.'

'That's your problem!' she says, raising her brows.

'What do you do for a living?'

'Cocktail waitress.'

'Where?'

'Arizona Center.'

'Which bar?'

'Why? You gonna stalk me?'

'*Huh!* Feisty one, aren't you? Look, you're welcome to continue this conversation in my room if you like.'

Unsure, she looks at ADD for guidance. 'Erm, I guess –'

'Do you mind if I steal Claudia from you for a minute?' I ask. 'Be my guest,' ADD says.

I unlock the door. 'Come on, Claudia. I don't bite.' I sit on the bed, Claudia on a chair, maintaining a safe distance.

'Your friend Skinner's not coming back here, is he?' she asks.

My ears twitch. 'No. Why?'

'He was freaking out about some woman he has a baby with –'

'Mari.'

'Yeah, Mari and girls in general. Then he looked at me and said, "You know what, I could throw you off the balcony right now."'

'When did this happen?'

'Earlier. I was outside on the balcony. I was so scared. He doesn't seem like the most sane person in the world,' Claudia says, her eyes wide.

'Don't worry. He won't try anything while I'm here.' *He knows I stay here. Would he attack this place?*

The door swings open – Claudia jumps. A bearish figure bursts in as if looking for someone to maul.

'Hello, la',' I say, rising off the bed.

'Hello, la'.' Wild Man gives me a hug.

'This is my new friend, Claudia,' I say.

'Hello, Claudia.' His hug raises Claudia off her feet.

'Not another English guy!' Claudia says.

'He's my best mate from my home town,' I say.

'I was hoping Skinner would be here, la',' Wild Man says, one brow arching.

'He threatened Claudia. You tell him, Claudia.'

'Yeah, and I'd only just met the guy,' Claudia says.

'What did he say?' Wild Man asks.

'He threatened to throw me off the balcony. I was so afraid of him. He isn't even big. He just looks scary. He almost has like a . . . like a devil look in his eyes,' she says, twiddling a lock of hair.

'Did he pull a gun on you?' Wild Man asks.

'No. But I knew he had one.'

For weeks, I call Claudia, but she refuses to go on a date. Eventually, she allows me to visit her place on Bell Road – a small one-bedroom apartment, the decor mostly pink and zebra print, the kitchen yellow. She serves veggie bacon on pink, blue and yellow flower-shaped plastic plates partially melted from microwave cooking. The next time I visit, I bring her a gift of glass plates. Unimpressed by money, she says she prefers thrift stores. It's months before she lets me stay the night and we start going out. She doesn't approve of my drug dealing, but I don't listen. She's such a good influence and so gentle in comparison to my exes, I fall in love with her.

One night in bed, I tell her, 'You're the golden-hearted woman I've been looking for all my life, but I've always chosen the wrong woman.'

'Shaun, I love you,' Claudia says, 'but this drug dealing is dangerous. I can't handle the thought of losing you if the cops arrest you. Since my parents got divorced, I've made a point of not getting involved with anyone I might lose. Dating a drug dealer wasn't something I wanted in my future. I'm giving my heart to you, and if you're going to continue to drug deal it's not something I want to stay involved with.'

'I want to stop dealing. There's just a lot of money owed right now.'

'You're silly! You're a day trader. You can make money doing that.'

'I do want to get back to that. I just can't stop the drug stuff overnight. I want to live a normal, healthy, happy life with you.'

'A normal, healthy life when you're running around with Wild Man and G Dog! They scare me, Shaun.'

'They're just my friends.'

'They come over here with guns. You disappear with them for days at a time, probably not up to any sort of good. Shaun, I need you to quit dealing drugs. There are two sides to it. Number one: our future. Number two: my family. My family life is so strong. When you disappear for days on end, I go to my mom or dad's house. I can't have my family know they raised somebody who's with a drug dealer. Aside from the world that is my family, you are the second part of my family. I want to start a family with you.'

Touched, I blush. 'OK. I promise I'm going to stop drug dealing, eventually,' I say, unconvinced.

'Will you come and meet my dad?'

'Yes, I'll meet your dad.'

The next day, we dress to meet her father: Claudia in a pink short-sleeve sweater and a knee-length skirt with a floral pattern, white, light green and pink. I put on bright-blue raver trousers and a black shirt. Before setting off, I drink a glass of wine to calm my nerves.

In Quartzsite, Claudia parks at a white one-storey house surrounded by a little wooden fence and khaki-coloured desert. We enter the gate. Greyhounds charge at us. Excited to see Claudia, they bark, smile and perform little sprints.

Inside, Claudia introduces me to Barry, a big man with long hair and biker tattoos. Behind round spectacles, his eyes, the same as Claudia's, are radiating good will. His demeanour and kind voice put me at ease.

'Pleased to meet you.'

Firmly, he shakes my hand. 'This is Callie,' he says, smiling at his wife, who has long dark hair and light-brown skin.

Lorna, their four-year-old blonde daughter, drags me away to show me her toys.

Over barbecued food, they ask about my job. Saying I trade the stock market, I feel guilty for fibbing. They ask for investment advice. I tell them to buy gold. We watch a comedy starring Ice Cube, laughing and joking all the way through it.

On the drive home, Claudia says, 'Don't ever tell any of your friends where my dad lives.'

'Of course not,' I say, offended. 'Why would you even say that?'

'Because Wild Man walked all the way to Buckeye and beat up a whole family. He could probably walk all the way to Quartzsite if he ever gets mad at me.'

'He won't ever get mad at you. It was so nice to be around your family, your dad especially. I don't know why I was so nervous beforehand.'

'They're always so funny and Lorna's so cute. Me and my brothers, we just laugh the whole way home after we visit Quartzsite.'

Claudia's joy starts to purge my soul. For a moment, I fill with sadness and don't know who I am. Shook up, I breathe deeply to steady myself. *How can I put this woman who loves me so much at risk by continuing to drug deal?* Gripped by an urge to do what's right for Claudia, for us, for my family, for her family, I say, 'You've been right all along. I'm going to stop drug dealing.' I watch, keen to see her reaction, my thoughts accelerating to figure out what must be done.

'Are you serious?' Claudia says, taking her eyes off the road to see if I'm telling the truth.

'Yes.'

Her brows leap and she beams.

'I love you and don't want to lose you,' I say, smiling.

Claudia takes a hand off the steering wheel and grips mine.

'What we need to do is rent a place together that nobody knows about. I won't tell any of my friends where we live.'

'My brother's moving out of his Scottsdale apartment. We can take that,' she says excitedly.

'Perfect! If we keep the lease in his name, no one will be able to trace us there.'

A month later, we move. I'm thrilled and nervous to put the English Shaun persona behind me. *It's the end of an era. At least I never got caught. My family will never know and what they don't know can't hurt them.* Claudia gets a job as a telesales consultant. I trade the stock market online. On weekdays, I try to live normally. Eating at Indian restaurants. Taking kickboxing and Spanish classes. Working out at the gym with Claudia, followed by smoothies at Jamba Juice. Even trips to the laundry room are fun, watching Claudia prance around in bumblebee-patterned pyjamas.

But on the weekends, I still hear the wolves howling that it's party time. I sneak off with Wild Man, getting high on GHB.

Aunt Mo – who started me out in America but returned to England in 1992 – flies to Phoenix. After a weekend of partying, I take Claudia to meet her at an Indian restaurant. Mo and Claudia get along right away. I sense an unspoken approval.

'How come you've lost so much weight, beloved nephew?' Mo asks. 'You look like shit!'

I almost drop a samosa. 'Long hours following the stock market in the US and London. I've not been getting much sleep.'

'Then either trade the US or London. You can't stay awake all day and night for both!'

'I know. You're right. I will,' I say, relieved she believes me.

'So what have you been taking to stay awake for so long?'

She knows! Caught off guard, I squirm and try to hide my guilt behind a smile.

Mo rolls her eyes and narrows them. 'Just remember, one way or another, it will catch up with you. One time, I had a line of coke to give me energy to play five-a-side football. It made me feel like I could take on the whole team alone. I managed to injure my ankle, but I was so high, I didn't think it was serious, so I kept playing. I got to the hospital the next day and the specialist asked me what I was on. Being honest, I jumped in with, "OK, I had a line of coke." He ignored me and continued with, "Were you on gravel or Astroturf?" I was laughing until he diagnosed me with a broken ankle.'

Mo asks more questions about my life, but out of fear word will get back to my parents, I clam up. I appreciate her concern, but I see no end to my drug use.

CHAPTER 56

SIX MONTHS LATER, I leave the Wild Ones' to drive home. I turn. So does the car behind. I turn. The car behind turns. *Following me or am I being paranoid?* I slow down. *Black car. Tinted windows. Driver has no hair.* I shiver. *The man Wild Woman described? Out to rob me. Aw shit! I'll show you what the RX7 can do!* I squeeze the wheel, lock my shoulders, screech off. The car speeds up, closes distance. I pump the brakes, turn too sharply, fishtail. *Screech!* He slows to turn. I speed away. Changing gears robotically, I zigzag down side streets. He pursues, drops distance. I ditch him and pull a U-turn, singeing the tyres. I turn off the lights, park, wait, my head throbbing. His lights appear. He roars past. Disappears. I put my lights on and head for the main road.

Minutes later, he's behind again. *How's that possible, you bastard?* Furious, I speed from Tempe to the outskirts of Phoenix, pursued all the way. I turn into a post office and arc around the car park. I get back on the road, cut into a neighbourhood, swing a U-turn and head in his direction. He slows down. I pass him. By the time he turns, I'm gone.

I run red lights and get on the freeway. *I'll soon be home.* I begin rehearsing what to tell Claudia.

Near Scottsdale, I notice cars in my mirror zooming towards me in the fast lane. I change to the middle lane, expecting them to overtake. They get behind, led by the black car. *No fucking way! No matter, I'll ditch them off the freeway.*

I take the exit. Four cars follow. *Mind's playing tricks on me.* I turn down a side street. All four turn. *Jesus Christ. I'm about to get killed or arrested!* I floor the pedal and roar away in low gear, the rev meter leaping towards the danger zone that shuts the car down before its engine explodes. *There's no way I'm leading these bastards to Claudia.* I shoot through a neighbourhood and run red lights until they're nowhere in sight. I cut back home.

I creep the car through the complex, scanning every vehicle for cops. It's a while before I feel safe enough to park. I get out, check the area and rush home in a sweat. I stab the key into the door and dash in. 'I just got followed!'

'You're sketching,' Claudia says, rising off the sofa. 'You've done way too many drugs in your lifetime.'

'No. Listen. I'm serious. Dead fucking serious,' I say, waving my arms. 'Four cars followed me from the freeway. When I turned up 78th Street, they all turned with me. It was like I had my own bloody motorcade.'

'There's no reason they'd want you now,' Claudia says, shaking her head. 'You've stopped dealing.'

'I don't know, love,' I say, hugging her. 'This shit really happened. It's serious. Really serious. I think we'd better move away.'

'Yes. Marry me and let's go to LA.'

I smile. 'Sooner rather than later. I'll see how much I've got in the stock accounts and we'll go.' We sit on the sofa and hug.

'Then I can put my acting classes to good use,' Claudia says. 'I want to go where there's a lot going on.'

'There's loads going on there.'

'And we can spend time by the water. Here we can't do that.'

'We'll rent a house by the beach. You can act and I'll trade stocks. We'll be like normal people. I just hope we have enough money.'

'You'd have enough money if you stopped paying everybody's bills,' Claudia says.

'I'm working on making the Wild Ones self-sufficient.'

'Shaun, the Wild Ones blow up house after house. I work this shitty job, so I pay my own part of the bills, so you know I'm not using you for money. But everyone else is.'

'I had so much money. I'm just so used to paying for everything for everybody.'

'And hanging out with the Wild Ones is dangerous,' Claudia says, throwing her arms up. 'We're trying to live a normal life, and they're getting more and more insane. What they do is dangerous for you. You'll get arrested. You think you're invincible. And these people you meet at the Wild Ones', how can you trust them?'

'That's what I'm trying to tell you: something's up. I'm getting followed around.'

'You're just being paranoid.'

'No I'm not! I'm going to call Cody. Have him take the RX7. It stands out way too much. It's obvious I've been identified in it.'

Two days later, Wild Woman pages me over.

In her living room, I sit on an old armchair. 'What's up?'

'The cops were here,' she says, on the sofa, her eyes exhausted, shoulders slumped.

'Detective Reid?'

'No. Regular cops. Wild Man came to the house demanding stuff and I wouldn't give him any. I told him, "You mean nothing to me no more. If you wannit, you'd better earn it. Go out collecting or something." I was being a right bitch and I just wouldn't give him the shit. So he started strangling me.'

'I keep telling you: he's going to kill you one of these days. I don't know why you guys stay together.'

'The cops came and said they'd had a report from the neighbours of domestic violence, but I don't see how they could have got here so fast. I'm wondering if they were watching me. Then they took us both to the police station and let us back out. That was dead sketchy. They ran our names, so why would they let us go?'

'If they've been looking for you ever since the raid, it doesn't make sense,' I say, shaking my head.

'I think we're in bigger trouble. They're coming for us. They're watching us. I'm telling you. I'm not stupid. I wasn't brought in on a banana boat.'

'They can watch me as much as they want, I'm not dealing any more. You'd better make sure they don't catch you in the act.'

'And another thing: Skinner's gone and fessed up to me that he did the firebombing.'

'What?' I ask, surprised.

'He asked me to go down and see him at his little flat. He was crying in his living room on his couch. Crying like he had a broken heart. I thought he was gonna kill himself. I was dead worried about him.'

'What did he say?'

'He said he was dead sorry about everything. I said, "I know it was you, Skinner. I know you done that with the bomb and all that." He said, "You don't understand what I'm going through." Money this, money that, blah, blah, blah, and all that. I said, "That's not my problem. You shouldn't have done that to me, 'cause I helped you out so many times." I gave him money and stuff when I shouldn't have done. I said, "Why'd you go and do that to me? I'm done with you." And that's when he told me he did it and said he was sorry. I never told Wild Man 'cause he would have just gone straight over there and murdered him.'

'Anything else I need to know about?'

'The black Impala's been round again. He's been going up and down the road. Grady went out there, knocked on his window and said, "Do you want something?" He chased him up Farmer. He followed the Impala.'

'How did that end up?'

'The Impala fucked off. Grady came back laughing his head off. He said, "I fucked him off, didn't I?"'

'It sounds like the car that followed me,' I say.

The next day, Mari calls: 'Skinner's left town.'

'Why?' I ask, peeping out of my living room window for suspicious cars. 'Did he say anything to you before he left?'

'Nothing. He was just crying. It's really weird 'cause he never leaves. Especially 'cause his little girl is here and he loves her. It's really weird that he was so willing to go, 'cause he's always sat there and said he'd never leave. I even gave him money 'cause I'm tired of his ass. He's shot at my windows, attacked me in the middle of the night. Too much craziness. I took him to the bus stop. He cried and said goodbye. I said goodbye and that was it.'

'Did he say why he was leaving?'

'He didn't. I told him I didn't want to be near him no more. I think it's just 'cause he has no place to go no more.'

'Do you think he's up to something?'

'He's so sneaky. He never talks about what's going on in his head, but he's always making plans. He ain't stupid. That kid was a gifted child.'

'I think Wild Man has put the fear of God in him and that's why he's took off.'

'Wild Man called me the other night. I'm lying there, and I've just put the baby to sleep, and I see it's Peter. He says, "I know, I know, I'm not supposed to call you after ten o'clock because of the baby, but can you come and pick me up 'cause I'm lost somewhere and the Mexicans are coming?" I'm like, "Are you fucking serious?"'

'He's more out of control than ever.'

Later that day, I return to Wild Woman's house, shocked by the debris and glass strewn across the living room. I take a seat. 'Why're all your windows smashed?'

'Wild Man went berserk again.'

'What over now?'

'He wanted more stuff. I said, "I'm not giving you stuff to put you in a frame of mind to do God knows what." I told everyone else, they so much as give him a sniff, I'll slit their throats, rip their heads off and shit down their fucking necks. They're more scared of me than him, 'cause they've seen me step to him. So they wouldn't give him anything, and he got pissed off and came to the house. I told him, "You're not getting none. Now get out." He kicked off and everyone scattered to their car. He comes out, picks up a boulder and throws it at the fucking car. It bounced off the bonnet and they screeched off. So he carried on. He put the boulder through all the front windows. I picked up a big blow fan and chased him down the drive with it. He said he was going off to kill Skinner.'

That night, Mari finds Wild Man at Skinner's flat and calls: 'Wild Man was sat there with a hammer, a golf club, a knife, a screwdriver, a chisel, a crowbar, a fork, all these weapons around him, waiting for Skinner in a chair, watching the front door. I told him Skinner had gone, but he wouldn't believe me. Joey Crack came in and Wild Man almost killed him with the crowbar. He said, "I thought you was someone else." He unplugged the freezer, so there was no noise, so he could hear Skinner coming. I just left him there, sweat dripping off him. I couldn't handle it any more.'

There are a few new faces at my kickboxing class, including an older man who insists I spar with him.

I put a helmet on, bite down on a mouth guard, get in the ring, assume the stance, raise my gloves. We skip around, sizing each other up, probing for openings. We close in. Kick. Punch. Block. Blow. Punch. Block. Kick. Kick. *Bam–bam–bam* . . . A few minutes later, we stop, exhausted, panting as if we've sprinted hundreds of yards, sweat pouring off us. I rip the helmet off, towel the sweat from my brow and watch the next two in the ring.

The dojo door opens. A hairless man enters with two children. He has a tough, creepy face and tattooed arms. *It's him!* I freeze.

He scans the dojo, avoiding looking directly at me. Perhaps sensing I've recognised him, he walks out.

'Hello!' says a girl I know.

'How're you?' I ask.

Before she can answer, an adult calls her away in a fearful tone, rousing my suspicion. My sparring partner hovers like my shadow until the class ends.

'Do you mind if I use your phone to order Indian food?' I ask the girl at the front.

Usually chatty and polite, she recoils as she hands me the phone.

Why's everyone treating me differently? What do they know? I make the call and leave.

Outside, a radio crackles. 'I see him,' someone says.

I'm obviously under surveillance. But if I'm not dealing drugs, what can they do?

On the road, I'm followed. I collect the food and drive around in circles until convinced the tails are gone.

At home, I burst into the apartment, trembling, and drop my gym bag. 'I was followed again.'

'You're crazy!' Claudia says, jumping off the sofa.

I raise my voice: 'Why do you always say that? Everyone was treating me differently at kickboxing. I saw the bald guy there that Wild Woman was going on about, which freaked me out. He must be an undercover cop. I heard a radio when I got out. Someone said he saw me. And then cars followed me again.'

'No they didn't! You're sketching out.'

'Claudia, I heard them outside on a police radio saying they saw me!'

'And that was at the kickboxing place?'

'Outside of it, yes.'

'*Hmmm.*' Claudia walks to the window and peers out. 'I don't see anybody. Stop sketching. Nobody's out there.'

'They're probably hiding out in a neighbour's place or in some kind of undercover van.'

'You're not doing anything wrong,' she says, turning to me. 'Nobody's trying to arrest you!'

'What's going to happen if I go to jail?'

'You're not!'

'Look, if they're following me around like this it must be something serious, even though I'm not doing anything.'

'I'm not worried. You have to be caught doing something wrong to get arrested.'

'I still don't think they're following me around for no reason.'

'Then let's just go to LA. Let's figure out the money thing, and let's just go.'

'You really want to do it? Just go?'

'Yes. If you think they're really following you, then we should.'

Over Indian food, we plan our move. We take showers. Make love.

'I love you, Bungle Bee,' I say in bed.

'Love you too, Shoggy Bee. Goodnight.'

We kiss.

Claudia falls asleep holding my hand, her other arm wrapped around Floppy, a pink and light-brown Build-A-Bear with long flat ears. Listening to her breathing, afraid to let go of her hand lest I wake her up, I replay the day's events. *Got to leave Arizona. Don't have enough time to organise a move to LA. Maybe get a plane to Hector's in Chicago until things calm down. But so what if I'm arrested: what can they do if I have no drugs? Surely they'll have to let me go.* Convinced something bad is going to happen but that there's time to avoid it, I fall asleep.

The next day – 16 May 2002 – I rise at 6.30 a.m. to place a trade. Snatching a quick $3,000 profit – money that'll help us move to LA – puts a smile on my face. I'm staring at the screen when banging shakes the door.

'Tempe Police Department! We have a warrant!'

My insides clench. I leap up. A voice echoes in my head: *Get the hell out!* I rush to the door. The peephole's blacked out. *Drug-dealer robbers posing as cops trying to stop me from seeing them? Want me at the door to shoot me first.* Feeling the threat from the other side of the door flare up, I back away. I run to the front window, glance out, quake. Police positioned behind cars. Marksmen aiming rifles. *Skinner, what have you done?* Afraid of getting shot, I duck. Blood surges to my head. *Hide in the attic – where there's hardly any room and they'll easily find you. Jump off the balcony – and break your legs and probably get shot. Shit! No. Let's not do that. But what?* I struggle to accept I'm trapped. My panic soars. I run to Claudia. *Maybe she'll know what to do.*

She scrambles from the bed – Floppy hits the floor – fixes her pink pyjamas, stares at me, shaking. 'What should we do?' she asks, her voice wavering.

PARTY TIME 271

The banging at the door reverberates through my body. My heart beats harder.

'Open the door!'

Maybe they'll go easier on us if we let them in. 'Better open it,' I say hurriedly, my jaw trembling.

We get halfway to the door – *boom!* – it leaps off its hinges. The folly of English Shaun hits me like a punch to the head from Wild Man. Dazed, I want to throw up. Aiming guns, the SWAT team hems us in with a wall of Plexiglas shields. Paralysed by fear of getting shot – instant death – I feel my chest seize up.

'Tempe Police Department! Get on the fucking ground now!'

I drop. I'm crushed, handcuffed, yanked to my feet.

A burly man with long hair puts his face up to mine. 'I'm Detective Reid. English Shaun, you're a big name from the rave scene . . .'

The wolves stop howling that it's party time.

WHERE ARE THEY NOW?

- Acid Joey was found dead in his swimming pool with his clothes on.
- Amy attempted suicide in Egypt by overdosing on pills and slashing her wrists, but was rescued. She is a schoolteacher in Shanghai.
- Carlos the Torturer is serving a life sentence.
- Claudia works as a department specialist in the corporate office of a chain of natural food stores.
- Cody – the sober one – resorted to heroin after our arrests and hanged himself at a rehab centre after he was put on medication with side effects that included suicidal feelings.
- Desirae lives in Phoenix with her husband and three kids.
- G Dog is serving a ten-year sentence for dealing crystal meth.
- Gangsta Dan is serving life for a murder committed in the hope of receiving insurance proceeds. His accomplice barricaded himself inside a house to keep the cops out, and stabbed himself to death.
- Hotwheelz lives near London – with me. He delivers produce to restaurants, shops and pubs, grows his own vegetables and is famous for his culinary and cider-making skills.
- Jaxson has heart problems due to his drug intake.
- Joey Crack got a job promotion, went out to celebrate and died from a heroin overdose.
- Kelly married, divorced and lives with her children.
- Keoki lives in Denver and performs internationally.
- Mari is a dental nurse.
- Raul is serving a life sentence.
- Sammy 'The Bull' Gravano is serving 20 years in a maximum-security federal prison. He has Graves' disease.
- Skinner never returned to Arizona.

- Sumiko never remarried and is a successful business owner.
- Wild Man married and has only had three fights since his release from prison, none of which he started – all of which he won.
- Wild Woman lives with her children in England. Daily, her heart beats irregularly, cramps and temporarily stops. She takes 14 different types of medication to stay alive.
- The wolves still howl from time to time, but Dr O, a brilliant psychotherapist (coming in *Prison Time*, the third instalment of the English Shaun trilogy), taught me how to deal with them.

LINKS

Blog: Jon's Jail Journal
Website: shaunattwood.com
Twitter: @shaunattwood
YouTube: derickatt
Facebook: Shaun Attwood
    Party Time (Shaun Attwood)
    Hard Time (Shaun Attwood)
    Prison Time (Shaun Attwood)
    Jon's Jail Journal
    T-Bone Appreciation Society

ACKNOWLEDGEMENTS

PROOFREADERS: **BARBARA ATTWOOD**, Karen Attwood, Gabriella Apicella, Shannon Clark, Sue Obaza, Isabelle Martinbeau, Tijana Timotijevic, Heather McQuaid, Clare White, Noshaba Malik, Amanda Stacey, Tonya Bowman.

Gabriella Apicella for structural advice and for reading the entire manuscript aloud for editing when I lost my voice.

Professor Brooks Landon for the cumulative sentence.

Stacey 'Pale and Interesting' Wood for the present tense.

Meg Rosoff for the quote.

Scott Alexander for permission to reprint extracts from his book *Rhinoceros Success* in Chapter 6.

Derick Attwood, Peter 'Wild Man' Mahoney, Tina Mahoney, Debbiy, Mike 'Hotwheelz' Richardson, Sean 'Hammy' Hamilton, Amber and Barry Holwegner, Kinkeroo, Vic Sibilla, Gerard Gravano, Margret Murphy, Andrea 'ADD' Swanson, Jessica and Jeremy 'Smiley' Arviso, Jacob Chavez, Caleb Hartman, Jill Cuomo, Andy Manning, Micah Gibson, Jerry 'The Prophet' Hoey, Nicholas Liberatore, Patrick Powers, Tina Powsey, Desirae, DJ Keoki, Gary Menichiello, Frankie Bones, Melissa Copen, Sarah Parry.

My readers, especially those who've provided guidance and feedback.

Robert Kirby – literary agent of the year – for launching my career.

Bill Campbell and the staff at Mainstream Publishing.

Tony McLellan and Emma Cole of the McLellan Practice for talks to schools.

Anne Mini for writing a brilliant introduction to *Hard Time* (US version) and for maintaining the only blog I read consistently, Author! Author!, which details everything a would-be writer needs to know to get published.

Tony Papa (*15 to Life*) for writing a foreword to *Hard Time* (US version) and the staff at Skyhorse Publishing.

Aunty Lily for hours of unpaid work at our sweatshop.

Andrew Donegan and Stephanie Senn for ebook artwork.

Heather McQuaid and Sarah Clark for brochure design.

Stephanie Senn, Jörg and Wm. Srite for IT help.

Libi Peddler and Andrew Parsons for photography.

Lynne and Gary Barnes for hosting the home-town book launch at the Eight Towers pub, and everyone who attended the Widnes and London launches.

Koestler Trust staff: Tim Robertson, Sarah Mathéve, Ben Monks, Vikki Elliot, Joyti Waswani.

Prisoners Abroad Staff: Pauline Crowe, Zainab Amer, Elga Batala, Caroline Beckman, Jo Bedingfield, Lorraine Cole, Theo Cresser, Jessica D'Cruz, Ola Fadojutimi, Theresa Gilson, Paul Keenlyside, Iris Lee, Elena Gonzalez-Conde Linares, Gayle Lyes, Laura Martin, Yann Paulain, Matthew Pinches, Kate Willmott.

Help and support at book signings: Waterstones staff, Mum (who instigated the signings, and whom I now begrudgingly allow snack breaks owing to pressure from my blog readers), Emily Brooks, Lydia Nicole Rainford, Charlotte Mount, 'Wild' John Wild, Natalie Mitchell, Iain Sambrook, Sue Fox, Gabriella Apicella, Tony Coker, Suzanne Collin, Helen Gowers, Noshaba Malik, Mick and Dawn and Micky Smith, Josephine and Simon Toms, Mary Brandon, Mark and Debra Sharman, Sadie Jones, Holly Parrish.

Media: Karen Attwood and Andrew Parsons (Parsons Media), Chris Summers (BBC), Susanna Reid (BBC), Jon Ronson (BBC Radio 4), David Hepworth (*Mixmag/The Word*), Dominic Herbert (*Sunday Mirror*), Martin Stanford (Sky News), Felicity Hannah (Yahoo!), Jeremy Vine (BBC Radio 2), Eddie Mair (BBC Radio 4), Catherine Whyte (Sheengate Publishing), Erwin James (*The Guardian/A Life Inside*), Quinn Norton (*Irish Times*), Tony Snell (BBC Radio Merseyside), Greg Mocker (CBS Channel 5), Marnie Wilson and Melanie Hall (*Surrey Advertiser*), Wesley Johnson (Press Association), Andrew Thorp and Sara Knowles (MojoLife TV), Donna Birrell (BBC Radio Cornwall), Mark Carter (BBC Radio Surrey), Nick Wallis (BBC Radio Surrey), Justin Dealey (BBC Three Counties Radio), Joe Talbot (BBC Radio Surrey), Stephen Lemons (*Phoenix New Times*), Adam Boulton (Sky News), Mike Peake (*FHM*), Chris Vallance (BBC Radio 5), Maurice Boland

(Talk Radio Europe), Paddy Shennan (*Liverpool Echo*), Paul Taylor (*Manchester Evening News*), Maryam Omidi (Dow Jones), Will Batchelor, Duncan Barkes (City Talk 105.9), Todd Landfried, Linda Bentley, Josi Standbrook (Kane FM), Hugh Stoddart (editor, *Not Shut Up*), Claire Richmond.

Other help: DJ Jay Wearden, Jonathan White, Dr Shapiro, Stephen Nash, Charlotte Knee, Charlie Ryder (Wormwood Scrubs Community Chaplaincy), Clayton Littlewood (*Dirty White Boy/ Goodbye to Soho*), Gem Rodgers of Waterstones Birkenhead, David Obaza, Eric Noi, Andrew Austin (*The Rainbow Machine*), Steven McLaughlin (*Squaddie*), Simon Eddisbury (*Lowlife*), Ian 'Aza' Harry, Alena and Jared Fiori, Suzanne Bayes, Amy Skaggs, Alesia 'Double A' Apodaca, Andy 'Mr Wolf' Stanley, Emma Cunningham, Stacey Wood, Jeff Svorc, Chris Barry, Daisy Harper, Danny Jurmann, Stuart Craig, Jonnel 'Posterboy' Sloane, Joshua Friedman, Ed Lieber, Lorna Millar, Cornel Grant, Warren Banks, Hazel Andrew, Nancy Buckland, Katarina Lukackova, Lorna Brookes, Natalie Ogden, Chris Hawthorne, John Davis and Robert Sockett, John Lawson, Laura Goulding, Craig Lam, Mo Hall, Pete Thompson, Mandy Melvin, Bucko and his daughters, Chloe and Ellie, Jess Parry, Daniel, Darby, Ste Dando, Steve Richard, Zara Zeb, Vicky Mortimer, Damion Redford, Karen Hampton, Tara Hall, Cindy Breau, Janet and Peter Strode, Gregory Haynes, Bruce Bettridge, Dave McNish, James and Dan Rose, Patty Harrison, Emma Freeman, Lynne Chapman, Richard Rowley and Sue Clifford (No Offence!).

Support over the years: Jose of San Diego, Zivi, Mike and Mick Kelly, Neil and Declan O'Connor, Julie Koningsor, Kathi Drafehn, Jayne and Steve and Michelle, Mr D, Alison Hicks, Tony Wimberley, Brian Block, Oliver Reed, Naomi Fox, Eric Young, Jessicat, Gareth Holmes, Sarah 'The Fair Surrah' Jane Gray, Pat Hamm, Linda Saville, Larry Florke, Glenda Hill, Alison George, Ed Lieber, Pearl Wilson, Gemma Lee, Karen Schwartz, Hannah Sassaman, Grace Avarne, Sandra Byrne, Rachel Baker, Denise Brousseau, Rosemarie Dombrowski, Marc Cupit, Clive Bratchell, James Halliday, Michal and Luke Jacobs, Georgina Hale, Katerina Kospanova, Alan Payne, Noelle Moeller, Terry Hackett, Misty Matonis, Barbara McDonald, Lorna Prestage, Pippa Ruesink, Sijia, John Williams, Joshua Friedman, Guida Rufino, Mary Wehring, Gavin Reedman, Donald Clark and Puggles, Zen, Lesley and Dave and Chris and Aidan Oakes, Jamie Andrews, Marc 'Cuban Boy' Bryon, Simon Austin, Chris Alexander, Andrea Bodman, Miss B. La Bamba, Lauren Better, Clare Bagley, Greg Bell, Celina Chico, Paul Claxton, John Burns, Jim Cozzolino, Scott Clouder, Fiona Dawson, Rachel Carpenter, Rosanne Cerello, Diarmuid Deeney, Howard Davidson, Srutadeva das, Laura Dabbs, Donald Felgar, Lisa Fagg, Helena Flint, Jason Foster, Finola Farrant, Rita Abraham, Andrea La Franca, Nichola Griffin, Karin Haems, Iain Dignall, Emily Robinson, Anthony Hanagan, Christine Gentry, Rebecca Greenhalgh, Mrs. S.F. Heming, Rachel Humphreys, Ingrid Hoflin, Melissa Takabayashi, Ross Thompson, Leah Simone Wickett, Mark Wright, Nathan Yost.

The Guildford Seiki-Juku Karate Club for constant inspiration and occasional injuries: Brian Shrubb, Steve Gurney, Mike Graham, Raquel Fulgoni, Damon von Styles, Martin Marshall, Bee Zeebee, Ashley Rowe, Nigel Cottrell, Steve and Jack Goodwin, Helen Gowers, Tijana Timotijevic, Philip Rambech, Ben Ayling, Ben Reynolds, Nick Murphy, Mick 'Iron Man' Channon, Alex Shannon, Clive Taylor, Mario Ragusa, Colin Brenton, Mark Hall.

For the ultimate natural high, BodyCombat at the Guildford Spectrum: Tony Coker, Tracey Debenham and Jon Hawkins.

To my mental-health team – oops, I mean my yoga instructors – for helping me stay stress-free and blissed out by encouraging me to bend like rubber, meditate and stand on my head: Natalie 'Yogini' Coleman (Poise Yoga Guildford), Yvette Meredith (Guildford Spectrum), Clive Bratchell (Infin8te Yoga Guildford), Callie 'The Queen of Yin Yoga' Meakin (DW Widnes), Swami John 'The Freestyle Master' Malloy (DW Widnes), Leela Miller (Triyoga Soho) and Sadhguru (Isha Foundation).

Cody Bates, Acid Joey and Joey Crack. RIP, my friends.

HARD TIME

Shaun Attwood

'Makes *The Shawshank Redemption* look like a holiday camp' – *News of the World*

'A searing indictment of the controversial penal tactics of Sheriff Joe Arpaio – who revels in the title of "America's Toughest Sheriff"' – BBC News website

'A tale of brutality and a lesson in behind-bars etiquette' – *Manchester Evening News*

'A gripping account of Attwood's time among lethal gangsters . . . and of living in fear amid sewage and cockroaches' – *City AM*

In *Hard Time*, Shaun Attwood tells the story of how he survived the jail with the highest death rate in America. Before being convicted of money laundering and dealing Ecstasy, he served 26 months on remand in the infamous Arizona jail system run by the notorious Sheriff Joe Arpaio.

Initially, Shaun goes into shock as he's submerged into a world where gang leaders dictate who lives and dies, the cells are so hot that bleeding skin infections are the norm and the food is green baloney with mouldy bread, or a mystery-meat slop known as 'red death', which sometimes has rats in it. And then there are the cockroaches . . .

Over time, Shaun learns to avoid violence and the predatory members of the Aryan Brotherhood prison gang by forming various alliances, including with the Italian Mafia. He increasingly uses his jail time for learning and introspection, taking up yoga and discovering philosophy.

Hard Time is a harrowing yet often darkly humorous account of the time Shaun spent submerged in a nightmarish world of gang violence, insect-infested cells and food unfit for animals. His remarkable story provides a revealing glimpse into the tragedy, brutality, comedy and eccentricity of prison life.

PRISON TIME

Shaun Attwood

Expected publication: 2014

Prison Time, the sequel to *Hard Time*, is the story of Shaun Attwood's journey through the Arizona Department of Corrections and his deportation to England.

Sentenced to 9½ years in Arizona's state prison for distributing Ecstasy, 'English Shaun' finds himself living among gang members, sexual predators and drug-crazed psychopaths. Shaun writes about the prisoners who befriend, protect and inspire him after he's attacked by a 20-stone California biker who's in for stabbing a girlfriend. They include T-Bone, a massive African American ex-Marine who risks his life saving vulnerable inmates from rape, and Two Tonys, an old-school Mafia murderer who left the corpses of his rivals from Tucson to Alaska. They teach Shaun how to turn incarceration to his advantage and learn from his mistakes.

Resigned to living alongside violent, mentally ill and drug-addicted inmates, Shaun immerses himself in psychology and philosophy to try to make sense of his past behaviour and begins applying what he learns as he adapts to prison life. Encouraged by Two Tonys to explore fiction as well, Shaun reads more than 1,000 books, which, with support from brilliant psychotherapist Dr O, speed along his personal development. As his ability to deflect daily threats improves, Shaun begins to look forward to his release – and a new love waiting for him – with optimism. Yet the words of Aristotle from one of Shaun's books will prove prophetic: 'We cannot learn without pain.'